GOD AND GOVERNMENT

Edited by
Nick Spencer
and
Jonathan Chaplin

SPCK

First published in Great Britain in 2009

Society for Promoting Christian Knowledge
36 Causton Street
London SW1P 4ST

British Library Cataloguing-in-Publication Data
A catalogue record for this book is available from the British Library

ISBN 978–0–281–06071–9

1 3 5 7 9 10 8 6 4 2

Typeset by Graphicraft Ltd, Hong Kong
Printed in Great Britain by Ashford Colour Press

Produced on paper from sustainable forests

Contents

About the authors iv

Foreword by the Archbishop of Canterbury ix

Introduction 1
Nick Spencer

1 Government as an ambiguous power 16
Nigel Wright

2 The nature and role of government in the Bible 40
Julian Rivers

3 Neither anarchy nor tyranny: Government and the New Testament 61
Tom Wright

4 The role of government in classical Christian political thought 81
David McIlroy

5 Government and social infrastructure 108
Nicholas Townsend

6 Government, solidarity and subsidiarity 134
Philip Booth

7 Government and the common good 159
Clifford Longley

8 Government and equality 180
Andrew Bradstock

Conclusion: Christian political wisdom 205
Jonathan Chaplin

Index 238

About the authors

Philip Booth is Editorial and Programme Director at the Institute of Economic Affairs and Professor of Insurance and Risk Management at Cass Business School, City University. He has previously worked at the Bank of England advising on financial stability issues. Philip writes and speaks widely on economic matters including on financial markets and regulation, pensions, and the relationship between Catholic Social Teaching and economics. He is editor and co-author of *Catholic Social Teaching and the Market Economy* and co-edited *The Road to Economic Freedom* – a compilation of the work of a number of Nobel Prize-winning economists. Philip is a Fellow of the Institute of Actuaries and editor of the journal *Economic Affairs*.

Andrew Bradstock was Director of the Christian Socialist Movement from 2005 to 2008 and before that served for five years as Secretary for Church and Society with the United Reformed Church. He is currently Howard Paterson Professor of Theology and Public Issues at the University of Otago in New Zealand. He has written widely on the relationship between faith and politics from both a contemporary and a historical perspective. His latest book is *Louder Than Words: Action for the 21st-Century Church* (Darton, Longman & Todd, 2007) and he is co-editor, with Chris Rowland, of *Radical Christian Writings: A Reader* (Blackwell, 2002).

Jonathan Chaplin is Director of the Kirby Laing Institute for Christian Ethics, Tyndale House, and a Member of the Cambridge University Divinity Faculty. He was Associate

Professor of Political Theory at the Institute for Christian Studies, Toronto from 1999 to 2006 and is a Senior Fellow of the Canadian think tank Cardus. He has edited or co-edited four books and published many articles on Christian political thought. His recent publications include 'Legal Monism and Religious Pluralism: Rowan Williams on Religion, Loyalty and Law', in *International Journal of Public Theology* and *Talking God: The Legitimacy of Religious Public Reasoning* (Theos, 2009).

Clifford Longley is an author, broadcaster and journalist with special interest in British and international moral and religious affairs. He acted as consultant to the Catholic Bishops' Conference of England and Wales for the production of *The Common Good and the Catholic Church's Social Teaching* (1996) and for *The Catholic Church and Human Rights* (1998). He was the principal author of *Prosperity with a Purpose* (Churches Together in Britain and Ireland, 2005) and has written, among other books, *The Worlock Archive* (Geoffrey Chapman, 1999) and *Chosen People* (Hodder, 2002). He has written extensively on religion, morality and culture in *The Times*, *Daily Telegraph* and *The Tablet* and is a panellist on Radio 4's *The Moral Maze* and a regular contributor to 'Thought for the Day'.

David McIlroy is a practising barrister, Visiting Senior Lecturer in Law at SOAS, University of London and Associate Research Fellow at Spurgeon's College. He is author of two books, *A Biblical View of Law and Justice* (Paternoster, 2004) and *A Trinitarian Theology of Law* (Paternoster, 2009), as well as numerous articles on Christianity and law, including 'What's at Stake in Natural Law?' (*New Blackfriars*, 2008), 'The Law of Love' (*Cambridge Papers*, 2008) and 'Towards a Relational and Trinitarian Theology of Atonement' (*Evangelical Quarterly*, 2008).

Julian Rivers has been Professor of Jurisprudence at the University of Bristol since 2007. He has taught a range of subjects in European and domestic constitutional and administrative law, human rights law and jurisprudence. His research interests lie mainly in the area of legal and constitutional theory, with a particular focus on legal reasoning and the relationship between law and religion. He has published widely and also translated Robert Alexy's *Theory of Constitutional Rights* (OUP, 2002). He has been on the writing group of *Cambridge Papers* since 1992 and has contributed essays to *Whitefield Briefings/Ethics in Brief* as well as the *Dictionary of Christian Apologetics* (IVP, 2006). He is a member of the Editorial Advisory Board of the *Ecclesiastical Law Journal*, on the advisory board of the Jubilee Centre, Cambridge and was also founding chairman of the Kirby Laing Institute for Christian Ethics at Tyndale House, Cambridge.

Nick Spencer is Director of Studies at the public theology think tank Theos, having previously worked for the Henley Centre, the London Institute for Contemporary Christianity and the Jubilee Centre. He researches and writes on issues of religion and society and is the author of a number of Theos reports including *Doing God: A Future for Faith in the Public Square* and *Neither Private nor Privileged: The Role of Christianity in Britain Today*. He has written a number of books, most recently *Darwin and God* (SPCK, 2009) and (with Professor Robert White) *Christianity, Climate Change and Sustainable Living* (SPCK, 2007). He has also written for *The Guardian, The Times, Church Times* and *The Tablet.*

Nicholas Townsend teaches Christian Ethics at the South East Institute for Theological Education and the University of Kent. Among other posts held, he has been Director of the Politics and Theology Programme at Sarum College in Salisbury and Head of Office for a Member of Parliament.

He has also worked for large and small companies in the private sector.

Nigel Wright has been the Principal of Spurgeon's College, London since 2000. He is an ordained minister with wide experience of both local church leadership and theological education and was President of the Baptist Union of Great Britain from 2002 to 2003. His particular interests have been in the theologies of radical Protestant movements and their implication for church–state relations. He is the author of many books and articles including *The Radical Evangelical* (SPCK, 1996), *Disavowing Constantine* (Paternoster, 2000), *A Theology of the Dark Side* (Paternoster, 2003) and *Free Church, Free State* (Paternoster, 2005).

Tom Wright is Bishop of Durham and is a regular broadcaster on radio and television. He is the author of over 40 books, including the popular For Everyone guides to the New Testament and the magisterial series entitled Christian Origins and the Question of God.

Foreword by the Archbishop of Canterbury

Never mind the crisis of religious faith for a moment; we have become painfully aware in these recent months of a deep crisis of faith in politics. The reputation of elected politicians plummeted in the wake of a series of sensational stories about expenses, and the effects were rapidly obvious in local and European elections.

The cost is great. It is deeply damaging for any society to get used to feeling cynical about its political representatives and leaders; it discourages people of passion and conscience from involvement in politics and helps to nourish a gloomy passivity about public life and shared purpose. And after a seismic shock to our economic life as well, it isn't surprising that the atmosphere in British society is anxious as well as cynical. Just as we needed (and still need) to be reminded to ask the question, 'What's wealth for?' so we need to be prodded into asking, 'What's politics for?'

Christian theology suggests two essential elements for an answer. First: if God's purpose for humanity is a common purpose, not just a set of individual blueprints for escape from a disaster area, we have a duty to ask how the organizing of society makes this purpose harder or easier, more or less attainable. It is not that the church approaches the wider society with a detailed programme which it expects government to enact. But it does offer a series of searching questions about what government can make possible for people and communities – and about what barriers to creative communal life it needs to take away. Second: if God's purpose is not only an idea but something revealed in the concrete events around the history of Jesus, if his purpose is 'incarnate', embodied, then the church is not simply an institution for religious enthusiasts, it is also a sign of possible human futures – in the New Testament's language, a 'pledge' or foretaste of what the grace of the Spirit can do with human material. The church doesn't just provide ideals for society to contemplate; it realizes, however patchily and temporarily, the new creation, the new humanity created out of formerly distant or alienated communities (Ephesians 2.14–15).

So a healthy relation between God and government is not one in which believers demand that the will of God (as they see it) should be enacted without protest by legal systems, nor is it one in which belief in God is treated by government as a probably rather regrettable private eccentricity. It is one in which government accepts that it needs to be challenged pretty constantly as to what it is doing to enable a morally serious project for life together to be taken forward, what it is doing to keep alive a sense of mutual responsibility; and one in which the church examines itself relentlessly as to whether it is being faithful to the fullness of the new humanity in Christ and, in the light of this self-examination, engages in the challenges that will keep society at large both critical and hopeful.

These essays trace some of the leading themes in Christian political theology – the limits and the responsibilities of government, the overriding need to keep working at definitions of the common good, the risks of looking to any one layer or segment of political life for a solution to fundamental human problems, the inescapably 'political' nature of the very existence of the church as embodying a loyalty beyond loyalty to Caesar (whoever happens to be 'Caesar' at any given time). It offers invaluable resources for what is now a sharply urgent task – thinking through the ethical and spiritual foundations of our democracy. If we are unable to do this, we are indeed in deep trouble. But the fact of the church's existence and persistence is, in spite of all, a sign against despair.

+ *Rowan Cantuar:*
from Lambeth Palace, September 2009

Introduction

NICK SPENCER

'This book doesn't have any answers!!!!'

So wails Homer Simpson as he tears through the Bible, looking for advice on what to do about his father who is rolling around on the floor, prophesying hysterically.

Christians engaged in politics, in whatever form, could be excused for agreeing with him.

That there are many Christians interested and engaged in political life is beyond dispute. Each of the mainstream UK political parties has an active Christian constituency and Christian political activity, in the form of lobbying and campaigning on issues as diverse as bioethics and religious freedom, climate change and family life is as animated as ever, perhaps more so. The list of politically active Christian groups – CAFOD, CARE, Christian Aid, Christian Concern for our Nation, Christian Institute, Evangelical Alliance, Faithworks, Salvation Army, Tearfund, World Vision – is long, as is the list of prominent Christian politicians.

There is no doubting the commitment, integrity, energy and faithfulness of these people and groups. Neither political loyalty nor religious commitment is particularly in vogue, and the British are notoriously nervous about mixing the things of God with those of Caesar. To be a 'political Christian', actively engaged in public affairs in contemporary Britain today from an openly Christian position, is likely to reflect a considered, personal decision. It's not the kind of thing you do by accident.

Unfortunately, the strength of that commitment is not always matched by opportunities to acquire great depth of theological analysis. In particular, there is a notable absence of serious thinking on the question of what political Christians should actually be trying to achieve *as political Christians.* Should they seek to maximize individual freedom, on the basis that freedom is a maximal human good and a fundamental achievement of the gospel? Should they try to implement the social vision of the Bible, using legislation and taxation to feed the hungry and house the homeless? Should they be trying to foster traditional Christian social structures, like the family, or values, like respect and social order?

The fact that there is no consensus on these questions, nor ever likely to be, reflects, in part, the contingent and elastic nature of all politics. Politics, especially today, is too technical and too circumstantial to lend itself to an obvious Christian template; or so it often appears. Politics is about developing flexible means towards often indiscernible ends. Christians might be expected to agree on some abstract definition of those ends but there is no earthly reason why they should agree on the means to them. Thus, some Christians have gone as far as to claim, 'It is part of the divine plan that [Christians] should be [politically] divided.'[1] We should not expect to secure Christian political unity or perhaps even convergence on substantive policy priorities. This book acknowledges that reality, with Jonathan Chaplin's conclusion exploring the sources of such political disagreement and tentatively suggesting a response.

Nevertheless, simply to accept that Christians are bound to disagree over the role of government and what they should be seeking to achieve in politics, and to leave it at that, would be to accord too much weight to pragmatic realities. It would also accord too little weight to the fact that, although the book through which Homer Simpson frantically searches doesn't provide technical answers to political questions, it does provide substantive guidance on how to frame and engage with such questions. Its guidance may not be particularly obvious, neatly assembled, focused on contemporary concerns, or framed in current terms, but the Bible has a wealth of serious and important material outlining the central purposes of government, material that has fed a long, rich and, sadly, largely unknown tradition of political theology.[2]

We say 'largely' unknown because, within academic spheres, the discipline of political theology is blooming. The journal *Studies in Christian Ethics* has been in existence since 1988, *Political Theology* since 2000, and the *International Journal of Public Theology* and *Evangelical Review of Society and Politics* since 2007. Such journals have published thoughtful and learned essays on a wide range of political issues, as has the recent *Blackwell Companion to Political Theology* (pub. 2006).

Inevitably, however, these academic resources rarely connect with those Christians who are actively and consciously engaged in the political process. This constitutes a serious omission, which needs addressing.

This book is an attempt to make such a connection. Rather than advocating one particular political position, thereby being a kind of theological Trojan Horse smuggling a particular party allegiance into the unsuspecting mind of the reader, it is a collection of essays, written by political theologians for political Christians, representing a *range* of Christian responses to one, central question: what, according to Christian theology, is the proper function of government? What, in other words, should those Christians engaged with politics, in whatever capacity, be aiming to achieve through their engagement? Each author, in the limited space available to him, articulates an answer to this question by drawing on particular theological positions and traditions, especially Catholic and Evangelical ones, in so doing attempting to persuade political Christians of its merit and validity for contemporary politics.

This is a hazardous task, not so much because it is likely to result in a call to civil disobedience or revolution (though the editors did not impose a three-line whip on such possibilities!), but because translating specialized academic discourse into language accessible to the busy practising politician is a challenging enterprise.

For this reason the guiding question – what, according to Christian theology, is the proper function of government? – is rooted, from the outset, in stubbornly concrete and contemporary terms.

At the time of writing, the state in Britain appropriates around 40 per cent of Gross Domestic Product (GDP).[3] In the mid-1970s this was nearly 50 per cent, on the eve of the Second World War 23 per cent and in 1900 9 per cent.[4] It employs around 20 per cent of the working population, as compared with 23 per cent in 1992 and nearly 28 per cent in 1977.[5] It spends around £189 billion on social protection, £119 billion on health, £88 billion on education and training and £38 billion on defence.[6] By comparison, in the USA total tax revenue as a percentage of GDP stands at 28 per cent. In Switzerland it is 30 per cent, in Germany 36 per cent, in France 44 per cent, in Sweden 48 per cent and in Denmark 49 per cent.[7] In the USA public sector employment accounts for 15 per cent of the population. In France it is around 20 per cent; in Sweden it is over 25 per cent.[8]

Government can also be measured by the volume of legislation that comes before it, recent UK trends of which are complex. The *volume* of primary legislation, that is, the number of Acts, has fallen since the 1950s. Between 1951 and 1955 there were 299 Acts passed, from 2001 to 2005 only 176. While the *number* of Acts has fallen, however, their average length has increased, so that whereas only 540 pages of primary legislation were passed in 1955, this had risen to 2,712 pages by 2005. The volume of secondary legislation, or Statutory Instruments, much of which is not considered by or laid before Parliament, has also increased over recent decades: 10,355 Statutory Instruments were passed between 1951 and 1955, rising to 17,823 between 2001 and 2005. This increase is also reflected in 2,340 pages of Statutory Instruments in 1955 and 11,868 pages 50 years later.[9]

It will seem odd, and perhaps naive, to ask which of these is 'right', and downright perverse to seek an answer from theology. Facts and figures, and the ideas relating to the role of government that shape them, alter over time and according to culture. How can anyone expect a definitive answer?

The answer, of course, is that you cannot and should not. But everyone with an interest in politics will have some sense of the direction in which they believe the answers should lie: what government should actually do, what services it should provide, what level of national income it should appropriate, how it should spend it, etc. It seems only sensible that Christians should form their answer by drawing on their religious convictions at least as much as on other ideological or practical commitments. Or, to put the point more positively: it is surely a matter of Christian faithfulness that our political standpoints are controlled as much as possible by our Christian convictions.

We should not, therefore, expect to derive percentages from the Bible or theological reflection. But we should be hopeful that it can provide us with guidelines that will enable us to arrive at those percentages wisely. How far is it government's duty to organize defence, healthcare, education or social support? How far is it its duty to provide, fund, subsidize or regulate transport, public order, housing or broadcasting? How far and in what way may government legitimately regulate/interfere in (delete according to political taste) the activity of private citizens or non-governmental institutions in each of these areas?

However we answer these questions, there is bound to remain ample room for disagreement, as the contributors to this volume illustrate. Nevertheless, if Christian theology *can* offer guidance on contemporary Christian political engagement – and the editors and contributors to this volume believe it can – it would be foolish to ignore it. It may not ultimately *make* political decisions but it can shape them.

This volume, then, is an attempt to bridge the gap between academic political theology and 'ordinary' political Christians, to translate the thought of the former for the benefit of the latter, thereby equipping them to think, deliberate and act in a way that is well informed by their religious faith. It aims to articulate a series of key principles and positions from within the Christian political tradition, each in response to the fundamental question: what, in the light of your reading of Christian political theology, should be the proper function of government in twenty-first century Britain?

God and Government separates loosely into two parts, the first four chapters exploring the biblical and theological foundations for Christian political thinking, and the second four outlining a series of distinct, sometimes overlapping, sometimes conflicting concepts for the role of government. In reality, there is more in common between the first and second halves than this suggests, as the key ideas that emerge in Chapters 1–4 relating to the legitimacy, limitations, accountability and purpose of government, remain central concerns in Chapters 5–8.

Nigel Wright, Principal of Spurgeon's College in London, opens the volume by exploring how government is fundamentally an ambiguous power, sharing humanity's own created, fallen and redeemed/able nature. In a chapter informed by the free-church tradition, Wright argues that Christians need to engage with government according to this complex, multilayered nature: positively but also sceptically, hopefully but also cautiously. Seeing government through this prism, Wright contends, helps guard against naive, cynical or idolatrous views of government, and orients us towards a view in which the role of government is to maintain orderly, just and prosperous societies – a role, he concludes, that demands the proper separation of church and state.

Julian Rivers, Professor of Jurisprudence at the University of Bristol, explores what the Bible has to say about the nature and role of government. He begins on a similar note to Wright, showing how, from the opening chapters of Genesis through to the closing vision of Revelation, the Bible is somewhat ambivalent about the nature of government. Within this ambivalence, there are discernible guidelines, however. Government is legitimate but should be limited, with Rivers detecting four key elements to that limitation. Government should reflect a commitment to a 'thick', material (rather than 'thin', legal) conception of human equality. It should be subject to law (rather than in control of it). It should operate within workable structures of accountability. And its powers should be divided among a wide range of independent institutions, offices and individuals. All in all, he concludes, the Bible lends considerable support to the idea of a constitution, in the sense of 'a collective commitment that we shall live together in *this* way as most conducive to our common freedom and well-being'.

Tom Wright, Bishop of Durham, then looks at the role of government in the light of the New Testament and particularly the imperial context in which it was written.

Emphasizing how 'Jesus is Lord' was a profoundly and provocatively *political* statement in a world in which Caesar's lordship was (often violently) enforced, Wright shows how Paul and the evangelists outline the gospel's powerful anti-imperial critique, while avoiding any anarchistic implications. He argues that governments operate within the space between tyranny and anarchy, ordained by God (even if unwittingly) to maintain peace and order but themselves fallen, tempted and under judgment, 'summoned to obedience to the Prince of Peace'.

David McIlroy, Visiting Senior Lecturer in Law at SOAS, moves the narrative on and examines the history of the idea of government in Christian political thought, from Augustine, Gregory of Nazianzus and Pope Gregory the Great, through Aquinas, Luther and Calvin to Karl Barth and Pope John XXIII. Recognizing that all these figures were of their time he argues that they still have much to teach us. In particular, he traces four key principles for government through the classical history of Christian political theology. First, that government is accountable to God; second, that government's role is limited; third, that government exists for the public good; and fourth, that the task of government is the wise execution of just judgment. He contends that understood together – government as (limited and accountable) just judgment in the cause of the public good – these principles provide a valid foundation for government today, going on to explore how they relate to questions of law and morality, and rights and responsibilities.

Although written independently of these first four chapters, the subsequent four, Chapters 5–8, draw on a number of shared themes in their attempts to articulate a clear Christian vision of what government should do. Nicholas Townsend, from the South East Institute for Theological

Education (SEITE) and the University of Kent, argues that government exists to provide the *social infrastructure* necessary for people to participate fully in the common good. He places the Christian conception of politics within its broader theological context, arguing that Christians can only come to understand what God expects of government if they have grasped God's fuller plan for human flourishing. Thus, he contends, 'the Christian polity . . . through its ministries of word, sacrament and pastoral care . . . is the primary mode by which God wishes to bring into being good relations among people'. The role of government, he argues, is to provide the infrastructure necessary for this to happen, such as by combating sins of commission (i.e. those crimes that actively prevent people's participation in the common good), and addressing sins of omission (i.e. giving people access to a range of basic goods such as food, water and healthcare that enable them to participate in the common good).

Although not writing from an explicitly Catholic position, Nick Townsend draws on the important resource of Catholic Social Teaching (CST) in formulating his idea that government should be about providing social infrastructure. CST is also central to the following two chapters. Philip Booth, Editorial and Programme Director at the Institute of Economic Affairs, draws on CST and in particular the twinned ideas of solidarity and subsidiarity. Solidarity, he argues, is primarily an 'attitude and virtue' which, translated into good works, should pervade *all* our actions, whether in the home, workplace or any social or community group. Subsidiarity, on the other hand, is a principle that insists that because action through the political sphere is necessarily coercive, thereby circumscribing individual and corporate creativity, it should be a last resort. Between them, these linked principles call for political structures that exist to aid the individual and the community, thereby promoting the common good.

Booth earths this discussion by exploring how subsidiarity and solidarity should operate together to shape our engagement with taxation and charity, arguing that 'Even a government of a distinctly Christian character should not take upon itself the duties of Christian communities to share goods, provide welfare and look after the aged and sick, except where efforts to provide these functions in other ways have failed.' He then applies the same logic to environmentalism, concluding that the solution to environmental problems, even international ones like climate change, lies in governments applying principles of subsidiarity within a framework of solidarity, such as by assigning 'polluting rights', like carbon credits, to individual polluters.

The following chapter, by the prominent Catholic social commentator Clifford Longley, also draws on CST, specifically the idea of the common good, and in doing so comes to rather different conclusions from Philip Booth. Longley argues that the common good is not one principle among many in Catholic Social Teaching, or even the first among equals, but rather the overarching principle against which *all* other principles should be measured. The principle of the common good puts to all policy proposals the simple question, 'Does this serve the common good?'

In understanding the principle of the common good in this way, Longley does not so much advocate a large or a small state (although, in practice, his vision for government is undoubtedly larger than Philip Booth's) as one that is responsive to particular circumstances. That is not to suggest that the government's role in enabling the common good is simply pragmatic, however. Longley concludes by exploring what the state's possible role in administering the common good might be, by comparing two strands of recent Catholic thinking on the topic. In the former, a tradition that Pope John Paul II seemed to be following, the common good was very much the business of the state; whereas in the latter, a tradition that followed the Second Vatican Council's *Declaration on Religious Liberty*, a more limited scope for the role of government was envisaged, confined primarily to the preservation of public order, rather than to active interventions to improve the lot of citizens. By way of conclusion, Longley underlines how this issue links into the question of what role *religion* should officially play vis-à-vis the state, thereby returning to issues raised by Nigel Wright in his chapter.

In the final chapter, Andrew Bradstock, Howard Paterson Professor of Theology and Public Issues at the University of Otago in New Zealand, explores how ensuring a degree of equality is a critically important task for any government informed by Christian principles. He identifies the idea of human beings' equal worth and status in the creation narratives of Genesis, and contends that a concern that none should be denied their basic needs pervades every book of the Bible, from the social arrangements in the Torah, through the warnings and visions of the prophets, the Magnificat, Jesus' teaching and ministry, right the way to the practice of the early church.

That established, Bradstock recognizes that there are many different ways of understanding equality and that 'equal' does not necessarily mean 'the same'. Eschewing the idea that society can somehow legislate to make people generous, let alone any thought of returning to the heavily bureaucratic 'command economy' models of the defunct Soviet bloc, he insists that government has a very real role to play in ensuring that meaningful equality (at least of opportunity if not of income) is achieved and maintained.

Thus, he advocates not only tax reform that reduces income inequality and an end to 'privileged education' which creates other unfair advantages, but also – in an idea redolent of Clifford Longley's treatment of the common good – an approach by means of which the equality question is asked of all policies. Political parties should thus undertake to 'poverty proof' all their policies to ensure that they are consistent with, for example, the goal of eradicating child poverty.

Between them, then, Chapters 5–8 put into concrete and contemporary terms some of the ideas explored in Chapters 1–4. Contributors do not agree entirely on the Christian idea of the role of government (although that was something of a *fait accompli* given the brief each contributor was assigned) but, as a rule, they do concur with the framework, set out in those early chapters, within which these ideas operate. This is outlined by Jonathan Chaplin, Director of the Kirby Laing Institute for Christian Ethics, who explores the framework, shared ideas and points of difference in his conclusion to the volume.

Chaplin recognizes that the contributors are reluctant to offer precise policy recommendations in their chapters, but argues that this is because the Christian principles on which they draw – like all political principles – do not generate such precision. Christians should no more expect to discern the 'correct' size of the public sector workforce from the pages of the Bible, than liberals to discern, from John Stuart Mill's *On Liberty*, whether the UK government is right to deny entry to controversial Dutch politicians, invited to present a film about Islam in Parliament.[10]

The ideas within each book can inform the thinking behind such decisions, of course, and that is precisely what *God and Government*'s contributors have done. Their work can help practitioners acquire political wisdom, understood as the skill of rightly applying a coherent body of Christian political principle.

Chaplin notes that there appears to be consensus among political theologians that the Christian understanding of government is that it is created, fallen, but open to redemption; legitimate, limited, accountable, diffused and representative; and, crucially, established to secure justice and the common good. Such commonality recognized, however, Chaplin also acknowledges that there are genuine and significant points of difference in various Christian political visions. In part these differences arise because of different understandings of the basic theological themes of creation, fall and redemption. But they also arise from different interpretations of political principles like justice and the common good, and in particular from contrasting readings of the principles of subsidiarity, solidarity and equality as is seen especially in Chapters 6, 7 and 8.

This is by no means an insuperable obstacle and, indeed, in some ways it is precisely what we should expect. It might be questionable whether political division is actually 'part of the divine plan', but it is undeniably the case that it is part of our earthly, fallen, waiting-to-be-redeemed reality. Christians should certainly not ignore points of difference or, worse, coerce one another into a particular political line, simply for the sake of order or unity. Yet they should work hard to establish points of agreement and to work together wherever they can.

The editors wish to extend their sincere thanks to each of the contributors to this volume. It is our sincere regret that they are all men – although it should be emphasized that was not for want of asking! Political theology is not an exclusively male discipline and there are a good number of very fine female political theologians working in the UK at the moment. Unfortunately, for various reasons, none that we approached felt able to contribute to this volume. Thankfully, the erudition, sophistication and accessibility of each of our eight contributors managed to make this omission less injurious than it might otherwise have been.

The book is the outcome of a joint project between Theos, the public theology think tank, and the Kirby Laing Institute for Christian Ethics. We would also like to extend our thanks to the staff at Theos, Paul Woolley, Paul Bickley and Jennie Pollock, for their valuable assistance throughout. This project was made possible by generous grants from the Hinchley Charitable Trust, the Jerusalem Trust, the Mercers' Trust, John Langlois, Crispin Odey, and Jeremy and Jo Sweetland, to whom we are immensely grateful.

It is our hope that this volume will play a serious role over the coming years in persuading Christians that politics is an honourable and worthwhile vocation (in spite of what the notorious parliamentary expenses scandal of 2009 has left many thinking); in showing them that there is a wealth of fruitful and relevant material in the Bible and Christian political thought on which they can draw in pursuing that vocation; and in fostering political wisdom that will contribute to the health of our political culture and the common good it seeks to advance.

Notes

1 Ann Widdecombe, Archbishop Worlock Memorial Lecture, 2006.

2 An omission that has begun to be rectified over recent years, not least through the publication of Oliver O'Donovan and Joan Lockwood O'Donovan's massive sourcebook in political theology, *From Irenaeus to Grotius: A Sourcebook in Christian Political Thought 100–1625* (Grand Rapids: Eerdmans, 1999).

3 HM Treasury, *Budget 2009: Building Britain's Future*, April 2009, Table C7 (<http://www.hm-treasury.gov.uk/d/Budget

2009/bud09_completereport_2520.pdf>). It should be noted that this figure is some way below the current figure for public spending, with the shortfall being made up by an unprecedentedly high level of borrowing.

4 Tom Clark and Andrew Dilnot, *Long-Term Trends in British Taxation and Spending*, Institute for Fiscal Studies, Briefing Note 25, 2002.

5 Stephen Hicks, *Trends in Public Sector Employment*, Office for National Statistics, Labour Market Trends, 2005, accessible at <http://www.statistics.gov.uk/articles/labour_market_trends/pub_sec_trend.pdf>.

6 HM Treasury, *Budget 2009: Building Britain's Future*, April 2009, Chart 1.1, accessible at <http://www.hm-treasury.gov.uk/d/Budget2009/bud09_completereport_2520.pdf>.

7 These data are from the OECD, <http://stats.oecd.org/WBOS/Index.aspx?DataSetCode=CSP2009> but, unlike the comparative UK data given above, refer to 2007 and so do not take into account changes made in response to the credit crisis and recession beginning in 2008.

8 OECD, *Employment in Government in the Perspective of the Production Costs of Goods and Services in the Public Domain* (2008), accessible at <http://www.olis.oecd.org/olis/2008doc.nsf/LinkTo/NT00000A16/$FILE/JT03239319.PDF> (data are from 2005).

9 Data from Office of Public Sector Information, <www.opsi.gov.uk>.

10 As the government did with the Dutch Freedom Party MP Geert Wilders in February 2009.

1

Government as an ambiguous power

NIGEL WRIGHT

The argument of this chapter is that governments and the process of governing must be regarded with ambivalence. It is appropriate, therefore, always to retain a degree of suspicion about them and, most particularly, for Christian communities, whether in their local, national or international forms of expression, to maintain a critical distance from them. However, this stance should not be seen as an attempt to be apolitical. Rather, it is in itself a form of political activity when this is broadly conceived. Critical distance enables churches to sustain their distinctive identity and therefore to offer a clearer witness to the 'powers that be' by means of an exemplary and prophetic way of life. In this way, churches can contribute to social improvement and transformation. Furthermore, individual Christians are encouraged to participate in the political process and in government itself and to do so in ways that are fully informed by Christian perspectives and ethics. But since the essence of political activity involves judgments that are themselves partial and limited, they do well not to overestimate their ability to put forward 'the Christian point of view'. In the history of Christian thought the ambiguity of government has been identified from a wide variety of Christian theological standpoints. This chapter is particularly informed by the history of the free churches which have stood at the radical end of the Reformation spectrum of churches.

The nature of Christian belief

Present-day Christians are the inheritors of a huge quantity of creative theological and philosophical thinking, so much so that any one of us will simply be scratching the surface of what has been thought and said by our forebears in the faith. This is certainly true when it comes to 'political theology', the impact of belief on the ways in which we conceive of government.[1] In addition, Christian belief is richly textured in that it requires us to hold together ideas that may be in tension with each other but whose value consists in the tension itself. To abolish the tension, or to stray towards one aspect of it to the detriment of the other, is to risk distorting and losing the belief.

One modern textbook on theology, by Roger Olson, makes the idea of tension the very lens through which Christian theology is to be seen. Christian belief repeatedly asserts *both/and* rather than *either/or*. When speaking of God, for instance, Christians insist that God is both *three* and *one* and end up with the classic doctrine of the Trinity by which they insist that the one God should be thought of as a 'triunity' of persons, Father, Son and Spirit. Likewise they insist that Jesus Christ is both *fully divine* and *fully human* and end up with the idea of the mediator who can act towards human beings on behalf of God, and towards God on behalf of human beings. Similarly, salvation is seen as both a *gift* and a *task*, something that is given to us by God through grace and yet which, once given, has to be worked out in a changed way of thinking and living. In all of these examples, to abolish the tension and insist, for instance, that God is one but not three, that Christ is fully human but not divine, or that salvation is the result of a task rather than in itself a gift, would be to depart from Christian belief as it has been normatively understood.[2]

Otherwise stated, at almost every point Christian belief invites us to think several thoughts simultaneously. This may be why across the spectrum of Christian believers there exists such diversity of belief. In large measure, this could be a question of diversity in unity and so a demonstration of the very idea we are illustrating.[3]

The point to which we are leading is that when we come to consider government, the state and politics we must, in keeping with the whole tenor of Christian belief, hold together several ideas simultaneously. We are in a both/and situation. To clarify this further, it is helpful to see how the both/and way of thinking applies to human beings and human nature.

Theological anthropology

According to Olson we live in a world which is both *good* and *fallen*.[4] Correspondingly, within this creation human beings should be understood as *essentially good* and yet *existentially estranged*.[5] These ideas will provide us with some necessary pointers to understanding the ambiguity of government.

Since the world has its origin in God it must be fundamentally and structurally good. So it is that in the opening creation narrative of Genesis 1 the Creator repeatedly affirms that the universe called into being is 'good'. Matter and earthly, finite existence are not evil but inherently good. This is a positive approach to the natural order and undergirds other Christian beliefs. The world is purposeful and productive and to live within it is a blessing. However, it also all too obviously contains suffering, pain and conflict. The good creation has been disrupted and distorted in some way, exactly how being a matter for debate. Either it has been diverted from its original created condition, such as by the sin and fall of human beings (the dominant approach of Christian tradition, although for some more difficult to hold in the light of scientific knowledge) or it has been suppressed in its onward progress towards peaceful perfection, such as by the failure of human beings to assume their proper place of stewardship and responsibility within the creation.[6]

Romans 8.20 is a pivotal verse here: 'For the creation was subjected to futility, not of its own will but by the will of the one who subjected it.' That the world is in 'bondage to decay' (v. 21) is not in question. It plainly is. What is not clear is how this subjection has come to be: is the agent of its subjection God, or 'Adam' or someone else, such as the devil? The verse leaves us wondering. However it has happened, there is universal agreement that the world as it is, is not the way it is supposed to be.[7] It has either fallen away from what it was when originally created by God, or it is falling short of what it is called to be, or both. Whichever way, this good world is also a fallen world, and both ideas need to be held together to gain perspective.

Human beings are clearly portrayed in the Christian scriptures and in Christian belief as pivotal to the whole creation and at the heart of its problems. They are 'shalom vandals'[8] in that they have violated the peace of the creation. But prior to this they are seen as creatures made in the image of God, who have been called to a unique place in creation as the apex of its development.[9] For this reason when they were created they were not only proclaimed to be 'good' but 'very good'. Like the creation itself, therefore, human beings are good but fallen, essentially good but existentially estranged from their true nature and vocation, unable and unwilling to rise to their proper calling to exist in God's image and likeness. It follows that everything that grows out of human nature and community reflects this same tension and shares the same condition. This is where we might address the question of government.

The powers

The New Testament has a surprising amount to say about 'the powers',[10] by which it may be understood to mean 'the invisible forces that determine human existence'.[11] Here is the recognition that human existence is not merely a matter of individuals who subsist in isolation but of an extensive matrix of real but unseen forces that shape human life and provide the context in which it exists. Governmental power, in whatever form, belongs to this matrix, and shares in the condition of being good but fallen. In a pivotal statement Walter Wink argues that the powers that constitute what he calls 'the Domination System' should be understood as being simultaneously good, fallen and to be redeemed.[12]

> It is precisely this simultaneity of creation, fall and redemption that delivers us from naivety regarding our personal or social powers for transformation. It liberates us from the illusion that at least some institutions are 'good' and viable and within human direction, or can be rendered so by discipline or reform or revolution or displacement. The powers are at one and the same time ordained by God and in the power of Satan. They can, to some degree, be open to transcendence but they will still do evil. They may be benign, but within a Domination System of general malignance.[13]

Here, then, is where we encounter the element of ambiguity. It is not as though the powers were initially good, then successively fallen and to be redeemed. Rather, they are to be regarded as all of these things simultaneously. This ambiguity needs always to be borne in mind when contemplating the relationship between God and government.

As this pattern of thought is crucial to the argument of this chapter it is worth developing in greater detail.

The powers as created

If the creation God has called into being and established is structurally and essentially good it ought to follow that whatever develops *legitimately* out of this creation is also good (sin and evil being deviant and illegitimate developments). The portrayal of God's creative work in the early chapters of Genesis leaves ample room for development within creation. God initiates creation and bestows on it the ability and the necessity to 'bring forth'.[14]

Creation is well understood as a divine work of calling all things into being, invested with the potential to become, to realize the potential which is inherent within the original creation and to share in a continuing creativity in which God lets creation be. Creation is not static and complete but a continuing process whereby God allows it to be fruitful and abundant. In response to the divine command creatures are active in co-creating with God. Nowhere is this more clearly stated than in relation to human beings who are placed under the divine command and have permission to 'Be fruitful and multiply, and fill the earth and subdue it; and have dominion over the fish of the sea and over the birds of the air and over every living thing that moves upon the earth.'[15]

These words plainly refer in the first instance to biological reproduction, but they should not be limited to this. In the calling to exercise dominion (which should not be understood as exploitation but as responsible stewardship) there is also the work of governing, directing and developing culture. This is sometimes described as the 'cultural mandate'. The building of societies, nations and cultures is thus understood as part of human responsibility before God, part of what we are called to do.

Human beings are the source of communities, institutions, governments and culture. These things do not exist in and of themselves as abstract or discrete entities but only as a product of human activity and ingenuity. They do not precede the human race but emerge from it. The potential to form and create them is part of what makes humans human and their purpose is the blessing and enhancement of human – and nonhuman – life. Governments and states are the product of human activity and would have no existence were it not for the human beings that constitute them. On the other hand, because they are the product of human communal existence they assume definite characters and have genuine power. The whole that is created out of human cooperation is certainly more than the sum of the individual parts. Experience suggests many examples of the ways in which humanly created laws, institutions and agencies can improve and empower individuals and foster human flourishing. All of this suggests that concern for human well-being and the search for the good life that goes with it must involve equal concern for the health of communal and corporate institutions which make such well-being possible. Whether these include the need to protect people from danger and harm, or to promote health, or to create wealth and share it so that all may benefit, or to make sure that all are fairly and humanely treated, the governmental task is an appropriate area for responsible Christian stewardship and activity.

In each of the above items – protecting people, promoting health, creating wealth and so on – we see that aspect of 'the powers' that can rightly be described as created and 'good'. There is a diversity of ways in which they can find expression. It is not as though there is a pre-ordained divine structure which exists outside human beings and into which they have to fit. To be sure, we all have to live out our lives within that which we inherit, but the 'state' is malleable in that it can take different forms at different times. It can change, as has frequently happened over time. But at its best the state should be understood as bestowing agency upon human communities. It might be understood as the way in which a whole community can act to achieve its goals, to do together what it would be impossible to achieve on its own. This is its great value. The vocation to politics and the shaping of public life is therefore a noble and constructive one which is a form of service for the well-being of all.

The powers as fallen

Noble though it may be, the picture just painted threatens to deceive, for 'government of the people, by the people, for the people'[16] is very rarely what government has ever succeeded in being. A review of the forms taken by the state in the Bible reveals a fairly typical sample, ranging from the oppressive regimes of the Pharaohs in Egypt, to the brutal empires of Assyria and Babylon, to the effective and ordered but often inhumane Roman Empire. Israel or the church suffered from each of these powers in turn. It is no surprise that both in the book of Daniel and in the book of Revelation the empires of this world are portrayed as ravaging beasts.[17] Not only so, but with some honourable exceptions the institution of kingship within Israel was itself a failure, as the prophet Samuel had warned from the beginning.[18] If governments and institutions grow out of communal human existence then they will not only express the created and therefore good aspect of human nature but will also reflect and reproduce the fallen and sinful nature to which those human beings have turned. It is inevitable therefore that governmental powers will be as corrupt as human beings have become.

Understood from this distinctively negative angle government has little to do with serving the people and a great deal to do with serving the interests of those who are in power. As Wink suggests, governments are an expression of domination, wielding power through violent means over the majority for the sake of the elite. Jesus offered his own critique when he said, 'The kings of the Gentiles lord it over them; and those in authority over them are called benefactors. But not so with you.'[19] Jesus apparently saw that the actual reality of kingship was the exercise of domination, but that this was cloaked with an ideology of benefaction.

The enjoyment of power and its fruits is usually concealed by some pretence that it is good for people. Jesus told his disciples to have nothing to do with this. Human governments invariably have their origins in conquest and domination. Only slowly and over long periods has this been qualified and modified to serve the interests of the many rather than the few. An absolute monarchy might be modified through time and conflict into a constitutional monarchy, or even no monarchy at all, but such changes come at a cost. Power is never easily given up. Even in the most democratic of countries it should be asked whether the people's interests are really paramount or whether the pretence that they are is simply another ideological device for keeping one elite or another in power. The dice will always be loaded in favour of the haves against the have-nots.

Government therefore is an ambiguous power, God-given and honourable from one angle, an arena for power games, self-enrichment and oppression from another. When the honourable aspect is to the fore governments can achieve much that is good. When the oppressive dimension is in view governments are capable of immense destruction and cruelty, as the dictatorial regimes of the twentieth century amply demonstrated.

The powers as 'to be redeemed'

This third dimension grows out of the fact that human beings are created by God, fallen from their vocation and yet capable of being redeemed. 'Fallenness' is not the last word about anything or anybody. Just as human beings can be redeemed so ought human institutions, including governments, to be redeemed to fulfil their life-enhancing, God-given roles.

A word of qualification is necessary here, however: the redemption of the state, just like the redemption of human beings, will only be accomplished fully in the fullness of time when God's purposes reach their fulfilment. It is only then that the song will go up, 'The kingdom of the world has become the kingdom of our Lord and of his Messiah.'[20] The redemption of government is best understood in this age as partial and limited.

Nevertheless, given the power of the state, any improvement in its ability to enhance life, promote justice and secure peace and prosperity for all is greatly to be welcomed. Drawing state power towards the service of justice and kindness is clearly in its own way both an expression of the created purpose of the powers and also a form of redemption. Yet this is where the concept of 'simultaneity' is to be recalled: governments never lose their character as fallen powers and are therefore never beyond reverting to type. Optimism needs to be tempered with realism. Hope is not to be placed in political leaders but in God. Still, not to seek to draw the powers towards a better way is to submit to complacency and despair. All humans have an interest in stable, competent and just government and governments need to be sufficiently strong to accomplish their objectives.

So far we have sought to establish the basic idea that government is an ambiguous power. To focus only on the created nature of the powers might result in naivety concerning their destructive potential. To focus only on their fallen nature might lead to a paranoia that neglects the good they might do. To overemphasize the capacity for redemption might lead to undue and deceptive optimism about what they might accomplish. To judge with accurate judgment it is essential to hold these three aspects of the powers together in tension. At any given time in any given place one or other aspect of the powers might be more in evidence. Christians in general and believing politicians in particular need to be alert to this. There have been times when governments have assumed a demonic character in whole or in part and are more to be resisted than obeyed. There are other times when there is opportunity for reform and reshaping and such opportunities should not be missed. Understanding the signs of the times is both a matter of spiritual discernment and of political judgment.

What now follows is an attempt to draw out some of the implications of the model we have been working with. These are particularly informed by the free-church tradition which has stood at the radical end of Protestantism.[21] The Protestant Reformation of the sixteenth century had very considerable political implications. In large measure this was because it shifted the locus of authority away from external institutions and their rulers towards the authority of the biblical text, and the right of believers to interpret it themselves rather than simply accept the interpretation handed down to them by the ecclesiastical authority. This opened the door to dissent and disobedience of authority wrongfully exercised.[22] In particular, Protestantism's rejection of the absolute power of the Church of Rome led potentially to a corresponding rejection of political absolutism.[23] The turn away from the teaching authority of the church to the right of every Christian to read and interpret the Bible has also been significant in revaluing the place of individual conscience and freedom within the political order.[24] The free churches were at the radical end of this positive dynamic.

The order of preservation

It might be true to say that the free-church tradition has been more negative towards governments and the state than others. However, this has generally only extended to attempts by governments to establish religious conformity and to override conscientiously held convictions. In all other respects, the functions of government have been regarded as legitimate. In particular, the need to maintain order and to punish wrongdoers has in principle been widely understood and welcomed as both biblical and necessary.[25] When government keeps within its proper limits there is every reason to obey its laws and, as opportunity presents itself, to participate at every level in its service. This might include in the legislature, in the executive, in administration and in the work of the magistracy. When government goes beyond its proper bounds to demand that which can only be demanded by God the watchword has always been, 'We must obey God rather than any human authority.'[26]

If interfering with consciences is an illegitimate activity taking governments beyond their proper sphere, the question needs to be asked, what are the proper tasks of government? Before answering this positively it is as well to examine another fundamentally important text which is often referred to when discussing the interface between faith and politics. This is Luke 20.25 (paralleled in Matthew 22.21 and Mark 12.17) where Jesus says, 'Then give to the emperor the things that are the emperor's, and to God the things that are God's.' This 'rendering unto Caesar' is not an attempt by Jesus to set out a neat political theology according to which Caesar exists in one circle and God in another, each with legitimate but separate demands. It is a characteristically enigmatic response by Jesus to a question designed to trap him, a non-answer in that it immediately invites a second question – namely, what does belong to Caesar?

The point is that *everything belongs to God, including Caesar*, and that the only thing that should be given to Caesar is what God apportions to him. Governments, like everything else in creation, are accountable to God. The emperor, or the government, is not an object of absolute devotion and for governments to claim such loyalty is to set themselves up as idols. Because the powers are fallen this is something they have often attempted to do. In fact, the refusal to call Caesar Lord or to offer worship to him was exactly what brought persecution on early Christians. Instead, governments and states are powers subordinate to God and ordered by God for certain specific purposes.

The first of these purposes concerns the maintenance of order. The alternative is tribal conflict, general anarchy and unfettered criminality. A fallen world in which people pursue their own self-interests to the detriment and oppression of others requires the maintenance of order. Another of the classic biblical texts concerning God and government states that 'those authorities that exist have been instituted by God' and goes on to say,

> Do you wish to have no fear of the authority? Then do what is good, and you will receive its approval; for it is God's servant for your good. But if you do what is wrong, you should be afraid, for the authority does not bear the sword in vain! It is the servant of God to execute wrath on the wrongdoer.[27]

This passage is not without problems for us in that it could be taken as a mandate to give unqualified support to any government. It needs to be read therefore in the light of what has already been said about obeying God above all. However, we can deduce the following principles: (1) government as such is to be respected as part of God's providential care of the world; (2) governments possess the power of 'the sword', which should be taken as the power to coerce and to punish crimes; (3) this power is to be used not against those who behave well but against wrongdoers; (4) when governments act in this way they are serving God in being agents of 'wrath', the divine hostility to wrong and destructive behaviour, and they are serving people in protecting and preserving them and avenging them when they have been wronged.

Although inevitably all of the above will be done imperfectly, the maintenance of a just and peaceful order is a primary function of government.

What is also striking about this verse is its use of the language of servanthood. The authority is 'God's servant for your good'. Governments are not called to domineer but to serve and to do this by seeking the welfare of those who are governed. This leads to the following two extensions.

First, governments serve the preservation of peace and assist the good of the people by fostering and supporting healthy institutions and community structures. Healthy and secure communities are less likely to turn to violence and crime. This by no means implies government ownership of such structures (often called 'intermediate'), but a recognition of their value in enabling human community and of the fact that governments with their power to coerce can help or hinder them.

Second, governments are called to serve God and people by promoting justice and well-being both in the exercise of criminal justice and in the development of societal structures which humanize and dignify rather than brutalize and oppress. This can be seen as an aspect of the redemption of the powers leading to the improvement of human society.

Together these various functions of government can be described as 'the order of preservation'. Government belongs to the order of preservation in that it serves to stabilize and maintain orderly, just and prosperous societies. In this framework people can live out their lives personally and communally and develop their potential. The degree to which any government achieves this high calling depends upon its acceptance of a servant status in which the management of power is seen as a stewardship to be exercised for the common good, rather than a means by which the few enrich themselves, materially and in other ways, at the expense of the many. The formation of such an ethos in government is bound up with the religious and ideological commitments of the communities out of which it arises and so inevitably links up with the discussion of religion and government.

The order of redemption

Even in the modern Western world, which has been marked by growing secularization, it is still clear that the relationship between religion and government is a live and contentious one. The free-church tradition has consistently argued for a clear distinction to be made between church and state, and therefore between all religions and governmental power. This has led to a doctrine, both theological and political, known as 'the separation of church and state'. Although accepted now as a staple of political theory, the origins of this doctrine lie in the call by early free-church pioneers for religious liberty and the rejection of the assumption that each state needed a religious authority to legitimate it.[28]

The state was understood to have its own integrity under God without the need for an 'established' or validating religion. This has been taken up on a wider front even by those who reject any form of religion. Throughout history worldly power has been assumed to require a religious validation to the extent that political dissent has been penalized as a form of irreligion or even of blasphemy. Through the free-church experience of persecution, it has gradually become established in many countries, but by no means all, that a person's standing and value as a citizen is not dependent on his or her religious beliefs. The latter should be left to personal conscience and not treated as a matter of public qualification or disqualification. This represents a shift from religious conformity to religious liberty and from a religious state to a plural, secular or non-sectarian state.[29] However, the separation of church and state remains a contested doctrine. It is helpful to set out what it is not before explaining what it is.

First, it does not imply *the separation of church from society*. Churches and other faith communities and the multiple institutions they generate are an integral part of community life and society at large. The state, or government, is not society itself, but the hard edge of society, given in order that society might be maintained. Separation of church and state does not therefore imply a strategy of withdrawal on the part of the church whereby it retreats into the private and mystical realm and takes no part in the public realm.

Granted that some religious groups do take this approach, they usually do so by overemphasizing the fallen rather than the created or redeemable dimensions of the powers.

Second, it cannot imply *the independence of the church from the state* as though what takes place in one can have no effect upon the other. To the contrary, institutions shape each other. State legislation, taxation policy, financial security, legal provisions for charities and the general well-being or otherwise of state institutions will make their impact upon faith communities. Traffic will also flow the other way as church initiatives, especially in the area of education and social care, will contribute to, supplement and sometimes replace government activity.

Third, it does not mean *the separation of the church from politics*. This is especially the case when 'politics' is understood more broadly than the central organs of state alone. All of life is political in that it involves processes of negotiating, agreeing and managing our common life. 'Politicalness'[30] is intrinsic to corporate life, whether this is in schools, trades unions, local councils, charities or congregations. Moreover, in all of these realms there is a continual discussion about what constitutes the goods that we have in common and how on the basis of shared or sometimes contested values we are to find the ground that will make life most fulfilling for all. This inevitably touches on the moral and existential beliefs we bring to the discussion, whether as people of religious or secular faith.[31]

Fourth, separation of church and state ought not to mean *the systematic exclusion of religion from public life*. This is what some have taken it to mean with a strong but negative emphasis, especially in the USA, on Thomas Jefferson's 'wall of separation' between the church and the state.[32] The complete exclusion of religion from the public realm is presumably based on the idea that religion is a poison.[33] This is clearly the goal of a certain kind of secularist. But it would simply signify the introduction of a different kind of established religion, the secularist version, with its own forms of priesthood and control. Hard secularism of this kind has already demonstrated that it is capable of greater atrocities than religion has ever managed to achieve.[34]

How, then, is the separation of church and state to be understood? It represents a clear desire to distinguish between the order of preservation served by government and the order of redemption served by the church.[35] Both are necessary but since the order of preservation requires the use of coercion and force, there needs at this point to be a clear separation between the way governments fulfil their mandate and the way the church (and indeed any religious movement) pursues its mission. Coercion, force or violence do not serve the coming of the kingdom of a God who is supremely revealed in a Messiah who gave himself up to death on a cross and taught his disciples to love their enemies and do good to those who persecuted them.[36] The preservation of human societies is an essential work but it cannot achieve human redemption. What it can do is provide the framework of peace and security within which the gospel of Christ can be proclaimed, and that gospel is the power of God for salvation.[37]

To separate church and state allows the church to be itself, and frees it for its prophetic task of witness. All Christians are called to be exemplary citizens and to seek the welfare of whatever society they belong to.[38] Since they are no longer subservient to the agenda of governments and the powerful, however, free churches are not under any obligation to give religious legitimation to the powers. This increases their value to society since communities of constructive dissent have the capacity to incubate new ways of living together and to stimulate social change. Reciprocally, freeing the state from religious control (if not religious influence) means that it can take its place as a modest instrument of the common good and can do so impartially and fairly. It need penalize none for their beliefs but can grant the space in which they can negotiate their own freely chosen religious decisions rather than acting out of fear of coercion should they fail to conform. In this way 'a free church in a free state' works both for the benefit of true religion and for a free, non-persecutory society.[39]

To separate religion and state in the way indicated suggests that churches should not have any form of established status nor should they seek any privileges for themselves that are not equally to be shared by other faiths and ideologies. This is a form of love for neighbour. Churches and religious bodies are wise not to enter into any binding or limiting arrangements with government but to maintain a critical distance from power. But individual members of the church should be free and encouraged to participate freely in all dimensions of government activity as conscience allows them. When they do so it is as citizens who happen to be Christians rather than Christians enjoying some kind of established privilege. If Jesus' metaphor of being 'salt and light' is to be followed, Christians have the capacity by their presence and quality of life both to work against any corruption that they find and to encourage and stimulate the good that they will also find.[40]

A possible biblical example of political action and witness along these lines comes from the accounts of Elijah recorded in 1 Kings 18. To follow this illustration it is important to see that Elijah was the official voice of the God of Israel, and known as such, whereas Obadiah was a faithful Israelite, but anonymously, perhaps even secretly so. Elijah was a prophetic voice in opposition to the then king, Ahab, who presided over a government hostile to Elijah's faith. Elijah was able to deliver his witness precisely because he was at a distance from the 'domination system' over which Ahab presided. Yet at the same time Obadiah, described as being 'in charge of the palace' and so one of Ahab's chief ministers, was working within the system to subvert it. In a time when the queen, Jezebel, was 'killing off the prophets of the LORD', Obadiah was able to take a hundred of them and shelter them in order to save their lives (vv. 3–4). Elijah's part in this as the 'official' representative of the faith depended on being at a critical distance. Yet Obadiah could only do what he did as an 'unofficial' representative of that same faith. Both were true to their calling and both had their place. The church as such, as an identifiable body, is most free to exercise its witness when it maintains a critical distance from power in a non-established position, dancing to its own tune rather than someone else's. Individual Christians, acting as citizens, are at liberty to work within and manage power structures, yet should do so with consciences shaped and informed by their Christian beliefs. Together these approaches maximize Christian witness.

Conclusion

Government is an ambiguous business that can be viewed negatively or positively, hopefully or pessimistically, depending whether its created, fallen or 'to be redeemed' dimensions are to the fore. In a world whose governments manifest every part of the possible spectrum, the model I have proposed is capable of considerable flexibility. The amount of space devoted to discussing the separation of church and state could be taken to mean that issues of faith and politics are very far from being past: they are alive and well and living in every country on earth.

This chapter offers few clues as to whose policies might be most 'Christian' but this is because politics and government are about complex decisions, always subject to the law of unintended consequences, often about the lesser of two evils and legislating in less than ideal ways for human 'hardness of heart'.[41] To recognize the ambiguity of governmental power is to provide the context in which theological and political wisdom might be exercised.[42]

Notes

1 Oliver and Joan Lockwood O'Donovan, *Bonds of Imperfection: Christian Politics, Past and Present* (Grand Rapids: Eerdmans, 2004).
2 Roger E. Olson, *The Mosaic of Christian Belief* (Leicester: Apollos, 2002), pp. 17–21 and throughout.
3 Olson, *Mosaic*, pp. 29–48.
4 Olson, *Mosaic*, pp. 155–75.
5 Olson, *Mosaic*, pp. 199–222.
6 These issues and alternative ways of thinking are explored at length in John Hick, *Evil and the God of Love* (London: Macmillan, 1966).
7 Cornelius Plantinga, Jr., *Not the Way it's Supposed to Be: A Breviary of Sin* (Leicester: Apollos, 1995), pp. 1–6.
8 Plantinga, *Not the Way it's Supposed to Be*, pp. 7–27.
9 Genesis 1.26–31.
10 As immediate examples Romans 8.38–39; Colossians 1.15. Walter Wink has subjected this language to careful analysis in *Naming the Powers: The Language of Power in the New Testament* (London: Marshall Pickering, 1988).
11 Walter Wink, *Unmasking the Powers: The Invisible Forces that Determine Human Existence* (Philadelphia: Fortress Press, 1986).
12 Walter Wink, *Engaging the Powers: Discernment and Resistance in a World of Domination* (Philadelphia: Fortress Press, 1992), p. 67.
13 Wink, *Engaging the Powers*, p. 70.

14 Genesis 1.11, 20, 24.
15 Genesis 1.28.
16 Abraham Lincoln, The Gettysburg Address, Gettysburg, Pennsylvania, 19 November 1863.
17 Daniel 2.31–45; 7.1–8; Revelation 13.
18 1 Samuel 8.1–18.
19 Luke 22.25, 26.
20 Revelation 11.15.
21 In the UK the so-called 'free churches' comprise about one-third of the church-attending population. For some of these movements, such as the Baptists and Congregationalists, free church convictions are a matter of theological principle and include the commitment to the disestablishment of religion. For others, such as some Methodists and Presbyterians, there is a greater willingness to consider the possibility of established or national church status and so being 'free church' is for them more a matter of historical and legal fact than theological principle. Most Congregationalists and English Presbyterians now belong to the United Reformed Church.
22 Alister McGrath, *Christianity's Dangerous Idea: The Protestant Revolution – A History from the Sixteenth Century to the Twenty-first* (London: SPCK, 2007), pp. 2–5.
23 It might reasonably be objected here that the English Protestant Reformation led not to a new order but simply to the despotism of Henry VIII. Henry's strategy was to refer to himself the ecclesiastical power of the Pope and to install himself as the Supreme Governor of the Church of England exercising, in effect, the old papal powers, only in more extreme form. But Henry was not acting here as a principled Protestant but in an opportunistic fashion for his own ends, and in this regard is not typical of the general political impact of Protestantism.
24 William G. Naphy, *The Protestant Revolution: From Martin Luther to Martin Luther King Jr* (London: BBC Books, 2007).
25 Romans 13.1–7.
26 Acts 5.29: this text occurs repeatedly in Christian statements relating to government.
27 Romans 13.1–7.

28 The first move in this direction is attributed to the Swiss-German Anabaptist Balthasar Hubmaier (*c.* 1480–1528) in his pamphlet, 'On Heretics and Those Who Burn Them' (1524). See H. Wayne Pipkin and John H. Yoder, *Balthasar Hubmaier: Theologian of Anabaptism* (Scottdale, PA: Herald Press, 1989), pp. 58–66. The first English-language call for religious freedom is that of Thomas Helwys (*c.* 1550–*c.* 1612), *A Short Declaration of the Mistery of Iniquity* (1612).

29 This shift in the English experience is charted by John Coffey, *Persecution and Toleration in Protestant England 1558–1689* (Edinburgh: Longman, 2000). See my treatment of this in *Free Church, Free State: The Positive Baptist Vision* (Carlisle: Paternoster, 2005), pp. 204–27.

30 Sheldon Wolin, *The Presence of the Past: Essays on the State and the Constitution* (Baltimore: Johns Hopkins University Press, 1989).

31 I put it like this because it is impossible to divide, as some people do, between voices that speak only out of 'reason' or only out of 'faith'. All secularists hold beliefs they cannot prove (the idea of the dignity of human life, for instance, is implicit in the claim to humanism) and all people of faith have their characteristic ways of reasoning.

32 Jefferson, who was a religious man, used this celebrated phrase in his 1802 reply to a letter from the Danbury Baptist Association, but it was first used by the Baptist theologian, and founder of the Rhode Island colony, Roger Williams: 'Mr. Cotton's Letter Lately Printed, Examined and Answered' (1644) in *The Complete Writings of Roger Williams*, Volume 1, p. 108.

33 It might be noted that the American version of Christopher Hitchens' atheistic bestseller, *God is Not Great: The Case against Religion* (London: Atlantic Books, 2007) carries the subtitle *How Religion Poisons Everything.*

34 There is an important distinction to be made between 'hard' and 'soft' secularism. The former is an atheistic ideology that is hostile to religious faith; the latter is a civil arrangement that is hospitable to faith and in order to facilitate it insists on the impartiality of the state and on principled pluralism. Soft

secularism can be and is embraced by people of faith, but hard secularism cannot be.

35 John Howard Yoder, *The Christian Witness to the State* (Newton, Kansas: Faith and Life Press, 1964), pp. 12–13.

36 Matthew 5.43–48.

37 Romans 1.16–17.

38 Jeremiah 29.7; Romans 13.7; 1 Peter 2.13–17.

39 The slogan 'a free church in a free society' is a useful one. It appears to have been coined by Camillo Cavour (1810–61), united Italy's first prime minister: see Wright, *Free Church, Free State*, pp. 206–7.

40 Matthew 5.13; apparently salt was used both to preserve and to fertilize.

41 Matthew 19.7–9.

42 Fuller statements of the content of this chapter can be found in my books, *Power and Discipleship: Towards a Baptist Theology of the State* (Didcot: Whitley Publications, 1996), *Disavowing Constantine: Mission, Church and the Social Order in the Theologies of Jürgen Moltmann and John Howard Yoder* (Carlisle: Paternoster, 2000) and *Free Church, Free State.*

2

The nature and role of government in the Bible

JULIAN RIVERS

Ambivalent about government

The Bible is profoundly ambivalent about government. In what must be the most well-known passage on the subject, Jesus is asked whether it is right to pay taxes to Caesar or not.[1] After drawing attention to Caesar's image on a denarius, he replies, 'Give to Caesar what is Caesar's, and to God what is God's.' A brilliantly enigmatic reply to a vicious question, but what exactly does it mean?

A common popular interpretation would have Jesus dividing the world up into a religious domain and a domain of government, with the political consequence that we should obey government in the things of government and obey God in the things of God. In its most pernicious version, the 'things of government' can then be applied to every aspect of our human material existence and 'the things of God' to the merely spiritual orientation of the soul. It has totalitarian tendencies. But Jesus cannot have meant this. 'The earth is the LORD's, and everything in it.'[2] God cannot be parallel to Caesar, he is far above him! On the other hand, and even in spite of his reference to the 'image of God' on the face of the coin,[3] it is not likely either that Jesus meant to assert ironically that Caesar had no authority at all. Rather, this passage parallels Jesus' reply to Pilate: 'You would have no power [i.e. authority] over me if it were not given to you from above.'[4] In these words, the right of the human judge is both recognized and limited. But even this is no easy solution to the dynamic, unsettling nature of Jesus' replies. How much authority can Caesar, or Pilate, rightfully claim?

This ambivalence about government is reflected repeatedly throughout the Bible. Take the theme of kingship. When Israel asked for a king they were rejecting God's rule and choosing oppression,[5] yet David was a king after God's own heart, whose throne would be established for ever.[6] The prophet Hosea captures this tension in his unrelenting critique of the kings of Israel, relieved by glimpses of reunification under a second David figure.[7] Or take the story of Esther. King Xerxes is caught between the machinations of wicked Haman and the wisdom of Mordecai. Justice only just prevails through the extraordinary beauty and courage of a Jewish girl. A decree is issued for the annihilation of the Jewish people, only to be annulled by another decree permitting an equally violent act of pre-emptive 'self-defence'.[8] And that was a good outcome?

The New Testament writers reflect this ambivalence too. In the Acts of the Apostles, Luke is keen to emphasize the lawfulness of the new Christian religion. Cornelius, the Roman centurion, is a key convert;[9] Gallio the proconsul judges the religion indistinguishable from Judaism (a permitted religion under Roman law);[10] Paul is proud of his citizenship and uses it to good effect.[11] After his arrest, if he had not appealed to Caesar, he could have been released;[12] when he finally gets to Rome the gospel is proclaimed boldly and without hindrance right at the heart of empire.[13] Yet the dark side of political authority is not ignored. Paul is repeatedly left in prison as a favour to his enemies.[14] The

Romans were 'wicked men' with whom Jews conspired to put the Christ to death;[15] King Herod refuses to give glory to God and is struck down by worms.[16]

Or take the Revelation of John. The first impression is one of overwhelming critique and rejection of this world. John is imprisoned on Patmos.[17] He sees Rome as the prostitute who sits on many waters, who is drunk with the blood of the saints,[18] whose politico-economic empire trades ultimately in the bodies and souls of men.[19] She is under judgment and will receive the full fury of the wrath of God.[20] Yet when the new Jerusalem is finally revealed from the heavens, the nations walk by her light and are healed by the leaves of the trees growing beside the river of life.[21] The kings of the earth bring their splendour into the heavenly city.[22] Here there is no simple final damnation of government, rather it is welcomed and transformed in the glorious unmediated presence of God.

Ambivalence about government is reflected in our reading of the creation narrative. Is government a 'creation ordinance', instituted like the family in the time of man's innocence, or is it purely remedial, a divine response of common grace to human sin after the fall? To be sure, the Eden narratives make no mention of human authorities; they have no cause to. But there was a law in Eden ('you must not eat from the tree'),[23] and it is hard to argue that all of the functions of government are related to human sinfulness. We can grant that in a society of perfect human beings there would be no need for armies or policemen, no prisons, no law courts, but is there still not a need for coordination and administration? Millions do not enjoy sanitation and clean water without someone taking responsibility. Street lighting stops me tripping over, as well as preserving me from the robber. Is it all a result of the fall? It seems more likely that government is a natural product of human society *made much harder* by sin; a good gift, like marriage, and like marriage easily distorted and subverted.

The Bible's ambivalence about government corresponds to our own experience. The biblical writers would have been astonished by the modern state. In its power, its competence, its efficiency and its rationality it far surpasses any ancient empire or kingdom. The modern state maintains armed forces and policing, administers courts, operates prisons, regulates trade and industry, protects public health and safety, provides utilities and transport systems, ensures healthcare and education, and in a myriad ways secures unprecedented levels of material prosperity. The contribution of the modern state to human well-being is phenomenal.

Yet at the same time, that power of technological and administrative efficiency has been put to the systematic torture and annihilation of millions upon millions, not only in the gas chambers of the 'Final Solution' and the prison camps of the Gulag, but in many states across the globe, to this very day. Perhaps more insidiously, and closer to home, the modern regulatory state extends its mentality of discipline and order into almost every aspect of human existence. We are governed as never before. These phenomenal levels of material protection are intended for our good, but are we not also deeply unfree as a result? The twentieth century was witness as never before to the good and the evil of big government.

In terms of political principle, the Bible's response to its own, and our own, ambivalence about government is to insist that government is both legitimate and limited. Within the unfolding story of the Bible, neither of these points is obvious. This explains why the history of Christian political thought has sometimes led to such divergent proposals. In order to understand what the Bible as a whole has to say about the nature and role of government, we need to see why it is arguable both that government is legitimate, and that it is limited.

Government is legitimate

The Old Testament writers were convinced that the Lord, the God who had created the heavens and the earth, and who had made himself known to Israel, was supreme over all other nations and all other 'gods'.[24] When King Nebuchadnezzar made an idol of himself and forced all others to worship him, he left the path of wisdom and chose foolishness. But God humbled him, and he was forced to acknowledge that the Lord's 'dominion is an eternal dominion; his kingdom endures from generation to generation'.[25]

The Psalmist recognized that God's Messiah, the anointed King of David's line, would exercise God's universal rule over the nations in person. Against all political opposition, 'The One enthroned in heaven laughs . . . "I have installed my King on Zion, my holy hill." '[26] Jesus came, claiming to be that Messiah, God's King coming into his kingdom. The apostles were gripped with the reality of Jesus' complete authority,[27] as they proclaimed him both Lord and Christ (Messiah).[28] He is the Lord himself, come in the person of his Son. They were easily understood to be claiming in Jesus a direct political rival to Caesar.[29] Nor was this obviously wrong. Writing from the depths of a Roman prison to the patriotic city of Philippi, Paul could insist that it was Jesus who was the Son of God, their Saviour and Lord, not Caesar as Philippian public inscriptions so proudly proclaimed.[30] Unlike Roman citizenship, the citizenship of the church is heavenly.[31] Christians are aliens and strangers in the world, constituted by God into a new chosen people, a new holy nation.[32] Again and again the language is deeply and unavoidably political, and it places a question mark against every other claim to political legitimacy.

It is against this background that we must place two key passages in the New Testament on government: 1 Peter 2.13–17 follows immediately after the assertion of the new nationhood of the people of God, and its language so closely parallels that of Romans 13.1–7 that both passages may well reflect a common source in the teaching of Jesus. It is certainly of a piece with that teaching. The authority of government is legitimate, established by God, so one should submit to it. Governments exist to restrain evil by punishing the wrongdoer, and to promote good by commending those who do right. Submission is thus not merely pragmatic; it is a matter of conscience. Governing is a work of God, and those who do the work of God are entitled to the support of his people.[33] So taxes are to be paid and respect accorded as they are due.[34] Note that the assertion of the legitimacy of human government comes right after texts which could (but should not) be taken to deny it.

It is worth observing the breadth of the apostles' conception of government. The modern state engages in a much wider range of activities than the Roman Empire, even if at the core there are similar functions: the administration of justice, defence and public order, the protection and promotion of trade and industry. Yet the function of government is cast in the broadest possible terms: commending the right and punishing the wrong.[35] The Roman Empire was also violent and oppressive to a high degree. Yet there is a robust realism about the apostles' teaching. Anyone who fulfils the task of government has a divine mandate for that task. At some point, presumably, a claim of authority loses its legitimacy, but that point is not identified here. Under Christ the King, human government is still legitimate.

Government is limited

If we discover, somewhat surprisingly, that government is legitimate, we also discover – again surprisingly – that government is limited. The difficulty here is that the categories of right and wrong seem almost too broad. Is government to pursue all good and prevent all evil?

We have got so used to a theory of limited government that we simply assume that it is not the role of government to promote true religion, to take the obvious and hardest case. But the Bible's vision of human well-being is holistic. All people are called to turn away from a life of self-worship to be reconciled to the one true God, who has revealed himself supremely in his Son, Jesus Christ, and who by his Spirit is building a kingdom that will fill the whole world. We live in the hope of resurrection, the complete transformation and renewal of the entire created order.[36] When Jesus came he announced the inauguration of this renewal: 'Today this scripture is fulfilled in your hearing.'[37] He is the first fruits of the harvest to come.[38] The Bible's vision of human blessing is both material and spiritual: each person 'will sit under his own vine and his own fig-tree'.[39] No more will one say to another, 'Know the Lord', because they will all know him.[40] 'Never again will there be in it an infant who lives but a few days, or an old man who does not live out his years.'[41] 'The wolf and the lamb will feed together.'[42] 'The infant will play near the hole of the cobra.'[43]

One might expect visions of future blessing in the Old Testament to be this-worldly, but the New Testament does not deny the materiality of future blessing either. 'Creation itself will be liberated from its bondage to decay and brought into the glorious freedom of the children of God.'[44] 'The body that is sown is perishable, it is raised imperishable.'[45]

'There will be no more death or mourning or crying or pain, for the old order of things has passed away.'[46] 'I am making everything new!'[47]

So it is not obvious that Christians – whether as politicians, judges, civil servants, police, tax collectors or citizens – are to do anything other than live in the light of the reality that is breaking into our world and give themselves wholly to the work of building Christ's kingdom.[48] Where, then, is the limitation of government?

And yet government is indeed limited in two key ways. First, government is limited by the existence of other human authorities, in particular, church, family and individual. The visible church in the New Testament is not simply a spiritual or ideological movement of like-minded people. It has an order and a social presence. It appoints to offices, involving teaching and pastoring, but also social welfare.[49] It administers sacraments.[50] It requires some mark of differentiation between those 'inside' and those 'outside'.[51] It resolves disputes between its members.[52] Its ultimate sanction is to put out of fellowship the unrepentant wrongdoer.[53] The authority of the church, administered by its office-holders, is not derived from government but from Christ.[54]

Once we have broken out of the pernicious assumption of state sovereignty (only God is sovereign!) to see that human authority is always plural, we quickly see that the Bible identifies several parallel authorities under God. The family – founded on the lifelong union of a man and a woman – is presented as the foundational social and political unit.[55] Its authority, the relationships between husband and wife, parent and child, is not taken away by Christ either.[56] Nor does it derive from government. One can even make a case for the independence of the commercial sphere, expressed in ancient times in the household economy.[57]

One can certainly see that self-government plays a central part in biblical ethics.[58] For my thoughts I am accountable to God alone, and I discipline myself to conformity to his will.

All this indicates that we should be cautious when talking about 'government', let alone the 'state'. Government, in general, is simply helmsmanship, and one may be steering the ship of state, but one may also be guiding a church, a family, or oneself. Older writers were correct to refer to 'civil government', precisely because there are other forms of government under God. Here, then, is one limit.

Second, government (that is, civil government, of course) is limited by the means at its disposal. 'Do not be afraid of those who kill the body but cannot kill the soul.'[59] The symbolic means of government is the sword;[60] its ultimate sanction is the deprivation of life, liberty or property. And this radically limits its serviceability to the King who eschewed the use of the sword.[61] It limits it, but it does not render it useless. Nowhere is the collaboration of church and state in the promotion of Christ's rule better captured than in 1 Timothy 2.1–4:

> I urge, then, first of all, that requests, prayers, intercession and thanksgiving be made for everyone – for kings and all those in authority, that we may live peaceful and quiet lives in all godliness and holiness. This is good, and pleases God our Saviour, who wants all people to be saved and to come to a knowledge of the truth.

With perhaps more than half an eye to the riot in Ephesus,[62] Paul assumes that government is to preserve peace and order, to let the church express through its love for God and neighbour the universal scope of God's desire for the whole world. That is the way 'the state' evangelizes.

So Christian politicians, judges or civil servants will not abuse their offices by behaving as if they were in church, or at home, or by imposing the standards they set for themselves. As servants of Christ, they have a good, but limited, work to do. And we should note that the Bible does not have much to say about where exactly the limits of government fall. To take one historical example, education was for centuries the exclusive preserve of the Christian church. It was rooted in the pursuit of the God who is truth. The period 1830–70 in the UK saw a concerted effort by the churches to provide universal elementary education, with increasing financial support from the government. But by the 1860s even the most ardent supporters of 'voluntaryism' had to admit defeat, and the rise of state-organized education dates from the Elementary Education Act 1870. Few would deny that universal education is a component of the common good, a central part of a Christian conception of human well-being. And it is hard to mount a convincing biblical argument that government should always have nothing to do with it. At the same time, there is clearly potential, witnessed through countless examples throughout the world, of governments co-opting education to promote an anti-Christian agenda, which is to say to promote falsehood and idolatry. So where, exactly, are the limits?

The Bible contends that government is legitimate, but limited. Government must take its cue from the one who has ultimate authority, who is a Prince of Peace,[63] who suffers to be servant of all.[64] Even if the precise boundaries of its limits are left unclear, the Bible offers us wisdom on the ways in which it should be limited, reflected in key political values running through many of the biblical writings. We can note four: equality, legality, diffusion and accountability. These keep government in its servant role.

Government should reflect a commitment to human equality

The Bible has a rich conception of equal human worth, which is given practical and material significance. This is implicit in the creation narrative, in which all are descendants of one couple.[65] We see it in the universality of sin and the universal need for redemption.[66] Jesus' ministry was radically inclusive, extending to rich and poor, men and women, foreigners and fellow-citizens, the socially excluded and the respectable.[67] In him all human hierarchies are overthrown.[68]

The story of Israel contains numerous and surprising instances of equality. The land was divided up according to tribes and families to ensure roughly proportionate access to the means of production.[69] The Jubilee system periodically reversed the accumulated debt and inequality in favour of the original distribution.[70] The law codes were distinguished from other contemporaneous codes of the ancient Near East by the absence of class-based punishments depending on the status of the parties.

Israel was not to choose a king, because God was their king who had entered into treaty with them, rescuing them from slavery and constituting them a people at Sinai. The hostility to kingship was also driven by concern about the inevitable accumulation of wealth implicit in ancient kingship. 'He will take your sons . . . and your daughters . . . the best of your fields and vineyards . . . the best of your cattle and donkeys . . . and you yourselves will become his slaves.'[71] God saved them from slavery and gave them a land. Human kings do the opposite. The prophets railed against those who heaped up wealth and estates and who sold the poor for a pair of sandals.[72] Grabbing the land of others is a central target of prophetic critique.[73]

In the church as well, Paul was concerned to wean the Thessalonians off their dependence on abusive client-patron relationships, encouraging each to work for themselves, so that they could in turn be generous to those in need.[74] As he asked the Corinthians to be more intentional about their financial support for the poverty-stricken church in Jerusalem he insisted that he was not seeking to reverse their fortunes – simply that there should be the equality of mutual support.[75] In doing so he appealed to yet another powerful Old Testament image, the provision of manna in the wilderness. 'He who gathered much did not have too much, and he who gathered little did not have too little.'[76]

What about equality of political power? The Bible does not make a case for representative democracy, and it certainly would reject any account of 'the sovereignty of the people' (repeat: only God is sovereign!). But it is deeply egalitarian, and to an extent which we in our equality-conscious material prosperity can still find challenging. The book of Deuteronomy, which recounts the creation of a polity by covenant freely entered into between a gracious God and a grateful people, has at its heart God's love for the disadvantaged.[77] It suggests that forms of government which reflect equal citizenship on the part of the government are preferable. It also suggests that our modern Western distinctions between formal, or legal, equality on the one hand and substantive, or material, equality on the other, which allow us to combine pride in our equalities agenda with blindness to devastating deprivation, are more than questionable. Our challenge is that material equality seems to require big government, with substantial intervention and redistribution. The genius of the Old Testament law was that it simultaneously combined material equality with small government. How can we pursue a fully rounded conception of equality without constructing an unlimited state?

Government should be subject to law

The Bible has a remarkably exalted view of law. Law is the way in which God reveals his will. Properly understood, it is the expression of a universal love,[78] and the exact opposite of sin.[79] The worst forms of law-breaking are obvious to all,[80] but good law is also a gift of God's grace, worthy of admiration and envy.[81]

Because law derives from God, kings are not above the law. While the Rule of Law is a staple of Western constitutional theory, standard accounts present it as an objective state of affairs, the situation that pertains when a government acts according to a scheme of justice expressed in settled rules, clear and well publicized, applied and enforced by an independent judiciary.

By contrast, the biblical view of law has a strong subjective dimension as well, rooting it in individual knowledge and motivation. The people were to put the law on their hearts, impress it on their children, talk about it at home and abroad, on sleeping and rising, binding it to their hands, their foreheads, their doorposts and gates.[82] The Psalms are full of the benefits of reflection upon the law of God, most notably that marathon of meditation, Psalm 119. It is the key to life, and Ezekiel foresaw a day in which God himself would write the law, not on tablets of stone, but on people's hearts.[83]

Not only is law to be internalized, it is to be 'done'. The language of walking is frequently used to express the regularity of daily action. 'Blessed are they whose ways are blameless, who walk according to the law of the Lord.'[84] Law is to be grounded in daily practice and experience, and is thus to be liveable. The Old Testament law was characterized not by technical rules to be applied by experts, but by rules of thumb expressive of an underlying value-orientation that could teach, and also required, wisdom. It was government by the people, for the people.

So the Bible does not contain a theory of the Rule of Law, but it does suggest that forms of government which are located within and not above law are preferable. Legislation is inevitable and important, but there must also be a widespread understanding of a law that is fundamental, not up for grabs in quite the same way.

And before we jump too quickly to ideas of fundamental human rights, valuable though these are, the fundamental law of a nation must be 'internalizable' and liveable – as relevant to my relations with my neighbour as to the constraint of government. Might there be more scope here for starting from a statement of truly universal duties, as opposed to rights against the state?

Governmental power should be diffuse

One of the most marked and sustained aspects of the Bible's teaching about government is its critique of imperialism. Babel is introduced in Genesis 11 as the supreme expression of human rebellion against God. God's response is to confuse the common human language and provoke national dispersal and diversity.[85] But Babylon continues to be the source of oppression to Israel and the place of her exile.[86] Babylon appears again in Revelation as the symbol of the Roman Empire, mighty and idolatrous.[87] Human beings are perennially tempted to look to concentrations of political power to provide a substitute for the security and authority found only in God.

Within Israel as well, institutional arrangements were diffuse. Although there was a focus for national unity in the centralized cult,[88] and even if a rudimentary judicial hierarchy existed from an early time,[89] it was essentially conceived as a tribal federation, with local law-enforcement and mutual obligations of self-defence. Even when the kingship was established, this was no absolute monarchy. The king was subject to the laws of kingship,[90] and the books of Kings contain the clear political message that God judges monarchical illegality. The king was not to exercise priestly functions,[91] and when later on the kingship attained considerable control over the priesthood, the prophets emerged as an office exercising a check on monarchy.[92] Ahab's sin in acquiring Naboth's vineyard was not simply greed for land and murder; it was the abuse of judicial process to concentrate power.[93]

Within the church there is a diversity of gifts and offices;[94] whatever may be the practical advantages of single oversight over many congregations, and whatever the extent to which this aspect of apostolic ministry should be perpetuated, the New Testament talks in terms of the church in a locality and presupposes a degree of independence for each local church. This model expresses not only the danger of concentrations of power, but also the goodness of different people perform-ing different functions.

The Bible does not present us with a worked-out theory of the separation of powers, but it does provide us with pointers in that direction. Evil is restrained and individuals flourish when authority is diffused. Are we paying too high a price for the efficiency and equity of modern government in terms of national and international centralization?

Governments should be held to account

The final biblical theme relevant to government is accountability. Each person is accountable to God for things he or she has done in this life, whether political or personal.[95] The judgment of God is envisaged not only at the end of time as the final judgment,[96] but also as an ongoing process of God's engagement with the world. Kings and emperors who defy God are brought low: Pharaoh,[97] Nebuchadnezzar[98] and Herod.[99] In the Old Testament, the fate of nations is likewise bound up with the fate of their rulers; divine accountability is both ongoing and collective.

Accountability is not simply a feature of our relationship to God. It shapes our human relations as well. In 1 Samuel 12.2–3, the prophet gives to the people an account of his life and work. The idea of a final account of a human being to the people he or she has served emerges again in Paul's address to the Ephesian elders: 'You know how I lived the whole time I was with you.'[100] This is not self-justification. It is accountability in practice. It is possible that there was an underlying principle of kingly accountability to the people which explains Saul's fear of David, as well as popular involvement in the accession of kings and the renewal of the covenant.[101] It is striking how many of the Israelite kings are provided with a prophet to encourage, challenge and rebuke them in their work. Nathan was sent to rebuke David;[102] Elijah to rebuke Ahab.[103] 1 Kings 22 warns against institutionalizing, or domesticating this critique, such that the powerful can pay lip-service to accountability while enjoying the flattery of their retainers.

Different offices require different forms of accountability. If the judiciary require security of tenure to ensure that they dispense justice fairly, they must also subject themselves to the bar of public opinion by justifying their actions with the most rigorous form of public reasoning we require of anyone. The Old Testament law ensured the accountability of its judges by another means: they had to be present at the corporal punishment they had ordered.[104] Witnesses were accountable for the testimony they offered.[105] If you can justify your action to your victim you are unlikely to commit an injustice.

Systems of accountability always struggle to find the right balance between distance and proximity. Come too close and you get co-opted; move too far away and you cannot tell what is going on. That is why God is the model for all accountability: he is wholly other, perfect in goodness, purity and love, yet he knows the secrets of our hearts, our thoughts before we have even uttered them. In the human context we have to settle for a range of institutions, but in each case we can ask: Is it too close? Is it too distant? Do our parliamentary select committees have enough access to departmental information? Are they sufficiently immune from executive pressure? Can the media find out what is going on? Can they resist co-option into the government's 'communication strategy'?

Conclusion: the Bible and the idea of a constitution

It is easy to assume that the Bible is a 'religious' book and that it therefore has little to say about 'politics'. Such a view is in part a reflection of a biblical distinction between the institutions of church and government, which is alien to other religions. But it also reflects a profoundly unchristian distinction between religious belief and true knowledge. Against all such forms of secularization, the Bible shows itself to be deeply political. It tells the story of a global kingdom, ruled over by one who is King of kings and Lord of lords,[106] one before whom every knee will ultimately bow and every tongue worship.[107] As we have seen, Christ places a permanent question mark after every other exercise of authority. This cannot avoid having political significance.

Surprisingly, we find that human institutions of civil government still have a place in God's purposes until the fulfilment of the ages. They are not the only form of human authority, but they take their place alongside other gifts of God's grace such as churches and families. They administer justice, preserve peace and order, and do whatever else is wise for the promotion of the common good. Even in their many flawed forms, they have a certain legitimacy, and are to be respected and obeyed. They are best arranged to reflect a commitment to a rich conception of human equality, they should be subject to law not in control of it, their powers should be divided among a wide range of independent institutions, offices and individuals, each of which should operate within workable structures of accountability. That is how government is our servant, not our master.

In short, the Bible as a whole lends considerable support to the idea of a constitution. Not necessarily a single written document – although that has advantages of accessibility and symbolic unity – but a constitution rooted in a collective commitment that we shall live together in this way as most conducive to our common freedom and well-being while we prepare for the return of the King.

Notes

1 Matthew 22.15–22.
2 Psalm 24.1.
3 Genesis 1.26.
4 John 19.11.
5 1 Samuel 8.
6 2 Samuel 7.5–16.
7 Hosea 1.11; 3.5.
8 Esther 9.15–17.
9 Acts 10.
10 Acts 18.12–17.
11 Acts 16.37–39; 22.23–29.

12 Acts 26.32.
13 Acts 28.30–31.
14 Acts 24.27; 25.9.
15 Acts 2.23.
16 Acts 12.19–23.
17 Revelation 1.9.
18 Revelation 17.
19 Revelation 18.11–13.
20 Revelation 18.21–24.
21 Revelation 22.2.
22 Revelation 21.24.
23 Genesis 2.17.
24 See, for example, Psalm 82.
25 Daniel 4.34.
26 Psalm 2.4–6.
27 Matthew 28.18.
28 Acts 2.36.
29 Acts 17.7.
30 Philippians 2.11.
31 Philippians 3.20.
32 1 Peter 2.9–12, echoing Exodus 19.6.
33 Compare 1 Timothy 5.17–18.
34 See also Titus 3.1–2.
35 Romans 13.3; 1 Peter 2.14.
36 Romans 8.18–21; 1 Corinthians 15.
37 Luke 4.16–21.
38 1 Corinthians 15.20.
39 Micah 4.4.
40 Jeremiah 31.34.
41 Isaiah 65.20.
42 Isaiah 65.25.
43 Isaiah 11.6–9.
44 Romans 8.21.
45 1 Corinthians 15.42.
46 Revelation 21.4.
47 Revelation 21.5.
48 1 Corinthians 15.58.
49 1 Timothy 3.1–12.

50 Acts 2.41–42.
51 1 Corinthians 5.9–13.
52 1 Corinthians 6.1–4.
53 1 Corinthians 5.13.
54 1 Peter 5.1–4.
55 Genesis 1.27–28; 2.20–24.
56 Matthew 19.4–6; Ephesians 5.22—6.4; Colossians 3.18–21; 1 Peter 3.1–7.
57 e.g. Ephesians 6.5–9.
58 1 Corinthians 9.24–27; Hebrews 12.1–12; James 3.1–6. See also the role of conscience in Romans 2.15.
59 Matthew 10.28.
60 Romans 13.4.
61 John 18.36.
62 Acts 19.23–41.
63 Isaiah 9.6.
64 Isaiah 52.13—53.12; Luke 22.25–27.
65 Genesis 3.20; Acts 17.26.
66 Romans 3.23–24.
67 One is tempted to reference all the Gospels. John 4 will suffice.
68 Galatians 3.26–28.
69 Deuteronomy 3.12–20; Joshua 13.2–12.
70 Leviticus 25.
71 1 Samuel 8.11–17.
72 Amos 6.1–7; 2.6.
73 1 Kings 21; Isaiah 5.8–10; Micah 2.1–2.
74 1 Thessalonians 4.11–12; 2 Thessalonians 3.6–10.
75 2 Corinthians 8.1–15.
76 Exodus 16.18.
77 Deuteronomy 10.12–22.
78 Matthew 5; John 15.9–10.
79 Romans 7.12.
80 Amos 1.3—2.3; Romans 1.18–32; 2.12–16.
81 Deuteronomy 4.1–8.
82 Deuteronomy 6.4–9.
83 Ezekiel 36.24–28; Jeremiah 31.31–34.
84 Psalm 119.1.

85 Genesis 11.8–9.
86 2 Kings 25; Jeremiah 29.
87 Revelation 18.
88 Deuteronomy 16.16.
89 Exodus 18.13–26.
90 Deuteronomy 17.14–20.
91 1 Samuel 13.7–14.
92 2 Samuel 12.1–15.
93 1 Kings 21.
94 Acts 6.1–7; 1 Corinthians 12.
95 Matthew 25.31–46; Romans 14.9–12; 2 Corinthians 5.10.
96 Revelation 20.11–15.
97 Exodus 9.13–19.
98 Daniel 4.28–32.
99 Acts 12.21–23.
100 Acts 20.18–35.
101 2 Samuel 5.3; 2 Kings 23.1–3.
102 2 Samuel 12.
103 1 Kings 21.
104 Deuteronomy 25.2.
105 Deuteronomy 19.16–19.
106 1 Timothy 6.15; Revelation 17.14; 19.16.
107 Philippians 2.10–11.

3

Neither anarchy nor tyranny Government and the New Testament

TOM WRIGHT[1]

The new imperialisms

There is a current debate as to whether what we see in today's world is really a form of empire. The hegemony wielded by the Western world, particularly by the United States as the current sole superpower, has some close affinities with earlier empires. But there are also considerable differences: the United States does not exercise direct governmental control over far-flung states in the way that, say, Queen Victoria ruled over a worldwide empire through viceroys, governors general and other imperial officials. Such differences are significant, but I would nevertheless side with those who use the word 'empire' to describe today's reality.[2]

Empires have a certain logic to them. If we have attained a new level of civilization, people think, we have a duty to share it with the world. This was exactly how the ancient Roman imperial rhetoric worked, as a glance at Cicero and similar thinkers reveals. We Romans are naturally free, we naturally possess 'justice', we believe in and maintain 'peace', and this gives us an obligation to share our unique gifts with everybody else. Of course, they come with a price tag, but that is only to be expected granted the great benefits that are being conferred. As with the Roman Empire, so with more modern ones, be they the British of the nineteenth century or the American of the twentieth and twenty-first. The political systems that evolved in the wake of the Enlightenment combined the ancient logic of imperial role with modern ideas of progress and made a potent story. Once the divine right of kings had been rejected as an obvious power-play, 'vox populi, vox Dei' provided an inexorable alternative, and with atheism on the increase the 'vox Dei' bit was set aside, leaving 'vox populi' as a law unto itself. If only the people's voice could be heard and harnessed, then the world would attain its long-denied utopia.

Many of today's political puzzlements arise, at least in part, from the failure of this expectation to materialize. We have all been voting for a long time now and utopia has failed to arrive on schedule. Modernist rhetoric kept up the pretence for a while, suggesting that a little more reform, better housing and healthcare, more appropriate foreign aid, the export of democratic freedoms to other countries, and so on, would enable us to turn the corner and bring about utopia at last. Yet this hasn't happened and isn't going to happen, a fact highlighted dramatically and tragically for us by events of recent years. The problem of evil – not the philosopher's puzzle about explanation, but the global puzzle about what to do – is the guilty secret that the rhetoric of empire seeks to hide.

This is not a uniquely modern problem. Paul had scathing words for the imperial delusion in 1 Thessalonians 5: 'When they say, "Peace and Security" [as the Romans did say to their subject peoples], then sudden destruction will overtake them, and there will be no escape.' Imperial protection rackets can only last so long. Sooner or later there will be a day of reckoning, as the system topples under its own lazy, top-heavy weight. Today's global empire is essentially an economic one, kept in place by electronic transactions rather than viceroys on the ground, but the same analysis remains true, as evidenced by today's global economic crisis.

And so long as we maintain the historic split of religion and politics, of faith and public life, we will be powerless to do more than lament before the errors of misplaced imperial ambition. The good news is that the great scriptural narrative, which we have for so long hushed up, tells a different story, one which calls all human empires – ancient or modern, military or economic – to account. This is the biblical story of the strange lordship of Jesus Christ. It has compelling implications for the conduct of British government today.

Jesus as Lord

One of the extraordinary reversals in scholarship over the course of the last 30 years has been the rediscovery of the political dimension to the New Testament. In the 1970s hardly anyone was writing about the Roman Empire in relation to early Christianity. It was assumed, partly because of the Lutheran 'two kingdoms' doctrine, that the early Christians were concerned with worshipping Jesus, living in the Spirit, being justified by faith, and explaining to one another how precisely to go to heaven, rather than with earthly politics. Paul's political views were dismissed with a wave at Romans 13, and Jesus' attitude to the state was summed up in the saying about rendering to Caesar, which was taken as marking a rigid separation of powers. The book of Revelation was thought of as a strange farrago of apocalyptic nightmares, which eager fundamentalists would systematize into end-times datelines and shocked liberals would dismiss as bloodthirsty fantasies. It was taken for granted that the early Christians were uninterested in serious political theology.

All that has changed in the last 30 years. In the Society of Biblical Literature[3] several groups have looked excitedly for critiques of empire in early Christianity. Matthew, Mark, Paul, John and especially Revelation are all deemed thoroughly counter-imperial. Indeed, the pendulum has swung so far so fast that it is in danger of flying off altogether into politically driven speculations with as little historical basis as the dualism they replace. Some assume, ridiculously, that since the New Testament now seems to be about politics it cannot after all be about theology. Somewhere in the middle of all this there is fresh wisdom to be found, and it comes both in the repeated assertion that Jesus is Lord – meaning, among other things, that Caesar is not – and in the emphasis that it is *Jesus*, the crucified one, who is Lord, thereby redefining the very notion of 'lordship' itself.

John's Gospel

It has often been remarked that, whatever we think of the historical value of the rest of the Gospel, the Johannine narrative of the trial before Pilate (John 18—19) offers a remarkably authentic picture of how a suspected rebel leader might be tried before a provincial governor.[4] But it is, of course, much more. It is the climax, within John's astonishingly skilful narrative, of the Gospel-long dialogue between Jesus and 'the world' (as introduced by the Prologue's statement that 'he was in the world, and the world was made by him, but the world knew him not') and also between Jesus and his fellow Jews (of whom the Prologue at once goes on to say that 'he came to his own, and his own received him not'). Pilate stands for the world, the world made by God but run by Caesar. Jesus stands for the kingdom of God, as announced by psalms and prophets, by Isaiah and Daniel.

The scene displays not just two kings but two types of kingdom. Here is Caesar's kingdom: a kingdom in which truth is relative to power. Jesus has come, he says, to bear witness to the truth, and Pilate's famous response, 'What is truth?', indicates the gulf between the two empires. Caesar's empire only knows the truth of Roman rule, the truth that comes out of the scabbard of a sword (or, as we would say, the barrel of a gun): the 'truth' of taxes and whips, of nails and crosses. But the kingdom Jesus comes to bring is not 'from this world'. If it were, he observes, his servants would have been fighting to stop him being handed over: that's what kingdoms originating in the present world always do.

This, we must insist, does not mean that Jesus' kingdom is a 'purely spiritual' one, a gnostic dream of escape that has nothing to do with the present world and hence has no challenge to offer to Caesar. No: Jesus' kingdom does not *derive from* this world, but it is *designed for* this world. But precisely because it is the kingdom of the wise Creator God who longs to heal his world, whose justice is aimed at restoration rather than punitive destruction, it can neither be advanced nor attained by the domineering, bullying, fighting kingdom-methods employed in merely earthly kingdoms. Jesus thus redefines what it means to be 'lord of the world' at the same time as he redefines, with heavy Johannine irony, what it means to be 'king of the Jews'. And the Jewish leaders, meanwhile, now with crowning irony, declare that Jesus cannot be their king, since they have 'no king but Caesar'.

In the middle of this extraordinary dialogue, Jesus says something yet more striking. Pilate has warned that he has the power to crucify or release him. Jesus comments that Pilate couldn't have this authority if it were not given him from above, so that the greater sin is ascribed to the one who handed him over – in other words, Caiaphas. It is truly remarkable, in the midst of the contrast between the two types of kingdom, to find this note, alerting us to the deeply Jewish perception, itself rooted in the doctrine of creation, that even in the present rebellious state of the world, God does not want anarchy or chaos. There must be rulers, even if they are bound to be themselves drawn from the ranks of the wicked. To have no rulers is even worse. The resulting paradox, that God-given rulers send the Son of God to his undeserved death, lies close to the heart both of the New Testament's doctrine of the principalities and powers, and of its multiple interpretations of the meaning of the cross.

Thus, when we read John's Gospel as a whole, and allow the confrontation with Pilate to shape the meaning John intends us to find in the story of the crucifixion and resurrection, we discover a deeper meaning to those climactic events than we get if we treat the political build-up as mere scene-setting for an essentially apolitical doctrine of redemption. Jesus has come not to destroy the world but to rescue it from evil, and if the structures of human authority are part of the good creation, the abuse of those structures constitutes a double evil. Jesus' task, driven not by the love of power but by the power of love, is to take the full force of that double evil upon himself, and thereby to complete the work of redemption just as the Father completed the work of creation at the end of the sixth day. The final cry from the cross in John ('It is accomplished!') resonates all the way back to God's *finishing* of creation on the sixth day.[5] The darkness of evening brings in the seventh day, the day of rest, before the arrival of the eighth day, 'the first day of the week', the day in which – if we are to allow John's massive build-up of imperial and counter-imperial themes to resonate as far as chapter 20 – the new creation is launched, and Jesus prepares to ascend, like the Son of Man in Daniel 7, to rule the world with a new kind of power, the transformative and healing power of suffering love.

The Synoptic Gospels

This spectacular Johannine political theology, routinely ignored by preachers and theologians alike, conforms closely to what we find in the Synoptics. Matthew's risen Jesus insists that all authority in heaven *and on earth* has been given to him, which deserves further exploration in terms of Matthew's plot and major themes. Luke contrasts the posturing of Augustus Caesar in Rome with the humble but decisive birth of Jesus. Then, in Acts, he describes what it means that the kingdom is indeed 'restored' to Jesus as Israel's king and to his followers acting as ambassadors. In Acts 17 we find Paul accused of heralding 'another king, namely Jesus'. The book ends with Paul in Rome itself, announcing God's kingdom and preaching Jesus Christ as Lord 'openly and unhindered'. No first-century reader would have missed the point, which was in any case implicit in the initial ascension narrative. Within modernism the ascension is merely a supernatural embarrassment, but within first-century worldviews (whether derived from Daniel 7, or based on Roman emperor-cult, or, like those of the early Christians, rooted in one and confronting the other) it clearly meant that Jesus was now constituted as the true, and divine, Lord of the world.

Mark's political theology has been variously explored,[6] and I simply focus on his redefinition of power in 10.35–45. James and John ask to sit at Jesus' right and left. Jesus responds that they don't know what they are talking about (though the reader will soon know, as two others end up in those positions when Jesus is at last labelled publicly as 'king of the Jews'). But then comes the great redefinition: the rulers of the earth lord it over their subjects, but with you, the greatest must be the servant, and the leader must be the slave of all – *because* 'the Son of Man came not to be served but to serve and to give his life a ransom for many'. That famous verse (10.45), drawing together Isaiah 53 and Daniel 7, is not, as so often imagined, a detached statement of atonement theology, but rather the clinching point in this devastatingly counter-imperial statement about power. That does not mean that it is *not* about (what we have come to call) 'atonement'. Rather, it is an invitation to understand atonement itself – God's dealing on the cross with the sin of the world – as involving God's victory not so much over the world and its powers (as though God were simply another cheerful 1960s anarchist) but over the worldly *ways of* power, the ways in which the powers that were created in, through and for Jesus Christ have rebelled and now themselves need to be led, beaten and bedraggled, in his triumphal procession, in order eventually to be reconciled.

Paul

That last sentence is a deliberate echo of Colossians 1 and 2, and points us to Paul. It used to be thought that Paul was a quietist, accepting magistrates and emperors with a shrug of the shoulders. I have argued elsewhere that this is a serious misreading of Romans 13, and that Romans as a whole, and for that matter Philippians too, offer a sustained if sometimes coded challenge to the absolute rule of Caesar.[7] Think of the opening of Romans (1.1–17): Jesus, for Paul, is the King, the *kyrios*, the Son of God, whose 'gospel' calls the whole world to loyal obedience, and generates a world of justice, freedom and peace. Paul was able, while deriving his gospel from a Christ-shaped re-reading of Psalms and prophets, to phrase it in such a way as to challenge, point by point, the normal rhetoric of Caesar's empire.

When Romans 8 offers a Christian variation on the Jewish eschatological hope for the renewal of creation, it upstages the boast of Rome that, under the emperor, the world was entering a new age of fruitfulness. Philippians 2 and 3 make the same point in different though related ways. 1 Thessalonians, as we saw, mocks the normal imperial boast of 'peace and security', and in chapter 4 provides a picture of the *parousia* of Jesus which seems designed to upstage the regular imperial panoply of the *parousia* of Caesar, 'arriving' at a city, or back in Rome after some great exploit, with the grateful citizens going out to meet him and escort him into the city. Of course, 1 Thessalonians 4 has become notorious as the proof-text for a 'rapture' in which God's people will be snatched away from earth to heaven, thereby leaving them without the promised new heavens and new earth, leaving Paul without one of his more powerful pieces of anti-Caesar rhetoric, and leaving us less able to mount any critique of empire.

Central to Paul, of course, as to John and Mark, is the theology of the cross, which is again to be seen not only in terms of traditional 'atonement' theology but also in terms of counter-imperial polemic. As any student of Roman history knows only too well, crucifixion was not just a very nasty mode of execution but also a clear statement of power. It warned subject peoples, slaves and insurgents that Rome ruled the world, that Caesar was Lord, and that resistance was both futile and very, very foolish. It made the theological point that the goddess Roma ran the world, and required her subjects – especially in the Middle East, which supplied the grain essential to the well-being of the overcrowded city of Rome itself – to do what they were told, when they were told. It took not only genius but considerable *chutzpah* to see, and to say, that the symbol which spoke of the horrible 'justice' of Caesar's empire could now speak of the restorative justice of the true God.

All this is based, of course, on the resurrection. If death is the ultimate weapon of the tyrant, then resurrection is the reassertion that the Creator God rules over the world which the tyrants claim as their own. To speak only of 'atonement' in the dehistoricized and depoliticized sense of 'Christ dying for my sins' as a kind of private transaction, while in itself highlighting one of the majestic truths at the heart of the Christian faith ('the Son of God loved *me* and gave himself for me'[8]), is to run the risk of colluding with empire, implying that the redemption that I enjoy will enable me to escape the world where imperial powers continue to behave as they always do. Equally, of course, to imagine that we can reduce Matthew, Mark, Luke, John or Paul to terms simply of 'politics', as though their political stance is not non-negotiably rooted in their theology of creation, atonement and new creation, is to reduce them to echoes of our own largely impotent political posturing.

It is the underlying theology, in fact, which enables the New Testament writers to avoid that kind of shallowness and lay the foundations for a mature political theology. We trace their thinking, through books such as the Wisdom of Solomon, all the way back to the biblical story of God's people under pagan rule. The line from Genesis 3 to the Tower of Babel in Genesis 11 then gives way to the call of Abraham; Abraham's family ends up in Egypt, rescued when God judges their pagan overlords; the decidedly ambiguous conquest of Canaan results in the still ambiguous kingdom of David and Solomon; and eventually we find ourselves back in Babel, in the Babylonian exile, which creates the context for those two most deeply political prophecies, Isaiah and Daniel. The Psalms, meanwhile, celebrate the kingship of

YHWH over the nations, and YHWH's placing of his Messiah as the one who will bring the kings of the earth to order. It is this story that formed the matrix within which the early Christians fashioned their own political stance.

At the heart of this stance we find the affirmation, the good news: Jesus is Lord. *Jesus*, the crucified one, is Lord; not another Caesar to bully and threaten, but the one whose life and death redefined power for ever. The book of Revelation is now widely and correctly seen as one of the great documents of early Christian political theology, offering a further account of the victory of the Creator God over the rebel powers of the world, a victory rooted in God's determination to restore and fulfil the creational intent and accomplished through the self-giving death of the Lamb. Revelation joins the rest of early Christianity in announcing that Jesus is Lord of earth as well as heaven, and that at his name every knee shall bow.

The Lordship of Jesus is thus to be understood in harmony with the larger theological themes of creation and judgment, themes that together constitute the good news of the Creator God over against the darkness of a world gone astray. Jesus' Lordship is not outside, or over against, the restorative purposes of the Creator God. Rather, he is exalted through his resurrection and ascension to the place where the God who made the world through him now rules the world through him. As Paul says, quoting Isaiah 11 at the final climax of his greatest letter, Jesus is the one 'who rises to rule the nations; and in him the nations shall hope'.[9] Only those who have lived with the hopelessness of human empire will fully appreciate that promise, just as only those who have lived with the violence of empire will fully appreciate the meaning of the victory over violence itself won on the cross.

The New Testament's theology of creation, resurrection and new creation thus forms the solid platform for the central gospel assertion that Jesus Christ is Lord, the good news for those in a newly imperial world. The good news is that this Lordship is not a mere heavenly lordship, distracting attention (and critique) from the tyrannies of the world, but a Lordship designed for earth as well as heaven, not only in the ultimate future when heaven and earth are one, but also in the penultimate future, in which Jesus' followers work to bring signs of his healing and hopeful rule to birth in the present time. It is to this task, difficult and complicated though it may seem, that we now turn.

Living in God's alternative empire

The last decade has forcibly reopened the question many in our world had considered closed for ever, that of the interrelation of faith and public life. It has never really gone away, of course, but for much of the last two centuries, particularly in the North Atlantic world, it has been regarded as effectively off limits. I have noticed that in America the idea that church and state might have anything to do with one another is often attacked with real venom, perhaps because of long memories of George III sending bishops to the colonies. Now, with the proliferation of multi-faith communities in many formerly monochrome parts of the world, and particularly with the rise of a militant Islam, we face old questions in new ways.[10]

Politicians and columnists to left, right and centre have chipped in with comments which indicate that we are totally unused to addressing questions of religion, culture and public life, and unaware that there might be some old maps which would help us find our way through countryside which is virgin territory to us but which was well known to many of our forebears in all the great world faiths. Two years running the *New Statesman* magazine has highlighted big features on 'God' which have shown, basically, that they know there is a question out there which needs addressing but don't know what it is – and that they are afraid of letting God get too close to public life. How can the early Christian political theology I have been exploring help us to think afresh about all of this, and navigate our way through this complex and dangerous territory?

The biblical theology which runs from Genesis and Exodus, through the ambiguous narratives of conquest and monarchy, through Isaiah and Daniel, through, indeed, the Maccabean literature and the Wisdom of Solomon, and out with a new focus into John, the Synoptics, Paul and Revelation – and for that matter Ignatius of Antioch, Polycarp of Smyrna and Irenaeus of Lyons – approaches questions of earthly power and the kingdom of God through the doctrines of the good creation, the promised new creation, and the Lordship of the crucified, risen and ascended Jesus. This invites us today to a massive task of retrieval, in implicit dialogue with political theologians of all sorts, but for which there is here only time for a short summary.

As I said above, it is part of the doctrine of creation that the Creator intends the world to be ordered and structured, with a harmony of its parts that enables flourishing, fruitfulness and the eventual fulfilment of the Creator's intention. From the beginning, according to the ancient poetic story, the Creator God gave to humans the task of reflecting the divine image into the world, being the bridge between the Creator and the creation, representing the presence of God within the creation and the presence of creation before God, and doing so with a rich awareness of both elements. The risk that the humans would rebel, and set up on their own, is a point in Genesis 1 which resonates deeply with several subsequent layers of the story: because, when evil enters the world, the Creator does not abandon it to chaos, does not unmake creation itself, but works from within to produce an eventual restoration.

It gradually emerges, throughout the Hebrew and Aramaic scriptures, that part of this divine purpose is to call and equip rulers, not only within Israel itself but within the pagan nations of the wider world, to bring a measure of order to the world – and even sometimes, as in Isaiah 10, judgment upon God's people! – even though they themselves remain part of the problem, abusing their vocation to further their own ambitions of violence, greed and hollow glory. The ambiguity of human power – the necessity of it on the one hand, and the inevitable temptations of it on the other – thus fleshes out the precarious position of the humans at the beginning and of Israel throughout the story, as the Israelites, like Adam and Eve (and that may be part of the point), rebel against the Creator and are eventually ejected from the garden, the promised land.

The promises to which Israel clung over the following centuries combined the two elements which give shape to early Christian political thought as well: first, God's use of non-Jewish powers to restore and give order and security to the post-exilic community; second, God's challenge to those very powers (and God's promise to the chosen people) that the coming Messiah, and/or the messianic community, would eventually put the whole world to rights, which would involve the demotion of all powers from the proud, arrogated position they routinely occupy.

Let me put it like this, in a threefold typology, based on the doctrines of creation and redemption: (1) God intends the world to be ordered, and will put it in proper order at the last; but (2) he doesn't want chaos between now and then, and uses human authorities, even when they don't acknowledge him, to bring a measure of his order in advance of the end; and (3) since that puts awful temptations in the way of the authorities, God's people have the vital calling to speak the truth to them and call them to account in anticipation of that same final day.

I hope it is clear that this gives to second-Temple Jewish thought, and thereby to early Christian thought, a complexity and density which does not correspond to the (over)simple political alternatives familiar in today's Western world. Perhaps it is also clear that this complexity corresponds much more closely to the way in which much of the rest of the world sees public life, and that if we are to engage with the world we live in, instead of assuming that our post-Enlightenment political mindsets are automatically superior, we would do well to think the matter through more fully.

The early Christian political theology includes the application to power of the achievement of Jesus Christ in his death and resurrection.[11] The problem of evil within the world cannot be reduced to the sum total of individual sin, hugely important though sin and forgiveness are. It includes, and the evangelists and apostles knew it included, the victory by the Creator God over all the powers that have rebelled within the world, and hence the announcement to the principalities and powers that their time is up, that Jesus is Lord and that they are not. (That, of course, is the message of Ephesians 3.10: the revelation of God's many-coloured wisdom to the rulers and authorities.) The rulers are therefore to be summoned to obedience to the Prince of Peace. The church was from the beginning entrusted with this dangerous message, and necessarily and inevitably suffered for it, but went on claiming, as in Acts, the moral and political high ground of reminding the authorities what their job really was, and holding them to it. The apostles found far less difficulty than we do in holding this package together. We, who have inherited the post-Enlightenment antithesis of anarchy and tyranny and have turned it into two-party systems of left and right, are called to relearn the more subtle, and more useful, biblical analysis of how the rule of Jesus Christ impacts upon the kingdoms of the world.

The church is therefore called to reject both tyranny – all rulers must bow before Jesus! – and also the anarchist dream of no powers, no 'order', no structure to God's world. In the promised new heavens and new earth there will be order. How much more, then, within the present world where evil still infects the human race, is it necessary that there be rulers and authorities who can hold it in check?

Equally, the church must also reject the Marxist dream of a simple inversion of power, of the rule of the previous underclass but by the same means as before. Rather, the church must affirm that the Creator God intends the world to be ruled by properly constituted authorities, but insists that they be held to account, and that it is part of the task of the church to do this, to speak the truth to power, to affirm power in its proper use and to critique it in its regular abuse.

Here, I think, we in the Western world have been too in love with our own modernist democratic processes, and have imagined that the only really important thing about power is how people attain it, since 'vox populi' will give them the absolute right to do what they want after being elected. Part of our difficulty today is precisely that this implicit belief is held so strongly that the idea of a democratic 'mandate' is, for many, part of an unchallengeable worldview, and far too much weight then attaches to all the expensive fuss and bother about elections.

The early Christians, like the Jews of the same period, were not particularly interested in how someone, or some system, came to power. They were much more interested in what people did with that power once they had it, and in holding up a mirror to power, like Daniel with Nebuchadnezzar or Darius, so that those in power might be reminded that they are responsible to the Creator God and that, ultimately, they are called to bow the knee to Jesus as Lord.

If the church could recapture this vision, there might emerge a more mature political theology that would avoid the sterile left/right polarization or the more recent but equally sterile centre/centre polarization (if that isn't too paradoxical) that has characterized so much Western politics. Our political discourses have become shallow and naive, not only in descending to spin and smear, but, more worryingly, in appealing to social and cultural feeling rather than to genuine issues of justice, power and freedom.

The church is called to bear witness to the promise of new heavens and new earth in which justice will dwell, to refuse to be conned by the rhetoric of either the new right or the new left, and to insist on bringing signs of that future to birth both in its own life and in the world around, based on the resurrection of Jesus and the power of the Spirit.

The church must, in short, learn from Jesus before Pilate how to speak the truth *to* power rather than *for* power or merely *against* power. This needs working out, of course, in economics both local and global; in ecology and stewardship of the whole creation; and, not least, in structures of global governance. Thus, for example, the suspicion or downright rejection of the United Nations on the part of some on the American right must be rejected if we are genuinely to work for justice and peace across the globe. Neither the USA nor the UK, nor some combination of the two, can ever again be as they stand a credible global police force, especially in the Middle East. Yet some kind of transnational policing is necessary in some parts of the world, and if the UN cannot currently provide it we must find ways of enabling it to do so.

To take another example, I am disappointed at the shallow level of engagement on many fronts over the question of establishment. From where I sit (i.e. in the House of Lords), it is clear that two regular objections to the present position are simply ill-informed. First, establishment does not mean that the church tells the state what to do; bishops have a voice, and often use that voice to speak up for the voiceless in their regions, and indeed for other denominations and other faiths, but we are not in any sense 'in charge'. Sometimes it is the representatives of other faiths who are the strongest supporters of establishment. Many Jews, for instance, have often said they would rather have someone speaking for God in public life than have a secular republic which could do what other secular republics have done in the past.

Equally, establishment does not mean that the state tells the church what to do. The cartoon on the cover of Theo Hobson's little book *Against Establishment*, with Her Majesty the Queen walking a dog on a lead, the dog's face being that of the Archbishop of Canterbury, is not only straightforwardly wrong (that simply isn't how establishment works), but ironically so: Hobson's own position is that the Church of England should reflect the mood and whim of the society in which it is set, going with the flow of contemporary moral positioning. In other words, for the Queen, substitute your favourite political columnist.

In fact, the present position does give the church (and those wider communities for whom it has a chance to speak up) a voice at the table; not the only voice, and not an easy voice to maintain in good order, but a voice none the less. There might well be other ways of achieving the same end, but there is an end there to be achieved, and the present system is at least a way of maintaining something of what ought to be done while the swirling currents of confused political rhetoric go round and round in circles.

The church now has a chance, granted the general decaying feel of Western democracy (think of the billions spent on elections in the USA; think of the refusal of the accountants to sign off on the European Union's accounts; think of the House of Commons' 2009 expense claims scandal and the British public's near-ubiquitous anger and cynicism towards all politicians . . .), to speak up about the big issues of justice, freedom, the very nature of government and democracy, the responsibility of all rulers not just to their own political backers or financiers but to those they rule.

God wants there to be good government, and the church – and Christian politicians – must bear public witness to that fact in every way possible. That, after all, is what Christians are doing when they pray, as Jesus himself taught us, for God's kingdom to come on earth as in heaven.

Notes

1 This chapter is adapted from the second Noble Lecture given at Harvard University on 24 October 2006.

2 Such as Niall Ferguson, *Colossus: The Rise and Fall of The American Empire* (Harmondsworth: Penguin, 2005) and *Empire: How Britain Made the Modern World* (Harmondsworth: Penguin, 2004).

3 An influential gathering of mostly American biblical scholars.

4 A. N. Sherwin-White, *Roman Society and Roman Law in the New Testament* (Oxford: Oxford University Press, 1963), pp. 24–47.

5 Genesis 2.2.

6 See, for example, Ched Myers, *Binding the Strong Man: A Political Reading of Mark's Story of Jesus* (Maryknoll, NY: Orbis, 1990).

7 See N. T. Wright, *Paul in Fresh Perspective* (London: SPCK, 2009), esp. Chapter 4.

8 Galatians 2.20.

9 Romans 15.12.

10 The question is now of urgent interest. See, for example, Jim Wallis, *God's Politics: Why the American Right Gets it Wrong and the Left Doesn't Get it* (Oxford: Lion, 2006).

11 See N. T. Wright, *Evil and the Justice of God* (London: SPCK, 2006).

4

The role of government in classical Christian political thought

DAVID McILROY

The awareness that the era of a close-knit relationship between church and state prevailing during the 'Christendom' period is over sometimes leads to the mistaken conclusion that the Christian thinkers who lived at that time have nothing to say to us in twenty-first-century Britain. This is a serious misjudgment. Although they made many mistakes from which we ought to learn, great thinkers such as Augustine, Aquinas, Luther, Calvin and Barth, at their best, offer us invaluable insight and perspective for dealing with contemporary political problems. The first three chapters of this book examined the resources of Scripture and biblical theology for guidance on the role of government. In this chapter I show how these biblical resources continued to guide the classical tradition of Christian political thought, shaping European ideas about government until the early modern era.[1]

It would be presumptuous to try to sum up over 1,500 years of Christian reflection on the role of government in a single chapter. Instead, I want to focus on four key principles recurring throughout classical Christian political thought: (1) government is accountable to God; (2) government's role is limited; (3) government exists for the public good; (4) the task of government is the wise execution of just judgment. Of those four principles, the first two are foundational (and their biblical and theological foundations were addressed in previous chapters), while the last two set out a framework for understanding the task and the purpose of government.

Government is accountable to God

Prime Minister Tony Blair's admission that he thought he would be accountable to God for his decision to take Britain into the Iraq war seemed to take political commentators by surprise.[2] After all, Alastair Campbell had insisted that New Labour 'didn't do God'. Blair was not, however, saying anything new within the Christian tradition. It has been a central claim of Christian political theology that kings are answerable to God for their actions.

In the fourth century AD, although the court theologian Eusebius declared the Emperor Constantine to be God's regent on earth, Gregory of Nazianzus insisted that precisely because Christians understand God to be Trinity, no human ruler can ever reflect God adequately.[3] Christians recognize one king, Jesus Christ, to be worthy of absolute honour and loyalty. The attempt to discern the implications of confessing the Lordship of Christ for the nature and role of government has been the defining question of Christian political thought ever since.

Among the various answers given to that question over the centuries, an important one has emphasized that Christian politicians should always remain mindful of the mercy of God shown through the life and death of Jesus Christ, and conscious of the future judgment they face before the throne of the ascended Christ. Remembering these things, it was urged, should have an impact on the way in which Christian rulers behave. Thus when in AD 390 the Roman

Emperor Theodosius ordered the massacre of 7,000 inhabitants of Thessalonica, Ambrose, Bishop of Milan, excommunicated him and Theodosius was only readmitted to the church when he had performed several months of public penance.[4]

Only a few years later, Augustine of Hippo wrote to Apringius, proconsul of Africa:

> I have no doubt that when you exercise the power that God has given you, a human being, over other human beings, you reflect upon the divine judgement, when judges too will stand to give an account of their own judgements.[5]

In a similar vein, in Book V, Chapter 24 of *The City of God*, Augustine wrote movingly about 'The State and Truth of a Christian Emperor's Felicity':

> But happy they are . . . if they reign justly . . . if they know themselves to be but men, and remember that; . . . if they use correction for the public good, and not for private hate; if their pardons promise not liberty of offending, but indeed only hope of reformation; if they counterpoise their enforced acts of severity with the like weight of bounty and clemency; . . . and if they do all things, not for glory, but for charity, and with all, and before all, give God the due sacrifice of prayer for their imperfections; such Christian emperors we call happy, here in hope, and hereafter when the time we look for comes, indeed.[6]

It was a repeated refrain among Christian political writers throughout the medieval and Reformation periods that kings were not free to behave as they chose, but were fully accountable to God for the ways in which they exercised their authority. Such an awareness should be a spur to the exercise of humility, mercy and charity in political decisions. Pope Gregory the Great warned that 'one should take great care, when defending justice, not to go too far and cross the threshold of arrogance; not, in an ill-judged love of right, to forfeit humility, the mistress of right'.[7]

The practical ways in which these virtues were thought to be demonstrated were many. One, often unnoticed today, was in the readiness to exercise flexibility in judgment. There is a strong current in Christian thought insisting on the importance of such flexibility.[8] This did not mean anything like modern pragmatism or relativism, but rather the virtue of attending with great care to the concrete particulars of a case in order that both justice and mercy be properly applied. Lawmakers simply could not know in advance all the circumstances in which the rules they laid down would end up being applied or interpreted. It would then be prudent to include the possibility of 'exceptional circumstances' which might require a departure from a general rule where this was what justice and mercy demanded. Today, for example, recognizing the limits of legislative foresight might lead to caution regarding the use of mandatory minimum sentences for particular crimes. This is an example of how the general norm of accountability to God lodged deep in the classical Christian tradition might make a quite specific difference to the daily discharge of the duty of political or judicial office today.

Not only humility and mercy, but also charity was upheld as a meaningful norm for a Christian ruler. Those who associate Calvin's political thought only with repression and rigidity might be surprised to hear him propose the following:

> If it is true that every nation has been left at liberty to enact the laws which it judges to be beneficial, still these are always to be tested by the rule of charity, so that while they vary in form, they must proceed on the same principle.[9]

Calvin even argued that the task of government endorsed in Romans 13.1–7 (punishing wrong and approving right) is one that should be understood as the attempt to put love into action.[10]

Clearly, the conviction that government is accountable to God runs directly counter to the suggestion, sometimes heard from the lips of Christian politicians, that 'God is on our side'. Many heard President George W. Bush to be implying such a claim in some of his pronouncements.[11] By contrast Republican presidential candidate Mike Huckabee, also a Christian, referred to such claims as the height of presumption.

Over time, and through many reverses and deviations, the tradition of Christian political thought came to emphasize increasingly that accountability to God should also be reflected in human structures of accountability for the use of political power. For example, the persistence of the church in asserting the right to criticize kings may be seen as having made an important contribution to the development of the principle of freedom of speech, eventually leading to an affirmation of the freedom of the press, which has proved in the modern era to be a vitally important way of holding governments to account. Equally importantly, classical thinkers informed by Christian natural law theory laid key foundations for what is probably the most fundamental modern constitutional principle, the 'rule of law' – which means that governments, and not only citizens, are subject to the law of the land and can be held legally accountable for breaches of it.

Government is limited

Pope Gelasius I (AD 492–6) established the distinction between secular political rule and ecclesiastical authority as fundamental to Christian thought. He argued that although Christ was the perfect priest-king, after Christ authority was distributed between secular rulers and the church, between secular power and spiritual power, between kings and priests. To keep them from pride, each had its own limited role and its own sphere of operation.

Ignoring Gelasius's lesson, Henry II appointed Thomas Becket as Archbishop of Canterbury, believing him to be a pliant instrument for his own purposes. Once installed, however, Becket proved to be unexpectedly independent. It was, ultimately, his insistence that the church had its own legitimate rights and that, accordingly, the powers of the king were limited, which led to his death. What is more, Becket's shrine became the most important in medieval England, so that, throughout the medieval period, the idea that the power of the king was limited was kept alive in England not only by Magna Carta but also by popular devotion.

Different classical Christian thinkers understood the limitation on government in contrasting ways. One fundamental distinction underlay most Christian treatments, namely that between the realms of the 'temporal' and the 'eternal'. Thomas Aquinas, for example, distinguished between temporal (temporary) things (i.e. 'secular' things, or things 'of this age') and eternal things (i.e. things 'of the age to come'). The church was responsible for eternal things; secular government only for temporary things. In parallel language, Calvin understood the role of government as the regulation of 'matters of the present life, not only . . . food and clothing, but . . . [also] the enacting of laws which require a man to live among his fellows purely, honestly, and modestly'.[12]

Calvin also implicitly operated with a further important distinction that allows us to express the tradition's view of the purpose of government in more specific terms. In a fallen world, he held, government had both a corrective or remedial role in restraining evil, and also a directive or coordinating role in providing for harmonious and equitable order in social relationships. I return to this distinction below, but it is helpful to refer here to Oliver O'Donovan's view of how the corrective function of government serves to limit its role. Seeking to express a central concern of the tradition, he holds that government action is only required if, were government to do nothing, some injustice, some public 'wrong', would occur. If no such wrong will happen if government does nothing then government should do nothing. O'Donovan goes so far as to suggest that it could be tyrannical for government to take action when private (i.e. non-governmental) initiative could address the issue equally well.

O'Donovan's principle would press governments today to identify very precisely the public wrong that their interventions are supposed to redress or prevent and to show why no other agency is equipped to address it adequately. By no means all current interventions of British government would necessarily survive such critical examination (and later chapters in this book engage in just such scrutiny – with contrasting results). On the other hand, O'Donovan's criterion of 'public wrong' would very likely justify governments in taking the sort of action that has seemed necessary to deal with the consequences of the 2008–9 credit crisis. In this sort of situation, even though government action is extensive, it is justified precisely because it is necessary to forestall a potentially catastrophic public wrong.

Having said that the role of government is limited, it is now almost universally recognized in Christian thought that the church's role is not to take over or dominate government either.[13] One reading of the Lutheran Reformation in Germany is that it was in part a reaction against the excessive interference of the Catholic Church in all aspects of people's lives, through the extensive reach of its canon law and its church courts. The logic of Luther's position was clear: only secular government has the right to use coercion to enforce its laws. Lutheran Protestantism thus led (albeit unintentionally) to the development of new forms of civil law in place of canon law, governing marriage, education, inheritance and other areas.[14]

There were, however, problems with the Lutheran reconceptualization of the relationship between church and government. There was a tendency for later Lutheranism to see government as above any human criticism, most evident in the declaration in Denmark in 1660 of an absolute monarchy. The same tendency is regarded by some as having contributed to the German church's general ineffectiveness in the face of Nazism.

There are, however, important exceptions to the picture of Protestant churches failing to provide an effective counterweight to government. The major Protestant theologian of the twentieth century, Swiss-German theologian Karl Barth, played a decisive part in the foundation of the Confessing Church, which insisted that submission to Nazism was incompatible with the confession of the Lordship of Christ. Barth believed that when the mission of the church to the state is faithfully carried out and when it is honoured by the state, then tyranny and anarchy 'will be dethroned; and the true order of human affairs – the justice, wisdom and peace, equity and care for human welfare which are necessary to that true order, will arise. Not as heaven (not even as a miniature heaven) on earth!'[15] If the government refuses to listen, then God will be glorified by the martyrs of the church.

Barth's theological roots were in Calvinism, which from its sixteenth-century inception generated a robust Christian critique of government. There were many serious deficiencies in the later Calvinist politics of John Knox and Oliver

Cromwell, but their overriding awareness that kings are accountable for the way in which they use their power and that such power is properly limited simply restated in rather more combative terms the central conviction of the Christian tradition. Indeed, the radical conclusion they drew – that a tyrannical government may even be toppled – was not without precedent itself. In the twelfth century, John of Salisbury argued, in line with the tradition, that rulers are accountable to God for governing justly and operating within a framework of divine law and natural right.[16] But then he ventured the radical implication that when a ruler grievously breaches that trust he has become a tyrant and may be deposed. Christians today who are declaring Robert Mugabe a tyrant for his attempts (continuing as I write) to cling on to power after the 2008 election in Zimbabwe, and urging his removal from office, are only reiterating a long-standing Christian political assertion.

The insistence that government has limits may be one of the most important services the church offers society. Simply by being itself and by defending its own institutional independence, the church reminds government that its citizens have other, and sometimes higher, loyalties than their membership of a state. Indeed, over time the assertion of what O'Donovan has called the 'doctrine of the two' laid the ground for the much wider claim that many other social authorities exist which do not derive from the state and to which the state must defer: families, educational institutions and many kinds of voluntary association, for example.[17] In that insight lay a vital foundation for what in the modern world we have come to refer to as the realm of 'civil society' – that network of intermediate bodies that serve to curtail the predatory instincts of the state.

Similarly, the church's affirmation that people belong finally to God and that God desires a direct relationship with each individual, strongly supports the recognition of individual civil liberty as an important Christian political principle. People require protected social and legal space in which to exercise personal responsibility for their lives under God.

The church's claims regarding the limits of government may also help to free government from the burden of impossible expectations. For example, it is very easy for politicians to get caught up in a cycle of punitive rhetoric about the need for tougher treatment of criminals. Proclaiming truths about eternal life, the church speaks of a judgment beyond that of any human court. Through its message of forgiveness, the church keeps alive the possibility of personal transformation. Through its declaration of God's mercy demonstrated on the cross, the church reminds society about the possibility of mercy in human judgment.

The recognition that government is limited should lead politicians to pause before expanding the field of government activity. Earlier I noted the distinction, implicit in Calvin's thought, between the corrective and coordinating roles of government. In the next two sections I elaborate on these two criteria for government action, beginning with the latter. I will suggest that, in line with the insights of the classical tradition, government should only act either in the execution of just judgment or the furtherance of the common good. The focus now will be on the contemporary outworking of these long-standing principles, though I will continue to call upon classical authors as my witnesses as I do so.

Government exists for the common good

Contemporary Western governments typically perform two distinct types of task (often very imperfectly). On the one hand, they promote a certain vision of the common good. For example, they may choose to promote marriage or child-rearing through the tax and benefits system. This need not involve coercing anyone to get married or to have children, but it does encourage people to regard these as socially valuable activities – as conducive to the common good. On the other hand, they seek to render what I shall call 'just judgment', responding to wrongs that arise within the public realm of society. For example, they protect individual freedom against arbitrary coercive restraint, or protect the natural environment against irreversible damage. Sometimes a particular government activity pursues both objectives at the same time, and sometimes it is not easy in practice to tell the two apart; nor is it always necessary to do so. The concepts of the common good and just judgment should be seen as complementary and mutually supporting rather than antagonistic or mutually exclusive.

In making these rather abstract concepts more concrete, it is helpful to distinguish between four types of government function: (1) association; (2) welfare; (3) defence; and (4) police. The idea of the common good is more to the fore in relation to the first two functions, while the idea of just judgment is more to the fore in relation to the latter two.

First, government provides stable conditions in which we can associate and communicate with one another – 'communication' here being intended in its older sense of sharing in a common life, or 'social participation'. In contemporary terms, government oversees networks of communications, monitors education, provides a regulatory framework for stable, well-ordered markets, and attempts to ensure that everyone has some access to the wider benefits of society.

Second, government ensures, whether directly or indirectly, that those who may be excluded from association and communication, through illness, unemployment or for other reasons, are given reasonable support and opportunities to take part in society once again.

Pursuant to the third and fourth functions, government has a responsibility for a country's defence against both external threats and internal disturbance. The modern distinction between the military and the police is necessary today to maintain clarity about their respective roles, but it ought not to obscure the fact that they are at root both concerned with protecting the peace of a particular territorially delimited social order.

I now want to explore further the role of government in promoting the common good. As government does so, two further aspects, each with roots deep in the tradition, are central: the ideal of public service, and the common good as the good of all.

The ideal of public service

Although the idea of the common good has subsequently been developed in a number of ways, for Thomas Aquinas it meant one important thing: government exists for the good of the people and not for the good of the ruler. This idea led to the coining of a new word in fifteenth-century England: 'commonwealth'. The word was used to describe the responsibility of the king to govern for the well-being of the people.

It is difficult for us in the UK today to grasp how far-reaching a historical advance this idea was. The idea that government exists for the good of the people is written into our very language of 'public service' and the description of our administration as 'the civil service'. This concept was hard-won, however. Charles I was executed for being a 'tyrant, traitor, murderer and public enemy'. His determination to defend his supposed right to rule without consulting

Parliament was seen by his opponents both as tyranny in the sense described earlier and as a rejection of a commitment to the common, i.e. public, good in favour of the promotion of the king's personal and private interests.

It is still of vital importance today to insist that politicians should not be seeking to advance their own private interests, or the narrow sectional interests of groups they may represent, but rather to serve the general public. A demonstrable commitment to the common good needs to remain a key component of governmental action. Lord Nolan, author of the 1995 Nolan Report on Standards in Public Life, formulated Seven Principles of Public Life, which summon politicians and officials to aspire to the highest standards of integrity and transparency in order to ensure that their actions are seen to serve the public good.[18] More broadly, in thinking about the reform of the funding of political parties, about standards of corporate behaviour in the financial and other sectors, in determining what to do about MPs' expenses, in deciding how best to address issues of corruption in high office and local government, we should be continually mindful of the need to develop and sustain systems which promote integrity and public service ahead of personal gain or sectional interest.

The common good as the good of all

The common good is more than the sum of its parts; it is a qualitative not an aggregative concept (as Nicholas Townsend explains further in Chapter 5). It expresses the value of community cohesion and solidarity, which comes from sharing a common life. It insists that society is more than a series of disconnected, isolated individuals. The insistence on the primacy of the common good is also an insistence that every member of society should find his or her place within it, that every member of society should have a stake in it and be able to exercise meaningful choices within it, and have access to the resources, education, housing, work and relational support which he or she needs to pursue a flourishing human life in all its dimensions.

The Christian tradition has affirmed both the value of the individual and the importance of individual choice on the one hand, and also the importance of community and the need for structures of association and community within which we can live fulfilled lives on the other. It is the duty of government to promote such structures, without either dominating them or marginalizing them. This aspect of the common good could be seen as supplying justification for policies as diverse as the promotion of the Welsh language in schools in Wales, the teaching of black history in state schools, the insistence that television corporations produce a significant proportion of British programmes reflecting life in Britain, or the provision of public support for a wide variety of arts projects (not promoting diversity for diversity's sake but honouring communities and subcultures which make a positive contribution to British society).[19] Government's aim in all these actions is to help UK citizens build a common public realm in which all have a real stake.

The norm of the common good also implies that no one should suffer permanent social exclusion. Thus a central and recurring theme in the tradition is that special attention must be paid to those who are most likely to be or to feel abandoned, notably those who are poor, whether financially or relationally. The prominent Old Testament concern for the socially and economically vulnerable – especially the widow, the orphan and the immigrant – has been continually reasserted in Christian political thought (even if too often ignored in practice).

In AD 257, when the Roman Emperor Valerian issued an order for the confiscation of all church property, the deacon

Laurence presented the sick, the aged and the poor, the widows and orphans of the congregation, and told the Roman officials: 'These are the treasures of the Church.'[20] In such a spirit, the church should insist that the interests of the poor be considered in all legislation and given special priority. The rich and powerful can hire lobbyists and organize campaigns and private meetings to pursue their agendas. Christian politicians must actively strive to listen to the voice of the poor. As Pope John XXIII argued:

> Considerations of justice and equity can at times demand that those in power pay more attention to the weaker members of society, since these are at a disadvantage when it comes to defending their own rights and asserting their legitimate interests.[21]

Christians may, of course, disagree about the extent to which the needs of the poor are best met by direct government action, by business enterprise, by promoting self-help, or by encouraging private philanthropy and the voluntary sector. Some of these questions are addressed in later chapters. But the weight of the classical tradition is solidly behind the prioritizing of the needs of the weakest, in whom it has been recognized that we see the face of Christ with special clarity.

The task of government as the wise execution of just judgment

Earlier I noted O'Donovan's proposal that the essential (corrective) function of government can be summed up as the rendering of just public judgment.[22] I now want to explain this important notion further. This notion is inspired by several key biblical terms. For example, there are two recurring words in the Hebrew Bible relating to justice. The first is *tsedeq* (often translated into English as 'righteousness'), referring to an order of right or just relationships and states of affairs. The second is *mishpat* (often translated into English as 'judgment'), referring to the ongoing practice of delivering justice. Combining these meanings, the term 'just judgment' means the concrete redressing of wrongs in ways that restore a divinely approved order of right relationships and states of affairs.[23]

Turning to the New Testament, we can (again following O'Donovan) interpret the classic passage in Romans 13.1–7 as affirming the same notion. There political authority is assigned the dual role of 'punishing wrong' and 'approving what is right' – rendering just judgment. In the sixth century AD, Pope Gregory the Great was voicing the settled standpoint of the Christian tradition in holding that the divinely assigned role of political authority was the exercise and execution of judgment.[24]

Gregory and many other classical Christian thinkers recognized that just judgment is an art, requiring practical wisdom so as to discern the most contextually appropriate response to the challenges of governing.[25] Often dismissed as 'rigid' and 'absolutist', the Christian tradition has long acknowledged that the Christian ruler must seek to discern the requirements of Christian moral teaching within and for the complex realities of the society that has to be governed. Augustine, for example, did not seek to resolve the inescapable ambiguities of governing. He knew that the conscientious ruler recognizes both the (sometimes) gruesome nature of the task he is called to undertake and also its moral necessity. The conscientious ruler will do what needs to be done to defend the state's territory, to maintain public order, to uphold property laws, to protect individuals from harm, and to enforce contracts.[26] He was fully aware that in doing so it would be naive to think that there will never be occasions when the only choices appear to be between thoroughly unpleasant options. These might include waging war in order to promote a just peace. Yet when force has to be used, it should be the minimum necessary to realize that end.[27] The complexity of government did not absolve rulers from realizing whatever degree of provisional justice (Augustine called it 'peace') they could in the earthly city. Thus, in Book IV, Chapter 4 of *The City of God*, Augustine declares famously that without justice, kingdoms are just like large-scale bands of robbers. It is the desire to act justly that distinguishes legitimate authorities from mere organized criminal gangs.

Governing, then, requires the application of wisdom to the task of judging justly. To see what this might mean in more contemporary terms, I want to refer to two questions: the relationship between rights and duties, and the relationship between law and morality.

Balancing individual rights and social responsibilities

It has often been argued, rightly, that Christian political thought provides a distinctive foundation for the ideas of human dignity and human rights.[28] Yet Oliver O'Donovan and Joan Lockwood O'Donovan have pointed to the difficulties surrounding the modern idea of *subjective* human rights – those rights supposedly possessed by each individual merely by virtue of being human, and construed as a type of property claim. Such an idea alone cannot provide an adequate criterion for the content of the just judgment which government is to render. Human rights, they hold, can at best be regarded as one (very important) type of legal claim on government action which must be arbitrated against others. Indeed, more generally, rights viewed as if they were subjective property entitlements do not provide a stable basis for a political society because they cannot account for those shared moral obligations, notably the common good, which make up the bonds of community that government must protect. A subjectivist concept of rights panders to the pursuit of individual self-interest, leading to a constant escalation of competing claims, expectations and demands. Far from providing a commonly agreed moral framework for the resolution of such claims, attempting to construct a legal system on the basis of subjective individual rights only increases conflict and undermines the ability of government to render just judgment or promote the common good. Yet the task of adjudicating among the competing legitimate claims of individual rights and public goods is by no means straightforward. Balancing individual rights against social responsibilities places great demands on the exercise of the virtue of wisdom. Political wisdom, in general, is the skill of rightly adjudicating among the competing and legitimate demands constantly made upon government. To do this requires knowing who is the source of a legitimate demand (that person or group may not have the loudest or the clearest voice) and whether and why that demand is in fact legitimate (some are spurious or even mischievous). Contrary to the myth sustained by modern secular liberalism, political wisdom thus understood is far more than the application of some neutral decision-making procedure; it involves the making of substantive moral discriminations. The acquisition of such political wisdom is sorely needed today, even though its content will be continually contested in a morally and religiously plural society.

The difference between law and morality

Christian political decision-making is not just a matter of taking propositions from the Bible or moral theology and translating them directly into law. The Christian political tradition has consistently recognized that there is a difference between the standards of Christian morality and what may be right to turn into law. Not everything that is seen (by Christians, or indeed everyone) as immoral ought to be made illegal.

Aquinas, who first systematized Christian natural law thinking, argued that human law is constrained by natural law in the sense that human law may not command what natural law forbids nor forbid what natural law commands.[29] Human law simply has no jurisdiction to order genocide or to outlaw marriage or family life. However, human law may have to tolerate what natural law forbids and in some instances must do so.[30] A classic example is divorce, for which it has long been recognized in the tradition that some legal provision must be made.

Aquinas counselled that law is only concerned with enforcing those matters of morality which belong to justice, that is, those which relate to right relations between persons.[31] We might refer to this as 'shallow justice', in distinction to the 'deep justice' which is the virtue that the Holy Spirit nurtures in Christians.[32] While the task of the church is to show people the path of true righteousness (deep justice), it is the role of government 'to bring about external peace and prevent evil deeds'.[33]

Whereas contemporary church pronouncements are sometimes criticized by politicians as being out of touch with political realities, Aquinas was clear about the difference between the morality that the church seeks to promote through its teaching and the laws that wise rulers should enact and apply. Attempting to prohibit all vices through human law would bring the law into contempt through the impossibility of adhering to it.[34] Human legislators must reckon with the realities of human sin, and this places a practical limit on what may be forbidden. Similarly, not everything that is morally right can be legislated. Even Christians, Aquinas realized, find it impossible to live morally perfect lives (as if anyone needed reminding). 'Laws should be possible both according to nature and according to the customs of the country.'[35] Well-framed human laws must take into account the fact that most people fall far short of divine standards of moral behaviour:

> Human law is established for the collectivity of human beings, most of whom have imperfect virtue . . . [so] human law does not prohibit every kind of vice, from which the virtuous abstain. Rather, human law prohibits only the more serious kinds of vice, from which most persons can abstain, and especially those vices that inflict harm on others, without the prohibition of which human society could not be preserved.[36]

While not everyone, and not even all Christians, will share the natural law approach on which Aquinas' proposal is based, it is the case that all politicians face the task of deciding which of the moral principles they subscribe to may be translated into law.[37] The general principles of morality need to be turned by politicians into specific, workable and enforceable laws and policies suited to the specific needs of their own political communities. For instance, politicians need to decide what counts in law as a valid marriage; to determine what counts as theft; to distinguish between tax avoidance and tax evasion; and to decide what punishments to impose in cases of breaches of the law in each case.[38] They also need to offer precise legal definitions of torture, and to decide, for example, whether or not the practice known as 'water-boarding' can sensibly be said to qualify.[39]

The classical Christian tradition, then, offers an important reminder today that the task of governing and lawmaking requires a distinctive virtue which is typically undervalued in contemporary society: the virtue of wisdom. And although politicians should never assume to themselves the role of society's moral tutors, it is nevertheless true that governing and lawmaking have an inescapable and necessary pedagogical impact. Consider, for instance, the way in which drink-driving campaigns have over time transformed society's attitudes towards the proper use of alcohol. When politicians discharge the task of judging wisely, they indirectly exercise moral leadership in society, whether they like that idea or not. The behaviours which law or policy promote and discourage, impose and forbid, help to shape what society holds up as worthy of moral praise or blame, as morally virtuous or vicious. In their acts of governance, therefore, politicians help to reinforce, to transform or to undermine a community's shared moral understandings.

This point needs to be kept in tension with a recognition of the inevitable limits of government's capability to promote the good. As O'Donovan puts it: 'Justice in human communities is only relatively just.'[40] This recognition can help Christians, as well as others, to come to terms with the need to accommodate aspiration to circumstance, to strive for workable agreements amid deep differences of conviction – to engage in what is often despised by those outside government as 'mere compromise'. So Christians should support the conscientious attempt by politicians to discern the best compromise between what ought to be done and what may practically be achieved. In O'Donovan's words:

> The exercise of political authority is the search for a compromise which, while bearing the fullest witness to the truth that can in the circumstances be borne will, nevertheless, lie within the scope of possible public action in the particular community of fallen men which it has to serve.[41]

Politics is difficult. Governing is hard work. The act of judging rightly requires both perspiration and inspiration. Indeed, in the Old Testament it was seen as a spiritual activity. In 2 Chronicles 19.6 Jehoshaphat encourages the judges he has appointed with these words: 'Consider what you do, for you judge not for man but for the LORD. He is with you in giving judgment.' Read through Christian eyes, we can take this to mean that judging justly can only be done in cooperation with the Holy Spirit.[42]

Conclusion

The church, at its best, performs four useful tasks for politicians. First, it expresses what it understands the content of God's just requirements for human society to be. Yet in enunciating a Christian morality it should do so in a way that reckons – as do Scripture and tradition – with the complexities and contingencies of the societies within which Christian politicians reach their judgments.

Second, it may indicate what approaches it believes would be principled accommodations and which would be unprincipled. For example, the Christian politician Ann Widdecombe voted in favour of amendments to the 1967 Abortion Act that reduced the normal time limit for abortion but allowed late abortions of handicapped babies. She did so because she believed that, on balance, the amendments would lead to fewer babies being aborted even though the change in the law meant that some handicapped babies were now at greater risk of abortion. In deciding how to vote on this issue of conscience, she was guided by the Catholic Church's teaching regarding the lesser of evils. The church's teaching gave her guidance on how to act in accordance with her Christian principles in a political context in which compromise is unavoidable. The political discernment of the right (just) thing to do in all the circumstances, which I have called 'shallow justice' and which the Bible calls 'just judgment', is a demanding task to which the church ought to offer its very best reflection.

Third, the church may, where the need demands it, offer sharp critique of government. Archbishop Desmond Tutu's stance against apartheid was both peaceable and yet uncompromising. Fourth, and by no means least, the church prays for politicians.

In return, government serves the church not in the first instance by handing out benefits or privileges, but rather by attending to its own functions of promoting the common good and executing just judgment. In providing a stable, relatively peaceful and relatively just society, government creates conditions and opportunities for the church to fulfil its own unique function – to witness freely to Jesus Christ.

Practical questions

What difference would attention to the insights of the classical tradition of Christian political thought considered above make to the practice of politics today? The answer to that is complex. I have briefly gestured towards some aspects of it here, and subsequent chapters address it in more detail. I conclude by suggesting that the classical tradition at least poses a series of pertinent and testing questions which individual Christian politicians might usefully ask themselves when considering any particular action: Am I prepared to answer to God for this action? Is this action necessary in order to prevent or to remedy a wrong? Is this a 'just judgment'? Should I adjust my action to take account of the possibility of unexpected circumstances? Does this action promote the common good? Whose interests does it benefit? What is its impact on the poor and the marginalized in society? Does this action strike an appropriate balance between morality and practicality? And, lastly, can I honestly say that this decision is an expression of love for my neighbours and of service to God?

Notes

1 By 'classical Christian tradition' I refer to the influential body of (mainly Latin) Christian political theologians represented, for example, in Oliver O'Donovan and Joan Lockwood O'Donovan, *From Irenaeus to Grotius: A Sourcebook in Christian Political Thought 100–1625* (Grand Rapids: Eerdmans, 1999). This is not to imply that thinkers on the margins of the classical tradition have nothing to teach us.

2 The remarks were made in an interview with Michael Parkinson, screened on ITV1 on Saturday 4 March 2006. Reaction to Blair's remarks can be found, among other places, at <http://news.bbc.co.uk/1/hi/uk_politics/4773124.stm>; <http://www.independent.co.uk/news/uk/politics/blair-god-will-be-my-judge-on-iraq-468512.html>; <http://www.telegraph.co.uk/. . ./news/2006/03/04/nblair04.xml&sSheet=/news/2006/03/04/ixnewstop.html>.

3 Gregory of Nazianzus, *Oration* XXIX.2, in P. Schaff and H. Wace (eds), *A Select Library of the Nicene and Post-Nicene Fathers*, Series II, Vol. VII (Grand Rapids: Eerdmans, 1989).

4 Theodoret, *Ecclesiastical History*, V.17–18, in William Stearns Davis (ed.), *Readings in Ancient History: Illustrative Extracts from the Sources*, 2 vols (Boston: Allyn and Bacon, 1912–13), Vol. II: *Rome and the West*, pp. 298–300.

5 Augustine, 'Letter 134: 411AD, Augustine to Apringius' in E. M. Atkins and R. J. Dodaro (eds), *Augustine: Political Writings* (Cambridge: Cambridge University Press, 2001), p. 63.

6 Augustine, *City of God* (New York: Modern Library, 1993), p. 178.

7 Pope Gregory the Great, *Moralia*, Book 25, Chapter 16, paragraph 36, in O'Donovan and Lockwood O'Donovan (eds), *From Irenaeus to Grotius*, p. 202.

8 Martin Luther, 'Temporal Authority: To What Extent It Should be Obeyed' (1523) in O'Donovan and Lockwood O'Donovan

(eds), *From Irenaeus to Grotius*, p. 593; S. Theron, 'St Thomas Aquinas and Epieicheia' in L. J. Elders and K. Hedwig (eds), *Lex et libertas: Freedom and Law according to St Thomas Aquinas* (Rome: Liberia Editrice Vaticana, 1987), pp. 171–82.

9 John Calvin, *Institutes of the Christian Religion* (1559), tr. F. L. Battles (London: SCM Press, 1961), Book 4, Chapter 20, paragraph 15.

10 John Calvin, *The Epistles of Paul the Apostle to the Romans and to the Thessalonians* (Edinburgh: St Andrew Press, 1961), p. 285.

11 See Rogers M. Smith, 'Religious Rhetoric and the Ethics of Public Discourse: The Case of George W. Bush', *Political Theory* 36(2) (2008), pp. 272–98.

12 Calvin, *Institutes*, Book 3, Chapter 19, paragraph 15.

13 Oliver O'Donovan, *On the Thirty Nine Articles: A Conversation with Tudor Christianity* (Carlisle: Paternoster, 1986), pp. 98–9.

14 John Witte, *Law and Protestantism: The Legal Teachings of the Lutheran Reformation* (Cambridge: Cambridge University Press, 2002), p. 64.

15 Karl Barth, *Church and State* (London: SCM, 1939), p. 84.

16 Michael Ovey, 'Beyond Scrutiny? Minorities, Majorities and Post-modern Tyranny', *Cambridge Papers* 13(2) (2004).

17 See John Courtney Murray, 'Are There Two or One?', in Murray, *We Hold These Truths: Catholic Reflections on the American Proposition* (Kansas City, MO: Sheed & Ward, 1960), Chapter 9.

18 *The First Report of the Committee on Standards in Public Life* (London: HMSO, 1995) (Cm 2850-I), accessible at <http://www.archive.official-documents.co.uk/document/parlment/nolan/nolan.htm>.

19 On some of the issues which this raises, see Julian Rivers, 'Multiculturalism', *Cambridge Papers* 10(4) (2001), and Jonathan Chaplin, 'Has Multiculturalism Had Its Day? Towards a Christian Assessment', *Ethics in Brief* 12(6) (Spring 2008).

20 Reported by Ambrose in *Three Books on the Duties of the Clergy*, Book II, Chapter XXVIII, in Schaff and Wace, *A Select Library of the Nicene and Post-Nicene Fathers*, Series II, Vol. X (Grand Rapids: Eerdmans, 1989).

21 John XXIII, *Pacem in terris*, tr. H. E. Winstone (London: Catholic Truth Society, 1963), p. 56.

22 Oliver O'Donovan, *The Desire of the Nations: Rediscovering the Roots of Political Theology* (Cambridge: Cambridge University Press, 1996).

23 Genesis 18.19; Deuteronomy 33.21; 2 Samuel 8.15; 1 Kings 10.9; 1 Chronicles 18.14; 2 Chronicles 9.8; Job 36.17; Psalms 89.14; 119.121; Proverbs 21.3; Isaiah 56.1; Jeremiah 22.15; Ezekiel 45.9.

24 Gregory, *Regula Pastoralis*, Part 2, Chapter 6, in O'Donovan and Lockwood O'Donovan (eds), *From Irenaeus to Grotius*, pp. 196–200.

25 See Proverbs 8.15–16.

26 Julian Rivers, 'Liberal Constitutionalism and Christian Political Thought' in P. Beaumont (ed.), *Christian Perspectives on the Limits of the Law* (Carlisle: Paternoster, 2002), p. 14.

27 One of the tragedies of Augustine's legacy is that, under pressure of circumstances, he agreed that the Roman state might coerce the Donatists, a rival church which was engaging in religious terrorism. This was later treated as a general mandate for the persecution of heretics, and Augustine's own teachings about the abhorrence of the death penalty and torture were ignored.

28 Witte traces this development in the Calvinist tradition in *The Reformation of Rights* (Cambridge: Cambridge University Press, 2007). For a powerful, and scholarly, assessment of human rights in relation to the Christian tradition, see Chapters 14 to 16 of Nicholas Wolsterstorff, *Justice: Rights and Wrongs* (Princeton: Princeton University Press, 2008).

29 Aquinas, *Summa Theologiae*, tr. the Fathers of the English Dominican Province, 1911 (5 vols, Allen, TX: Christian Classics, 2000), I–II.95.2.

30 Aquinas, *Summa Theologiae*, I–II.96.2.

31 Aquinas, *Summa Theologiae*, I–II.99.5 ad.1.

32 See David McIlroy, *A Trinitarian Theology of Law: In Conversation with Jürgen Moltmann, Oliver O'Donovan, and Thomas Aquinas* (Milton Keynes: Paternoster, 2009), pp. 198, 216, 232–4, 237.

33 Luther, 'Temporal Authority', in O'Donovan and Lockwood O'Donovan (eds), *From Irenaeus to Grotius*, p. 587.

34 Aquinas, *Summa Theologiae*, I–II.96.2 ad.2.
35 Aquinas, *Summa Theologiae*, I–II.96.2; 97.1.
36 Aquinas, *Summa Theologiae*, I–II.96.2; II–II.69.2 ad.1; 77.1 ad.1.
37 Pamela Hall, *Narrative and the Natural Law: An Interpretation of Thomistic Ethics* (Notre Dame: University of Notre Dame Press, 1994), p. 41.
38 Aquinas, *Summa Theologiae*, I–II.95.2; John Finnis, *Aquinas: Moral, Political, and Legal Theory* (Oxford: Oxford University Press, 1999), p. 266.
39 They do not, however, have a totally free hand in doing so. If water-boarding is torture on any rational view, then it is torture whatever politicians may say. See Christopher Hitchens, 'Believe Me, It's Torture', *Vanity Fair*, August 2008, accessible at <http://www.vanityfair.com/politics/features/2008/08/hitchens200808>.
40 Oliver O'Donovan, *Resurrection and Moral Order* (Leicester: Apollos, 1986), p. 130.
41 O'Donovan, *Resurrection and Moral Order*, p. 130.
42 This is not to imply, however, that only Christians can truly judge.

5

Government and social infrastructure

NICHOLAS TOWNSEND

Introduction

'Politics' refers to decision-making for a whole, geographically defined community by means of enforceable law, together with all the activities directed towards that – elections, lobbying, opposition and so on. At least, this is a working definition that corresponds with the main use of the word in British public life.

There are three main questions we can ask about what *should* be done in politics.

The first concerns the role of political authority: What is the proper purpose or end, and thereby the role, of political authority? In short, what should government *do*? The present chapter tackles this question.

The second concerns political obligation: Why should people see themselves as obliged to accept political authority and generally to obey its decisions? Putting this another way, what is the source of government's authority? In answering this, Christians have usually included reference to Romans 13.1–7.

The third concerns the form of government: How should the institutions through which political authority acts be constituted? Should they, for example, be monarchical or democratic? Should there be a separation of powers? The issue of the relationship between religious and state institutions arises under this third question.

These questions ask, respectively: What? Why? How? In various ways, all three are addressed in this book. They give the main headings under which almost all practical issues about what should happen in politics arise.

A very rich resource for addressing them is the extraordinary body of documents known as the 'social teaching' of the Roman Catholic Church. It is précised conveniently in the recent *Compendium of the Social Doctrine of the Church*.[1] But reading this isn't really a substitute for study of major earlier texts, such as *Populorum progressio* of 1967 and *Centesimus annus* of 1991. This body of teaching cannot be digested in a single sitting – the *Compendium* alone has 400 pages – but is a storehouse on which all can draw. Nothing quite comparable has emerged in Protestant or Orthodox Christianity.

Yet Protestants tend to find some frustration with Catholic Social Teaching (CST) because the roots in biblical and theological sources of positions it affirms are sometimes not as clear as they might be. This is despite the very evident turn to Scripture in the encyclicals of Pope John Paul II. This chapter aims to answer the first question above in a way that connects the New Testament with what we find in CST.[2]

We can clarify the question of the role of political authority by looking at its current context. The central political debate of the twentieth century – and one suddenly revived by the 2008 financial crisis – focused on it in relation to one area of policy, the economy. To what extent is it government's role to direct economic activity or should this be left to free markets? A legacy of that focus on economic policy may be that people tend to see the wider question through the lens of this issue. But it arises in different ways in each major area of public policy – criminal and civil justice, ecological protection, social security, healthcare, education, to list a few. To come to a general answer through just one policy area is risky as it could lead to highly inappropriate policy-making in others. Politicians need a general, 'macro' view of what government is to do so that they can deliberate well in each policy area. Otherwise they will not have good reasons for deciding what to advocate.

There are a number of 'ready-made' answers in the main schools of modern Western political thought. In briefest summary, liberalism holds that the role of political authority is to secure equal individual freedom for all. The differences in the liberal tradition turn on how 'freedom' in this formula is understood. Traditional conservatism holds that government's role is to enable us to sustain our present way of life by dealing with inevitable change in ways that avoid losing more than we gain. 'Old' social democracy sought to use political authority to bring about, as far as practicable, equality of economic resources and political power. In Britain, the advent of New Labour in the 1990s symbolized a shift beyond relatively sharp distinctions among such stances, to what some see as post-modern, liquid politics. This may have made answering the question more difficult, but it also gives an opportunity to overcome some of the difficulties in the main modern 'ideologies'.

CST speaks of the role of political authority in terms of a much older concept, the common good. We start with a short exposition of this.

'Good government' and 'bad government'

> . . . the common good is the reason that . . . political authority exists . . . To ensure [it], the government of each country

> has the specific duty to harmonize the different sectoral interests with the requirements of justice.
>
> (*Compendium*, 168–9)

The first point that describing government's role in terms of the common good entails is basic, yet always needs restating. The exercise of political authority, whether at local, national or international level, is to be for the *whole* of the respective community. It ought never to be only for some sectional interest, such as the ruler's financial backers or C2 voters in marginal seats. This contrast is none other than the fundamental difference between good and bad government and is as old as Western political thought. The principle is expressed in the convention at UK general elections that, after each result is declared, the winning candidate's speech makes clear that he or she will serve the whole constituency, however divisive the campaign might have been.

Human well-being: an 'irreducibly common good'

> The common good does not consist in the simple sum of the particular goods of each subject of a social entity. Belonging to everyone and to each person, it is and remains 'common' because it is indivisible and because only together is it possible to attain it. (*Compendium*, 164)

The next point is equally important but less easy to grasp, and certainly more controversial. It is that for each person, human well-being consists essentially in the simultaneous generation and enjoyment of the good of the whole society, as we participate in multiple ways in this. The human good is, this means, *inherently* or *irreducibly* common. It is analogous to the good of a concert, a football match or a great feast of celebration – it can exist for anyone only as all participate in the shared action in which they produce and benefit from it simultaneously.[3]

That claim is controversial because it denies certain other views about human well-being. It is contrary to individualistic views, using this term for those according to which you or I could enjoy the good life irrespective of whether our neighbour also does. It denies, for example, that well-being consists in each individual maximizing pleasure or freedom, although of course pleasure and free agency are goods. It denies also that society is only an arena for dealing instrumentally with others in order to gain the means to private satisfactions (as consumerism tends to assume). Rather, like a great celebration, society is an irreducibly common good, in living within which the human good for each of us is found – or it can be to the extent that we participate in ways that generate this.

This is to affirm a 'communitarian' position – a term liable to strike fear and scepticism into some liberal readers. They will, understandably, hear echoes of authoritarian uses of power to attempt to bring about community goals that many citizens do not endorse. But later we shall notice how such a politics of the common good requires full protection of each person's human rights.

The common good: what is political authority's distinct role?

> The common good . . . involves all members of society; no-one is exempt from co-operating, according to each one's possibilities, in attaining it . . . [This] responsibility . . . besides falling to individual persons, belongs . . . to the State, since the common good is the reason that political authority exists . . . The goal of life in society is in fact the historically attainable common good.
>
> (*Compendium*, 167–8)

According to CST, all have responsibility to act for the common good. Our participation in business, family life and the arts, for example, can and should engender it. However, political authority is presented as having a role in which the common good is its specific *raison d'être*. Whereas for business people or musicians to give proper attention to their own activities can be sufficient for these to contribute to the common good, governments have to focus on its requirements directly. Yet the texts of CST are not especially clear on exactly what the relationship is between the specific role of political authority and the common good.[4] This chapter aims to clarify this. In doing so it sets out a conception of the role of government that can constitute a basis for policy deliberation.

Politics and the Christian gospel

Taking up the working definition with which I began, the Christian gospel is not about politics – a risky statement! I mean that the gospel as such is not about making things happen by the ordinary means of political power, enforceable law. This point enables us to identify one pitfall to which Christians can be prone. When we realize that God isn't just concerned about private spiritual lives, we might think that what God wants is for the whole of Christian morality to become the nation's laws and support political campaigns to this end. Certainly, God longs for and calls all humanity to live in the way for which he has created and redeemed us. But God's route to bringing this about is not politics in that sense. Rather, it is the gospel.

How can we describe the Christian gospel? Here is one way. By the coming to Israel and all the world of God's Son, by his becoming human, namely the Jew Jesus of Nazareth, the reign of God has been renewed and begun to be made real in this age. It is a reign in which righteousness, justice and peace replace sin, oppression and violence. This is what happened through Jesus' incarnation, death, resurrection and ascension. The people who came to faith that Jesus is the Christ and repented of sin were thereby brought within this reign. Here they found forgiveness and, in their new common life, astonishing signs of blessing. But all this did not happen by the standard means of political power. On the contrary, God's reign came by his Son being the servant of the people in a way that repudiated such means. Jesus called his followers to the same kind of service, to lives together that were formed by and manifested his way.

How could this be possible once Jesus of Nazareth was no longer among them? There were two, equally important factors. The first was the supreme authority given to Christ that was even over death.[5] This meant that there was no worldly power they needed ultimately to fear. They were freed from all the overbearing claims of lower authorities, even Caesar, to live under the just and gentle rule of Jesus Christ. Second, there was the Holy Spirit – the Spirit of God's Son, as St Paul put it in Galatians 4.6 – who had been given to them and enabled them to go on living in the way of Jesus. St Paul emphasized (also in Galatians) that their identity now lay in faith in Christ, not in Israel's law, and their moral practice was free, not subject to such law. As the Spirit of Christ made possible this life of faith and freedom, they would manifest the Spirit's fruit, the moral qualities of imitators of Jesus.[6] This community 'in Christ' would go on making real the renewed reign of God.

The Christian gospel is that this has happened, and that still anyone may 'repent and believe'[7] and begin to 'live by the Spirit'.[8]

That is just one way to summarize the gospel.[9] It is incomplete – it does not describe, for example, *how* Christ's death and resurrection effected forgiveness for us, or the Christians' gradual discovery that God's Son and the Spirit are both fully divine. Nor does it refer to the actual history of Christianity, with its highs and despicable lows. But it will do, I hope, for the purpose here.

For Christians, then, to take hold of the ordinary instruments of political power in order to try to bring about what the gospel requires would be totally contradictory to it. Such politics would necessarily make a society unchristian. In this sense, the gospel is not about politics.

But, as numerous writers have pointed out in recent decades, Jesus' own proclamation of the gospel was inherently political. When he came into Galilee announcing that God's reign was at hand, both Jews and Romans would have heard a political message. Israel's God was again becoming king! 'Kingdom' or 'reign' was not the only political term. 'Gospel' itself, *evangelion* in Greek, was the news trumpeted across the Roman Empire to mark military victory or the accession of a new emperor. And so on: messiah – an anointed royal figure; lord (*kyrios* in Greek) – the one in authority, not least Caesar; church (*ekklesia* in Greek) – in one meaning a gathering of Roman citizens who worked for the community's welfare.

The gospel was political – it was all about a kind of reign or rule, a way of being a people, a city, that was an alternative to the then dominant Israelite, Greek and Roman forms. The church was a public or outward body under a distinct rule, in short a polity. Recognition of this is now very wide among scholars, to the point of almost becoming a commonplace.

The gospel is not about politics. The gospel is political. The latter is true even though the way of Jesus involved repudiation of the ordinary, coercive means of politics. The paradox that produces the apparent contradiction is that the Christian polity was so radically alternative that the more it was faithful to its founder the sooner it could appear not political at all. This strange polity shows the need for a different definition, according to which politics is about how people live together and the common good this generates, even though the people are not defined by geographical boundaries and there is no dependence on enforced law. Yet this definition cannot simply displace the other: we have two meanings of one word (nothing unusual about that) and the initial one will remain useful.

Having identified one pitfall to which Christians are prone, we need to notice another. The first occurs *before* people see that the gospel is political, whereas the second comes *after* that. This is perhaps more understandable because, as much recent writing shows, for example by Stanley Hauerwas, William Cavanaugh and Samuel Wells, recovery of recognition that the Christian community is a polity can lead to astonishingly fertile insights about its life and witness.[10] Yet these writers, who may fairly be called the Hauerwas school, seem to have been slightly blinkered by those very insights. They appear not to see that, *from the perspective of church as public body*, Christians may and must address another agenda too, about Christian participation in a geographically defined society. This includes seeking to answer theologically the three questions distinguished at the start of the chapter – about politics in the sense given there. Such writers barely reach these questions.[11] Their writing is often brilliant, but what they seem to say to those Christian people who seek to participate faithfully in secular politics is, at best, 'On this one, you're on your own.'

This second pitfall can be described essentially in this way. The New Testament itself makes clear enough that the *two* political strands that run through the Hebrew scriptures, the 'authority' strand and the 'prophetic' strand, continue after Christ, both renewed, under God's authority. If this is true, and 'the powers that be' are given by God, it would be a refusal of vocation, for some, to stand back. With the pastoral support of their local church, they are to be in there, by God's grace working with others to ensure those powers are exercised justly, rather than abused to exploit or torture, or left unused in the face of poverty or genocide.

'Government as social infrastructure' in theory

We come to the main argument. To begin we need to see a connection between the earlier two sections of the chapter. 'The common good' and 'the reign of God' are different ways of referring to the same thing. The ultimate or perfected common good is the same as the final reign of God, a connection which comes out clearly in Augustine of Hippo's famous use of the biblical metaphor of 'city of God'. In the end this will be the 'new Jerusalem, coming down out of heaven', when God's reign will be complete.[12]

Similarly, the penultimate or temporal common good is nothing other than the reign of God being made real now. Certainly the world as we know it is pervasively corrupted by sin and distorted by suffering. Yet to the extent that people live in ways that manifest among us the diverse goods that God graciously gives, they live within God's reign and contribute to the temporal common good.

Granted this connection, I shall mainly speak of the common good in the rest of the chapter. In line with the normal usage in CST, I shall mean this in its temporal sense, the 'historically attainable common good' (as quoted earlier). Of course, CST remains perfectly clear that such unqualified reference implies no downplaying of the recognition that what is in view is not the final city of God.[13]

The summary of the gospel at the start of the second section referred to Paul's call to 'live by the Spirit' in Galatians 5—6. Romans 12 is partly parallel to those chapters, but there is no equivalent to Romans 13 in Galatians. In Romans 12 Paul presents, through a series of exhortations, an extraordinary vision of how the Christian community in Rome is to live. He goes on to advise on how they should act in relation to the imperial authorities. Does the new life 'in Christ' which he has urged them to live out mean they no longer need see a place for worldly authority? His emphatic answer is no. Chapter 13 begins, 'Every person must be subject to the ruling authorities [KJV: 'the powers that be']. There is no authority, you see, except from God . . .'

This passage gives 'ethical instruction ("be subject . . .")', rather than 'theological or philosophical reflection on the nature of government', as Pilgrim puts it.[14] Tom Wright too emphasizes the relatively limited scope of Paul's purpose in this passage.[15] Yet we can identify from Romans 12—13, read against the background of the earlier letter, some clear pointers to a more general Christian theological understanding of government. It is as though Paul is saying: 'The main thing you need to grasp, to appreciate, to live in light of, is all that God has done in his Son, Jesus the Christ, and the Holy Spirit. This is what the whole letter has been about. But you also need to keep in mind another, more mundane way in which, still, the same God is acting: through the Roman authorities.'

So these passages portray two related but distinct ways in which God acts for our good. The first is that described in Galatians 3—6 and Romans 12, 'life by the Spirit', which is equally the way of God's Son, Jesus Christ. The second is that of Romans 13.1–7, temporal or secular rule, which does depend on the ordinary means of political power and therefore on possible resort to what in Paul's day was 'the sword'.

Paul doesn't imply that somehow the kingship of Christ is not over the emperor and his governors. On the contrary it was the Christians' profession that Christ is Lord of lords that got them into trouble and for some led to martyrdom. What Paul conveys is that, under God, the emperor and his governors have their own place. I suggest we may distinguish these complementary ways in which God is working after the coming of Jesus Christ and the giving of his Spirit as primary/direct and secondary/indirect. It is by looking at how these are related that we find a route to describing the role of political authority.

The New Testament story of the coming of God's reign and formation of the Christian polity – the church – suggests the following theological affirmation. God's primary agency for bringing into being good relations among people, the good society, the common good, is the way of human living which that community itself is supposed to make real.

Granted which, we may ask: what remains left for political authority, acting through law that is when necessary enforced, to achieve? To show the basic shape of the answer, two fundamental points may be made, relating respectively to those two ways in which God acts.

First, if that 'primary agency' were to be usurped by political authority seeking directly to bring into being the common good, this would be wholly contradictory to God's way revealed in the gospel. Therefore, governments must never take over the Christian community's mission, as could happen if they were to try to make any aspect of this a matter of law that is enforced by 'the sword'.

The second point follows: we need to conceive of any role for political authority as secondary or indirect in relation to the common good. What does this mean? Its role must refer to *social conditions* which don't themselves constitute the full temporal common good that God intends, but which have to be in place if there is to be the very possibility of this existing for anyone.

To illustrate, imagine the launch conference for this book – if you're reading this, it has taken place. The venue, the chairs, the lighting, the transport network; the conditions of human living of those who attend: food and water, good enough health, freedom to come – all those constitute the preconditions of actually holding the event. Together they form an infrastructure that establishes the very possibility of this social good. But for the event itself actually to take place, it is not just the infrastructure that is required. People need actually to be there, to speak, to listen. The presentations need to be more or less coherent. Responses need to be to the point, and so on. In short, communication needs to take place. These things form the good itself, of which the infrastructure is only the necessary condition. Here is a distinction between two modes or levels of action: the common agency that constitutes the event itself, and establishment of the infrastructure. Holding this illustration in mind can assist us as we now unpack the two fundamental points above.

The Christian polity is the primary mode by which God wishes to bring into being good relations among people, the common good – through its ministries of word, sacrament and pastoral care. But if there are social preconditions of this happening, conditions of the possibility of the common good, establishing them must be the role of political authority in the secular polity, acting through law that is enforced.

Now the life of faith, freedom and the fruit of the Spirit, the community of love of God and neighbour, is open to all: the common good is for all, of course. So if there are social preconditions of its possibility, they must be secured for all – irrespective of, say, religious profession, ethnicity or economic status. If some lack such conditions of living, they are being excluded from the very possibility of the life God intends for them – even though establishing those conditions is not the same thing as directly generating the common good itself.

In light of the gospel, what remains left for political authority to achieve? We can now state the formal answer: *to secure the social conditions necessary for the possibility of the common good.*

This may seem an abstract argument, but it doesn't take much further thought to see that it is to do with non-abstract and often urgent human needs: food, somewhere people can live, access to healthcare, at least some education, some freedom to form views on such claims as the gospel of Jesus Christ and that 'there is no God but God and Muhammad is his prophet', water supply, power, roads, sewage systems. I say it is 'to do with' these very concrete goods, as I don't want to prejudge exactly what will follow in practice but only to convey a sense of this idea of the conditions of the possibility of the common good. Of course, each of those areas of possible political practice would need to be considered directly and in appropriate detail to establish what would fall within a description of those conditions (and the remaining chapters take up aspects of that task).

The concept of 'infrastructure' is not just useful for the earlier illustration, but can be a label for this view of the role of political authority. People need a 'social infrastructure' that secures for them the preconditions of living with one another well in the way God intends. It is for government to establish these conditions for all equally.

But what this role *doesn't* include is the renewal of human relations that is to be made real in the Christian polity. Secular governments acting through law are to establish only some outward conditions. What is required for the good of all and each is a going beyond this, the common agency of simultaneous generation and enjoyment of the common good.

In the light of the New Testament, here is a *Christian theological* account of the role of political authority and, inherently, of the limits to that role. Supposing, as would be necessary, that this could be set out for the various major areas of public policy (e.g. ecological protection, economic policy, social policy, home affairs, foreign affairs), we would have a substantive account of *political justice*. Governments' responsibility 'to render what is due', to do justice, is to establish and sustain the 'social infrastructure' that is necessary for the possibility of anyone enjoying the common good.[16]

How does the argument of this section connect with Roman Catholic Social Teaching? It describes the role of political authority in a way that corresponds with several statements in CST, for example:

> Political power . . . must have as its aim the achievement of the common good. While respecting the legitimate liberties of individuals, families and subsidiary groups, it acts in such a way as to create, effectively and for the well-being of all, the conditions required for attaining humanity's true and complete good.[17]

Yet the argument also shows how the Christian gospel itself, as we discover it in the New Testament, lies behind this view of the role of political authority. It brings out a connection between this aspect of contemporary CST and biblical sources in a way not found in the documents themselves.[18]

'Government as social infrastructure' in practice

This section will put some flesh on the bones of the theory of 'government as social infrastructure' by beginning to show what it would mean in practice. Along the way I shall give pointers to how it is related to other political positions.

What kinds of government action will be needed in practice to establish and sustain the social infrastructure? Uncontroversially, a first kind is stopping people committing wrongs that prevent the possibility of others' participation in the common good. Obvious examples include murder, assault, rape and theft. Governments must use law to end and prevent those sins of commission that preclude such participation. This aspect of government's role is a response to human sin, so it can be called remedial.

A second, parallel aspect of what governments must do is in response to sins of omission. To have the possibility of participating in the common good, people need access to a range of basic goods such as food, water, healthcare and income in old age. To the extent to which people provide and share such goods in the ordinary contexts of family life, local communities and exchanges in markets, as they should, no government action to ensure people have them is necessary.

But in fact many lack such goods, and this is essentially because of sins of omission, coming from, for example, complacency or selfishness. To the extent that this is so, the preconditions of the possibility of the common good are not in place. So government must act in ways that ensure that people have access to such goods, although this certainly does not entail that state agencies are the best equipped to provide them directly. This second kind of action is also remedial.[19]

A third kind of practical action is not remedial but is directive to the common good. Think here of rail networks and sewage systems. To the extent that there are certain things that the 'social infrastructure' positively requires which, by their nature, can only be *either this way or that* within any geographical community, it is within government's role to decide them. The question of where, if anywhere, the airport or the new city park should be located can in the end be answered in only one way: here and not there. So those who can determine things for a particular community as a whole, the political authorities, have to decide. This is the *directive* or *coordinating* aspect of government's role. Human sin might make this more difficult, but it is not what makes it necessary.

In a perfect world, such direction would be all that government need do. In 'fallen' human society, however, it is the additional remedial role that usually is the most prominent. Recognition of the directive role points to a warning. 'Government as social infrastructure' justifies only such coordination as is needed to establish the preconditions for the common good. This is in massive contrast to statist forms of government, whether 'old' socialism on the left or Italian and Spanish Fascism on the right, in which there was no clear sense of limit and, instead, an assumption that state action would *directly* bring about the good society. The concept of social infrastructure can give a basis for discerning what is within the role of government and what is not.

While the distinction of these three kinds of government action emerges within an explicitly Christian theological argument, it has a correspondence with contemporary non-theological analysis of duties and rights. The sins of commission against which government must act are failures of duty to respect people's 'freedom rights', including their so-called 'basic liberties' (notably bodily integrity, movement, association, worship, speech and personal property). The sins of omission against which government must also act are failures of duty to meet people's 'benefit rights'. These are rights to obtain such goods as fresh water, healthcare, some level of education, and enough income to live off. So the first two aspects of government's role involve upholding, respectively, *freedom rights* and *benefit rights*, which are also known as 'first generation' and 'second generation' rights. While the match is not exact, the third, directive kind of government action has some affinity with so-called 'third generation' rights, those to do with participation in a society's wider cultural life.[20]

Recognizing such correspondence does not imply that fuller articulation of it would be unproblematic. The language of rights is not a reverse prism through which moral disagreement suddenly becomes agreement. This is because there are substantively different philosophical and theological views about human beings and therefore of duties and rights. The particular way in which 'government as social infrastructure' leads to affirmation of human rights will in some respects differ from how other perspectives do so. To give an example, which inevitably is controversial: in relation to the growth of the human foetus in the womb (leaving aside discussion about the very early human embryo), most Christian teaching differs from voluntarist liberalism in not seeing the point of viability outside the womb as morally significant for when the life of a person with rights begins.

We now look at what 'government as social infrastructure' would mean more concretely by brief remarks on one area of public policy (limited space precludes addressing more than one), namely the economy and business. In the aftermath of the 2008 financial crisis, the need to draw on the wealth of resources in Scripture and the Christian tradition that address the basic moral issues in this area is overwhelming. The first thing to be said is that these are moral issues. There has been no deeper cause of the economic crisis than the explicit denial in the neoliberal capitalism which has dominated recent decades that what people do in markets should be subject to moral analysis.

Second, business activity should never be subjected to an *overriding* imperative of maximizing profit. Rather, it can and should be a hard-headed form of love of neighbour, in which the *end* is to supply goods and services – things that are good for and of service to people – and the wholly necessary *means* is making a profit. In neoliberal capitalism, ends and means have been mistaken for each other.

Third, to anyone who *has* subjected themselves to mere financial return as the overriding end, to an idol, Christians simply announce the gospel's message. 'Repent! Worship the true God. Accept forgiveness. By God's Spirit, practise love of neighbour, even in business.'

Fourth, while businesses can be run in a way that puts right neoliberalism's reversing of means and ends, we human beings are pervasively sinful and the reality will always fall short of that pure vision. While this gives no excuse, the economy has always been and will be 'mixed', manifesting virtue and vice.

All of which points to the respective roles of the Christian polity and the secular polity. Good business is engendered essentially by the former: it is possible as people act in line with that message. They might do this because of actual Christian faith, or through an ongoing moral legacy of Christianity in largely secularized societies, or on common ground with other philosophies or faiths.[21] Those with the talents and skills – entrepreneurial flair, strategic vision, imagination, precision with numbers, speed, marketing nous, creativity, attention to detail, sharp antennae, leadership gifts – surely could employ them in practice of that hard-headed love of neighbour. But political authority can't bring this shift about. Rather, it is for the ministry of the word to do so, both the word made flesh – the examples that Christian business people are to give – and the word preached. Local, national and international business communities should be able to witness it in their colleagues and competitors, and hear it from the public platforms that pulpits always are.[22]

It is not for governments to effect such moral transformation by imposition. Rather, the role of the secular polity is to establish the preconditions for good business. As in all areas of policy, government must remedy the sins of commission and omission that preclude people from participating in the common good. A few examples of the former are: contributing to unsustainable ecological damage; supplying dangerous products; selling loans to people who obviously can't repay them; and preventing people from having a weekly day off. Examples of the latter are: wilfully not fulfilling the terms of one's employment; not ensuring safe conditions for workers; and paying mere subsistence wages. Good business people, whether employers or workers, will avoid these. But to the extent that in practice businesses don't, it is plainly government's role to ensure by enforced law that such sins do not exclude people on economic grounds from the social infrastructure.

I hope that this short discussion suggests the potential that 'government as social infrastructure' has for generating discussion about policy. For it to inform practice a great deal of work would be needed, as is proper and inevitable. But part of its appeal, I suggest, is its generality, which makes it highly fertile for policy thinking. In this it is comparable with, for example, John Stuart Mill's harm principle or John Rawls's two principles of justice. Of course, unlike these two positions, it is explicitly a Christian understanding. The argument for it arises from the gospel. Therefore it makes no claim to neutrality in relation to different philosophical or religious stances.

To conclude, we return briefly to the context of contemporary debate about government's role. To traditional conservatism, 'government as social infrastructure' brings a conception of justice that necessitates challenge to hierarchical and oppressive social orders. To socialism it brings a basis for principled limitation of the state's role. To the various individualistic forms of liberalism, it brings a communitarian vision of the good life, without loss of a robust conception of human rights. To the particular version most influential in recent times, neoliberalism, with its ideological tendency to minimize state activity, it offers the sharpest moral critique and an alternative vision that could re-energize business. This Christian theory of the role of political authority could be called a 'fourth way'.

Acknowledgement: I am very grateful to the editors and also to Nigel Biggar, Jonathan Boston, Séverine Deneulin and Lincoln Harvey for comments on drafts of this chapter. Sincere thanks too to the students of Sarum College and to several year-groups of CARE's Leadership Programme, in sessions with whom the position argued for here has been tested.

Notes

1 Pontifical Council for Justice and Peace, *Compendium of the Social Doctrine of the Church* (London: Burns & Oates, 2004), hereafter *Compendium*. The full texts of this and other documents mentioned in this paragraph are accessible at <www.vatican.va>. References to the *Compendium* and other Vatican documents give section numbers, not page numbers. An introduction to Catholic Social Teaching that is both helpful and provocative is S. Hauerwas and J. Bennett, 'Catholic Social Teaching', in G. Meilaender and W. Werpehowski (eds), *The Oxford Handbook of Theological Ethics* (Oxford: Oxford University Press, 2005), pp. 520–37.

2 An important background source for the argument of this chapter is the set of articles by John Courtney Murray SJ, edited by Leon Hooper SJ as *Religious Liberty: Catholic Struggles with Pluralism* (Louisville, Kentucky: WJKP, 1994). The position to be advocated here can be seen as a development of Murray's.

3 This way of explaining the common good draws on Charles Taylor, 'Irreducibly Social Goods', in Taylor, *Philosophical Arguments* (Cambridge, MA: Harvard University Press, 1995). Section 3 of the following article outlines the concept of the common good more rigorously: S. Deneulin and N. Townsend, 'Public Goods, Global Public Goods and the Common Good', *International Journal of Social Economics* 34 (1/2) (2007), pp. 19–36, accessible (Feb. 2009) at <http://www.welldev.org.uk/research/workingpaperpdf/wed18.pdf>.

4 This is despite the 'principle of subsidiarity' (*Compendium*, 185–8), which there is not space to bring into this discussion but which is addressed in the next two chapters. On the lack of clarity I refer to, see further note 18 below.

5 Matthew 28.18.

6 Galatians 5.22.

7 Mark 1.15.

8 Galatians 5.16.

9 This summary of the gospel draws on many sources. In addition to the NT texts cited, see Tom Wright, *Surprised by Hope* (London: SPCK, 2007), pp. 213–17, for one helpful short statement. See also *Compendium*, Chapter 1. The phrase 'just and gentle rule' is from the church's liturgy; see e.g. the Collect for the Third Sunday before Advent in the Church of England's *Common Worship*.

10 To see that, just read Wells' book *God's Companions: Reimagining Christian Ethics* (Oxford: Blackwell, 2006).

11 Not all of the authors of the seven chapters presented under the promising heading 'Constructive Political Theology' in Peter Scott and William Cavanaugh (eds), *The Blackwell Companion to Political Theology* (Oxford: Blackwell, 2004), could be identified with 'the Hauerwas school', although broadly the *Companion* can be. Some of those chapters are excellent – yet

none of them directly addresses any of those three questions. Thank goodness for the Roman Catholic Church's social teaching and the few contemporary writers who do so. Among the latter, especially notable examples are O'Donovan in the global North and Villa-Vicencio in the South. See Oliver O'Donovan, *The Desire of the Nations: Rediscovering the Roots of Political Theology* (Cambridge: Cambridge University Press, 1995) and *The Ways of Judgment* (Grand Rapids: Eerdmans, 2005); C. Villa-Vicencio, *A Theology of Reconstruction: Nation-building and Human Rights* (Cambridge: Cambridge University Press, 1992).

12 Revelation 21.

13 See *Compendium*, 170.

14 W. Pilgrim, *Uneasy Neighbors: Church and State in the New Testament* (Minneapolis: Fortress, 1999), p. 8. Pilgrim identifies some weaknesses in the 'sharp and provocative' interpretation of Romans 13 by J. H. Yoder that 'reflects his pacifist stance' (Pilgrim, *Uneasy Neighbors*, pp. 9, 11).

15 Wright summarizes what Paul is getting at here as follows: 'He has just said, strongly and repeatedly, that private vengeance is absolutely forbidden for Christians. But this doesn't mean on one hand, that God doesn't care about evil, or, on the other, that God wants society to collapse into a chaos where the bullies and the power-brokers do what they like and get away with it . . . That is almost all that Paul is saying . . . ', Tom Wright, *Paul for Everyone: Romans Part 2* (London: SPCK, 2004), p. 85. The translation of Romans 13.1 at the end of the last paragraph is from the same source, p. 82. See more fully N. T. Wright, *The Letter to the Romans*, in *The New Interpreter's Bible: A Commentary in Twelve Volumes*, Vol. 10 (Nashville: Abingdon, 2002), pp. 712–23.

16 Although I refer to ecological protection in this paragraph, limited space means that this chapter does not articulate what needs to be said about non-human nature. Ecological sustainability for its own sake (that is, not just as a resource for humans) is a basic prerequisite of the common good, and my use of 'social infrastructure' presumes that throughout. While

clumsier, 'eco-social infrastructure' would capture the needed sense better.

17 *Octogesima adveniens* (1971), 46. See further e.g. US Catholic Bishops, *Economic Justice for All*, 1986, 122; this is accessible at <www.osjspm.org>.

18 Moreover the argument gives enough clarity to overcome an apparent confusion in CST. Whereas most of its documents present the common good as the *end* of human life in society, that is, the highest temporal good there can be (cf. *Compendium*, 168), one frequently quoted definition gives a different impression. This is that the common good is 'the sum total of social conditions which allow people, either as groups or individuals, to reach their fulfilment more fully and more easily' (*Compendium*, 164, citing *Gaudium et spes*, 26; there are a few other similar statements, e.g. in *Mater et magistra* of 1961). Here the common good is not described as the *end*, but as a state of preparation for it, a set of circumstances necessary if it is to be possible. This seems confusing because it begs the question: what is the end *beyond* the common good, viewed as a set of 'social conditions', which it serves? However, this difficulty can be overcome if we see that statement as giving a fair description, not of the common good as such, but of the specific role of political authority in acting for it. When government deliberates and acts, it must have the common good explicitly in view, but the role of political authority can only ever be *indirect*, *secondary*, in relation to it. The argument outlined in the main text enables us not only to connect New Testament sources with CST but also to resolve this apparent tension in the latter.

19 For those interested in the writing of Oliver O'Donovan, I note that the shape of the argument for 'government as social infrastructure' is broadly similar to that in his work, although there are differences. (See *Desire*, especially Chapters 3–6. It is not only similar but is greatly indebted to it.) O'Donovan argues that the whole of the role of political authority can be placed under the heading, 'judgment'. One thing he means in using this label is that government's role is, in one way or

another, made necessary by sin. Therefore, both kinds of action just outlined would fit within both 'government as social infrastructure' and O'Donovan's view of 'government as judgment'. Yet one difference is that the former conveys a clear recognition of a principled limit to the role of government, as suggested already: its remedial task extends only to acting against those wrongs that preclude people from the possibility of the common good. While a fuller discussion would be necessary to delineate the boundary this limit sets, it is not easy to see how in principle O'Donovan's category of 'judgment' generates such a limit. *Prima facie* the more political authority brings judgment on sin the more it attains its end. At stake here also is the major question of whether it should be part of the role of political authority to *intend* to 'make people moral', by disciplining people in the virtues, as the dominant pre-modern Western Christian tradition (in e.g. Aquinas and at least some Calvinism) held. I am inclined to think that this view represented a significant usurpation by political power of what is properly within the Christian community's own ministries, not least of word. Of course, even if this is right, such moral disciplining will to some extent take place *de facto* as a 'side effect' of governments' remedial action to establish the 'social infrastructure'.

20 An outstanding Christian statement about duties and rights, to which the perspective presented in this chapter corresponds, I think, is the papal encyclical *Pacem in terris* of 1963.

21 For Christian understanding of business that is very close to that expressed here, see e.g. *Compendium*, Chapter 7; for corresponding practice, see <www.tbnetwork.org>. For astonishingly rich accounts of Western modernity that bring out the extent of the legacy of Christianity in its ways of living, see Charles Taylor, *Sources of the Self: The Making of Modern Identity* (Cambridge: Cambridge University Press, 1989) and *A Secular Age* (Cambridge, MA: Harvard University Press, 2007). In relation to other faiths, substantially the same stance on business as outlined here has been powerfully articulated by Jonathan Sacks, the Chief Rabbi, and it is advocated by the Muslim economist Muhammad Yunus, founder of the

Grameen Bank, in Claire Foster and Edmund Newell, *The Worlds We Live In: Dialogues with Rowan Williams on Global Economics and Politics* (London: Darton, Longman & Todd, 2005).

22 Before modernity's mass media, speaking from a pulpit was like issuing a press release. To a large extent churches have acquiesced in their own privatization by reducing preaching to talking to a club; cf. Nick Spencer, *Neither Private nor Privileged: The Role of Christianity in Britain Today* (London: Theos, 2008), pp. 32ff. That does not imply that speaking well in public debate on controversial topics is easy. See Keith Clements, *Learning to Speak: The Church's Voice in Public Affairs* (Edinburgh: T. & T. Clark, 1995).

6

Government, solidarity and subsidiarity

PHILIP BOOTH

Subsidiarity and solidarity: an introduction

Christians, and especially Catholics, frequently use the phrases 'solidarity' and 'subsidiarity' to describe the extent to which a free-market economic policy should be balanced by government intervention. Sometimes these concepts, which are discussed widely in Catholic Social Teaching,[1] are regarded as being in competition – as if the application of one should be balanced by the other in any thinking about public policy. But when these concepts are properly understood, it is only in extreme cases that their application can lead to the necessity to balance one against the other, thus trading off, say, a decrease in subsidiarity for an increase in solidarity.

One way of thinking about solidarity is to consider it to be the duty of the political authorities to pursue what is sometimes called a 'preferential option for the poor'[2] through government intervention, redistribution and so on. The argument would continue that such intervention should be limited because of the principle of subsidiarity, which requires that government intervention should take place at the lowest level of government and, preferably, that autonomy should remain with voluntary groups and the family.

This way of thinking tends to lead to a moderate left or a moderate conservative view of politics. According to this view, the state should redistribute income and wealth but protect private property. It should also devolve responsibility to lower levels of government where possible, thus giving the family autonomy in fields such as healthcare, education and so on. This produces an out-turn rather like some of the Christian Democratic states of the European Union (EU). However, from the point of view of political economy, such an equilibrium is not stable. The reality of the fallen nature of humanity can lead to the accumulation of increasing responsibilities within an increasingly centralized state, unless we actively try to restrain it.[3]

In fact, we need to think of both the concepts of subsidiarity and solidarity in a richer context. If we do so, it leads to conclusions about the appropriate role of government in economic life that are less obviously clear but more sustainable. If one reads Vatican statements that use the word solidarity, it is clear that only one aspect of the concept relates to the pursuit of ends through the means of the political system – in other words government action to help the poor, the homeless and so on.[4]

So, what do we mean by 'solidarity' and from where does the term arise? Properly understood, solidarity is an attitude and virtue. It relates, first, to how we view our neighbours. It is an attitude that is then translated into good works through our actions as employers, within our families and extended families, through professional associations, community groups, schools, parishes and so on. Finally, in Catholic Social Teaching, there is action through the political sphere – where the state has a role, though not the primary role, of overseeing the exercise of human rights in the economic sector.[5]

Action through the political sphere is coercive and thus circumscribes the freedom and creativity of those trying to address social problems: it is therefore just one aspect and not the most important aspect of the exercise of solidarity. The idea of solidarity has been used throughout Catholic Social Teaching but John Paul II's encyclicals have a particular emphasis on the theme. The principle is rooted in the biblical values of awareness of the needs of others and of our common humanity as children of God, as well as in our obligations to those in need, which are clearly stated in both the Old and New Testaments. As a virtue, solidarity is grounded in rational free choice and is about choosing the good of our neighbour wherever we encounter him or her. In this context, it can be seen how relatively unimportant the political dimension is intended to be.

In turn, the application of the principle of subsidiarity does not generally involve a crude balancing act with solidarity. Among other things, it aids us in developing the philosophy by which we should judge *how* to implement public policy in the economic sphere. The principle of subsidiarity demands that government and coercive measures in the economic sphere are a *last* resort. As the *Catechism of the Catholic Church* puts it, 'The principle of subsidiarity is opposed to all forms of collectivism. It sets limits to state intervention.'[6] The application of the principle demands that government *helps* or *assists* lower levels of community – and especially families – in achieving their legitimate objectives.[7] In the words of the Rio Declaration on the Family: 'Subsidiarity means that the family, not the State, not large organizations, must be given responsibility in managing and developing its own economy.'[8]

We have seen the principle of subsidiarity enshrined in the EU – especially in the Treaty of Maastricht. In EU governance, subsidiarity means that lower levels of government are responsible before higher levels of government for implementing EU policy. However, in its proper context, subsidiarity means that there should be intervention in economic life only where it is deemed necessary; it also means that voluntary associations have responsibility to meet economic ends before any level of government. But, crucially, subsidiarity is the process by which the state helps private and intermediate groups attain *their* legitimate ends, never supplanting their initiative, only facilitating it. This is very important and quite distinct from the interpretation of subsidiarity within the EU where the EU sets the policy objectives. A good example of the proper application of this principle would be in education where the church has often proposed a role for the state in financing education, but always asserted that this finance should be provided in such a way that parents' wishes are never supplanted and that private education – including that provided by the church – is not discriminated against.

The principle of subsidiarity, like the principle of solidarity, is not just plucked out of thin air. It has long been a key part of Catholic Social Teaching, if not always explicit. It arises from the idea that the individual has free will and is of infinite value to God. The individual is by nature social and the community is more than just the sum of its parts. However, political structures exist to aid the individual and the community – and in doing so promote the common good. The state should be subservient to individuals, families and communities – not the other way round. This is drawn from the church's understanding of the nature of humankind, and its special place in creation, an understanding that is shared by all Christians.

Of course, debates between Christians on the appropriate scope of the market and the domain of the state in economic life are legitimate. There are occasions where we are asked to balance the principles of solidarity and subsidiarity.[9] Application of the principle of solidarity sometimes implies action by the state, just as the application of the principle of subsidiarity calls for that action to be limited and designed in a particular way. But neither the Catholic Church nor Scripture exhibits a bias in favour of the general use of socialized, political mechanisms to achieve the sorts of objectives (protection of the poor, sheltering the homeless, provision of health and education, etc.) that Christian communities and others hold dear.

In the words of the *Compendium of the Social Doctrine of the* [Catholic] *Church*:

> Experience shows that the denial of subsidiarity, or its limitation in the name of an alleged democratization or equality of all members of society, limits and sometimes even destroys the spirit of freedom and initiative . . . state action in the economic sphere should also be withdrawn when the special circumstances that necessitate it end.[10]

There is, of course, legitimate debate to be had on what those special circumstances are and when they have ended. We look at that debate with regard to two different policy applications in the remainder of this chapter. The first is in the field of taxation – perhaps the most enduring topic that helps determine the extent to which economic power is centralized within government. The second is the subject of the environment – a policy area that many would feel comes into the category of giving rise to the special circumstances that permit intervention by government.

Taxation and charity – the distinction

In his encyclical *Deus caritas est*, Pope Benedict XVI confirmed the message of John Paul II's encyclical, *Centesimus annus*, that a state that tried to provide for all material need would become a mere bureaucracy. He also notes that charitable need is not just material and that, even in the most just state, charity will be necessary – it meets needs in a way that is more fully human than a welfare state can. The principle of solidarity is not a call to put a cross on a ballot paper to elect a party that will tax our rich next-door neighbour to give to the poor person across the road – it is a call to action to help those in need. This call to action should resonate within our hearts and should be applied at the individual and family levels, and also collectively – though this collective application is not to be exercised principally through the political system but through the rich tapestry of voluntary collective institutions.

Too much Christian discussion on economic matters is dogged by a belief that Christian concepts of charity and mercy should be translated directly into political policy. Some Christians seem unable to see a poor person without calling on government action to help him or her. They ignore both the philosophical problems of favouring action through the political sphere and, also, the empirical problem that such government action frequently does not achieve the desired results: indeed, it often achieves the opposite of the desired results. Charity and mercy are virtues that have no limit in their application. Government, however, is naturally limited in its capacity to act because it can only take resources from one group in society and transfer them to others, and because its distance from the real needs of individuals naturally limits its effectiveness. Government is therefore not an appropriate vehicle for exercising charity and mercy. It is, rather, for the government to administer justice, thus setting the framework within which all Christians can pursue their vocation.[11]

Even a government of a distinctly Christian character should not take upon itself the duties of Christian communities to share goods, provide welfare and look after the aged and sick, except where efforts to provide these functions in other ways have failed. If a government undertakes these functions, it undermines the free will, dignity and genuine love and charity of individuals within their communities: government action in these fields crowds out the voluntary action and personal response that should be key characteristics of Christian communities motivated by true love.[12]

This distinction between the role and responsibilities of Christian communities on the one hand and the distinct role of government on the other has a long heritage in Catholic Social Teaching. Five hundred years ago the Late Scholastics warned against the dangers of taxation. In the early social encyclicals strong statements were made against taxation of the poor and the pursuit of equality for its own sake. Referring back to Pope Leo XIII's encyclical of 1891, Pope Pius XI wrote: 'Wherefore the wise Pontiff [Pope Leo] declared that it is grossly unjust for a State to exhaust private wealth through the weight of imposts and taxes.'[13] And then, in the same encyclical, he himself stated, 'the rich are bound by a very grave precept to practice almsgiving, beneficence, and munificence',[14] and, 'How completely deceived, therefore, are those rash reformers who . . . in their pride reject the assistance of charity.'[15] Charity is not a marginal activity for those with an excess of goods, it is fundamental to Christian living.

That does not mean that the state should be absent from the economic sector. Catholic Social Teaching is clear that government must redistribute income to the extent that it is necessary for all to have the necessities of life, where other means fail. As one writer puts it: 'Under general or social justice all are entitled to access to the necessities of life, and it is the duty of the State to see that this is the case.'[16] Interestingly, he adds, 'the citizen in return being prepared to work for his needs'. This thinking about the distinct characteristics of charity on the one hand and redistribution by the state on the other is, of course, quite compatible with the teaching about subsidiarity and solidarity discussed above.

These points about the dangers of an all-embracing welfare state and a misunderstanding of the role of the state and voluntary activity in meeting human need were perhaps best summed up by Pope John Paul II in his encyclical, *Centesimus annus*:

> In recent years the range of such intervention has vastly expanded, to the point of creating a new type of State, the so-called 'Welfare State'. This has happened in some countries in order to respond better to many needs and demands, by remedying forms of poverty and deprivation unworthy of the human person. However, excesses and abuses, especially in recent years, have provoked very harsh criticisms of the Welfare State, dubbed the 'Social Assistance State'. Malfunctions and defects in the Social Assistance State are the result of an inadequate understanding of the tasks proper to the State . . . By intervening directly and depriving society of its responsibility, the Social Assistance State leads to a loss of human energies and an inordinate increase in public agencies, which are dominated more by bureaucratic ways of thinking . . . and which are accompanied by an enormous increase in spending.[17]

Average tax burdens today are very high throughout the developed world by historical standards, reflecting to a large degree the development of 'social assistance states' throughout the Western world. In the UK, the total tax burden (when government borrowing which is merely deferred taxation is included) is around 50 per cent. This represents, to a considerable extent, the denial of the principle of subsidiarity arising from the government taking upon itself the responsibility of welfare provider of first, rather than last, resort.

How government finance is delivered

It is legitimate for Christians to disagree on the size of the state, as measured by the tax take. However, for a given level of government spending on welfare, also important is how a government delivers that spending. The Catholic Church has always emphasized strongly the role of the family in the provision of health, education and other welfare services. Pope John Paul II's 1981 apostolic exhortation, *Familiaris consortio*, for example, suggests that the state should provide families with aid to meet their educational needs and that aid must be in proportion to the needs of the family. This would seem to suggest some form of means-tested assistance to help with the finance of education. However, the duty to provide education is clearly laid upon the family, the church and other intermediate institutions and not the government. Indeed, the church goes as far as suggesting that it is an injustice for the state not to support attendance at non-state schools, that a state monopoly of education offends justice and that the state cannot *merely tolerate* private schools.[18]

This is very important in contemporary political debate. The principle of solidarity arguably requires that support may be given through the tax system to those families who cannot afford an education for their children. However, the principle of subsidiarity *demands* that the state is limited to providing help. There is no need for the state to provide education or to dictate how that education should be delivered. This is a long way from the form of education provision in the UK at present – though it is an approach which sits more comfortably with policies pursued in some European countries such as Sweden and, perhaps, Holland.

Subsidiarity and solidarity: the environment

The second major area of policy that we will discuss in the subsidiarity/solidarity framework is that of the environment. There should be a natural affinity among Christians for economic frameworks that are effective in preserving the environment – after all, the environment is part of God's creation. Notions of 'stewardship' come easily to mind when Christians consider this subject, though this does not necessarily help us determine the legitimate role of public policy. As it happens, however, it does seem that the modern economic way of thinking about environmental problems is quite compatible with a Christian approach that applies the ideas of 'subsidiarity' and 'solidarity'. This framework though has implications for policy that are quite different from those implied in the statements of many Christian groups on environmental matters.

While the subject of the environment has not had the same attention in Catholic Social Teaching as, say, the problems of underdevelopment, clear statements have been made regarding the responsibility of all Christians to the created environment. In *Octogesima adveniens*, an apostolic letter published in 1971, the exploitation of nature was raised as a problem. Also, a letter from the bishops, assembled at a synod in Rome, published in the same year, suggested that it was not possible for all countries to have the same kind of development that had been pursued by the then rich nations, with obvious implications relating to the exploitation of natural resources.[19]

More particularly, there have also been statements in Catholic teaching about the environmental responsibilities of businesses and consumers. A business must 'contribute to the common good also by protecting the environment'.[20] Businesses are told that they must see that their environmental impact is factored into their costs.[21] Consumers are warned about creating lifestyles that involve pillaging the natural environment from future generations and are called to temperance and restraint.[22] As well as consumers and businesses having a responsibility, states are also asked to draw up juridical frameworks to ensure that the natural environment is protected.[23]

The above statements are carefully crafted and they are not intended to lead people to accept a reductionist interpretation whereby all laws and regulations that restrict business activity and consumption to the apparent benefit of the environment are to be welcomed. Indeed, statements of a specific policy nature in key teaching documents of the Catholic Church are generally sparse and this is particularly so in relation to the environment.

In the first place, in an expression of solidarity, we are called to conservation as consumers and producers – we should be careful and act with restraint and moderation in our consumption patterns. Indeed, Christians should act with restraint and moderation in all areas of their lives. Also, in solidarity, the state should develop an appropriate juridical framework that ensures the appropriate protection of the environment, which may well involve calling businesses and consumers to account, *in one way or another*, for the impact of their actions on the environment. It does not follow that this should involve direct regulation to restrict business activities – Christians are free to disagree about such matters. I shall argue below that extending the realm of private property, so ensuring that those who consume environmental resources are held to account in their production and consumption decisions, together with an effectively functioning market price mechanism, is an approach to this problem that simultaneously applies the concepts of subsidiarity and solidarity while also providing good economic and environmental outcomes. This does not, of course, rule out more specific intervention in some circumstances. However, the primary goal should be for public policy to provide the framework within which individuals, families and communities can deal with environmental problems in ways that are appropriate given their circumstances.

Private property and environmental protection

Private property has long been regarded by the church as the essential building block of a sustainable society.[24] It is interesting, therefore, that economists regard environmental problems as symptoms of poorly defined or incompletely defined property rights. For example, if the property rights to my house include a right to a view, then my neighbour is not able to build a block of flats that obstructs my view without first purchasing that right from me. On the other hand, if I have no property right to a view and the legal system prevents me from obtaining one, then it is much more difficult to resolve this environmental problem satisfactorily.

In practice, strong private property rights provide effective incentives to preserve the environment. An interesting real-life case study is given in *Saving Our Streams: The Role of the Anglers' Conservation Association in Protecting English and Welsh Rivers* by Roger Bate.[25] He shows how a voluntary group, the Anglers' Conservation Association (ACA), acting in solidarity and using the courts, ensure that people do not pollute rivers that they do not own. The ACA have been able to assert their property rights and prevent individuals, firms and often government bodies from polluting and destroying rivers.

Perhaps more pertinent, given the concern about environmental problems in the developing world, is an example from Nigeria. As is noted below, forest destruction in Africa is a serious problem. A detailed report in *The New York Times*[26] provides an extraordinary story of how trees in the Niger valley gradually came to be regarded as the property of local farmers. Instead of illegally logging for firewood farmers had an incentive, once they became owners, to nurture the trees and sell their products. In turn, the significantly increased forest density helped to keep the soil more fertile.[27]

The more effective establishment and enforcement of private property, especially where property is widely owned, is an essential aspect of the principle of subsidiarity. The existence of private property does not mean that there will not be abuses of the environment, but abuses can most effectively be resolved, whether by negotiation or by government action, once ownership of environmental resources is well defined.

In response, it might be argued that the institution of private property would allow people to destroy those parts of the natural environment which they owned, even if this had no direct effect on other persons, and that this is incompatible with the notion of persons being stewards of creation. However, it should be noted that there is no Christian imperative to simply *preserve* the environment in its natural state. As is stated in the *Compendium*, 'God entrusted to man the task of exercising dominion over the earth, subduing it and cultivating it.'[28] Moreover, the extension of private ownership would seem to provide strong incentives to cultivate and use environmental goods productively and sustainably because the value of land, rivers and other environmental resources at any given time will depend on their sustained productivity into the indefinite future.[29] Indeed, countries where governments uphold property rights effectively have much better environmental protection than those that do not.

One interesting example in this respect is that of forest destruction.[30] Forest burning simultaneously involves the production of greenhouse gases and the destruction of what is known as a carbon sink – as well as having local impacts on towns and villages close to forests. There is growing evidence that a general environment of economic development and strong property rights is effective in limiting deforestation. United Nations figures suggest that the global rate of net deforestation has fallen from nine million to seven million hectares per year, comparing the last decade of the twentieth century with the first few years of the twenty-first century (despite an increase in world population).[31] More pertinently, nearly all the net loss is now confined to South America and Africa: the USA, Europe and Asia are now reforesting on balance. There is also a very strong correlation between economic growth and reforestation. No nation with an annual GDP per capita of more than $4,600 per annum had net forest loss in the period 2000–5. Of course, there is also a strong correlation between effective property rights protection and national income. Thus it seems that strong property rights protection, national income growth and a nurturing of the local environment can go hand in hand.[32]

International environmental problems

More challenging, however, are environmental problems that cross national boundaries. There are many situations where the effective definition and trading of private property rights has not arisen for one reason or another and these provide particularly good examples of environmental degradation or even catastrophe. One such example is fishing rights in European Union waters, such as the North Sea. Nobody owns the North Sea and, though the community of fishermen as a whole has an incentive to maximize fish stocks in the long term, no individual trawler owner has an incentive to do other than to extract as many fish as possible. If we can imagine an entity that owned the North Sea and that was able to sell fishing rights, then that entity would wish to keep fish stocks high over the long term in order to raise the value of the asset. The owner would have an incentive to sell fishing rights in such a way that conservation was promoted. The owner would also have an incentive to ensure that any entity polluting the sea was prevented from doing so or was required to pay compensation. Private ownership should lead to conservation and a better husbandry of the marine environment.

We can, indeed, envisage private property rights in the sea, just as we have in land – or at least we can envisage mechanisms set up by government, such as are used in Alaska and Iceland, that mimic private ownership in fishing rights.[33] Such systems provide a good example of the application of the concepts of solidarity and subsidiarity. Subsidiarity demands that higher-order communities (the government, or supranational body in the case of the EU) should help lower-order communities pursue *the latter's* legitimate ends where they cannot be pursued by individual or voluntary action. The legitimate end of the lower-order communities in this case is sustainable fishing. It may not be feasible for individuals to resolve this problem through individual action.[34] So, ultimately, we may look to institutions of government to help set up systems whereby fishing rights can be defined and traded. This is quite compatible with the responsibilities laid upon government in Catholic Social Teaching, as discussed above. Once such a system is set up, individuals and lower-order communities themselves decide how to operate and earn their living within the framework set by the higher-order community in accordance with the principle of subsidiarity.

The state or supranational authority should step in to help when lower-order communities are clearly incapable of achieving, for whatever legal, economic or institutional reason, their legitimate ends – sustainable fishing in this example. It is not, if we apply the principle of subsidiarity, for the higher-order political community to define the desired ends and neither should the higher-order political community simply step in and regulate to achieve the ends of a particular elite or pressure group. But, in solidarity, the government, if no other entity is capable, should ensure that the community can achieve its legitimate aims.

Fishing is, perhaps, an 'intermediate' example of an environmental problem – it is neither local nor global. Problems such as man-made global warming arising from the emission of greenhouse gases are global in nature.[35] Let us assume that greenhouse gas emissions are a problem and that the problem can be ameliorated by policy action. The creation of property rights in the atmosphere is obviously difficult. If we accept the scientific evidence, there are clear effects of carbon dioxide emissions on certain groups of people that arise from the behaviour of other groups of people – and there is no practical way of ensuring that only people who emit CO_2 suffer from the effects of global warming. In solidarity, people emitting large amounts of greenhouse gases should, in the first place, out of concern for the plight of fellow humans, be prudent in their behaviour and try to limit their impact. Such a voluntary approach, which may well extend far beyond individual action to action by intermediate groups within society, may, however, not be sufficient to deal with the problem.

Thus, also in solidarity, we may, as Christians, propose that action is taken at the political level, perhaps on a supranational basis. This should be a last resort as far as Catholic Social Teaching is concerned. Christians can legitimately disagree whether political action is appropriate – it is a matter for prudential judgment. No Christian should speak as if government action here (or government inaction, for that matter) is a Christian imperative.

Furthermore, the motivation for the decision to take action at the governmental or intergovernmental level should always be driven by recognition that the lower-order communities genuinely wish for some sort of action, for example to stabilize CO_2 emissions, but economic and institutional constraints prevent them from taking such action voluntarily. This may seem obvious but it is a thought process that policymakers should go through explicitly – rather than being influenced to too great an extent by campaign groups and those who have a vested interest in political action.

It would also seem appropriate that mechanisms to alleviate the problem are chosen that leave room for the greatest freedom of action at the individual level. Tradable quotas or carbon taxes would seem to be the obvious instruments, but this would lead us into a technical economic area that cannot be explored within the constraints of this chapter. However, the point is that different communities in different situations may wish to achieve a reduction in carbon emissions in different ways. Some may be able to develop and sell alternative methods of producing energy (such as wind or solar power); others may wish to explicitly cut energy consumption. Tradable quota systems and taxes allow individuals, families and lower-order communities, in accordance with the principle of subsidiarity, to make these decisions in ways that direct regulation of economic activity does not.

Slogans and muddled thinking

In this way, the application of the principles of subsidiarity and solidarity can take us a long way towards understanding how Christians should approach environmental problems and provides us with a framework for considering the issues. Though the approach above is quite compatible with serious works on Catholic Social Teaching such as the *Compendium*, the *Catechism* (1994) and Rodger Charles's analysis of Catholic Social Teaching, it is a long way from the sloganizing of many campaign groups. Indeed, it sits uneasily with statements of the local Catholic Bishops' Conference in England and Wales.[36] To take an example of the former, the diocesan newspaper of Arundel and Brighton, in its lead article in February 2008, quoted, uncritically and without qualification, radical campaigner George Monbiot stating that the capitalist system could not protect the environment and 'it has to go'. Such a statement cannot be justified given the evidence, nor can it be justified in terms of Catholic Social Teaching. Indeed, the appalling environmental performance of communist countries and countries that do not have functioning market economies is now a matter of undisputed record.

While some Christians may feel that a market economy does not provide all the answers to environmental problems, there is no justification for assuming that an economy without a functioning market system will do so. Most indicators of environmental quality have been improving dramatically in the last 40 years in those developed countries that have systems of secure property rights and market economies. This is because the institution of property rights and the application of the principle of subsidiarity, which are basic features of market economies, ensure that all resources are used more efficiently, including environmental resources. Conservation is built into the system of incentives when resources are owned because their use has to be paid for. A well-functioning market system, together with the price mechanism, promotes conservation and the development of alternatives to finite resources in the face of scarcity.

It can be perfectly legitimate to examine the facts and theory and, through a process of reason, prudentially come to a view that an interventionist approach to environmental problems is necessary. However, not to go through that careful process can lead to the creation of policy through the adoption of slogans rather than the use of deep analysis. All Christian groups have a duty to consider these issues carefully, but they should also understand the consequences of different approaches to policy because it is quite possible to develop policies in this field in such a way that the cure is worse than the disease.

Pope Benedict's World Peace Day message is important to bear in mind in this regard: '[It is] important for assessments . . . to be carried out prudently, in dialogue with experts and people of wisdom, uninhibited by ideological pressure to draw hasty conclusions.'[37]

In general, the Christian message should be one of hope. We should avoid the atmosphere of despair that leads us to ignore environmental problems; we should not be facile optimists and idealists; and we should not be pessimistic to the extent that we accept evils such as population control which is promoted by many environmental groups as a mechanism for protecting the environment. God has not only endowed the world with great natural resources but has also endowed human beings with great technical ability to overcome environmental problems.

Personal and business responsibility for the environment

So far, the discussion has focused entirely on the framework in which we might think about government policy. However, in concluding, it is important to consider the comments that Catholic Social Teaching has made about the environmental impact of consumers and producers. This is particularly so, as they take us back to our discussion of the proper meaning of solidarity.

I have argued above that environmental problems arise mainly where property rights are poorly defined and price mechanisms do not function properly. Any approach to policy – whether interventionist in nature or based on a comprehensive role for private property rights in protecting the environment – will produce outcomes that are far from perfect. Individuals, businesses and voluntary communities should, in solidarity, go further than their legal obligations in terms of their care for the environment. How far they go is a matter left for prudential, personal judgment. Some people might choose to adopt very simple lifestyles but they should not assume that they should require others to follow them in such a way of living.[38] In a similar way some Christians may wish, out of charity, to give away all the income they do not need for essential goods, but they should not set up political systems which involve taking away the income of all other citizens, through punitive taxation, as this completely undermines the nature of the charitable act and the dignity of the person from whom money is taken.

A more difficult problem is that of how businesses should behave in areas of the world where the sorts of structures of law and property rights that we take for granted in the West do not exist and where it is possible that environmental destruction will result from business activity. This takes us into the field of corporate social responsibility, one in which there is much muddled thinking.[39] I shall simply end with a comment that corporations should, in solidarity, not simply assume that, if they behave in accordance with the law in the countries in which they operate, they have discharged their moral responsibilities (whether towards the environment or otherwise) – particularly where property rights are not protected properly by the law.

At the same time, it can be counterproductive to impose upon corporations that operate abroad business practices that are normal in the West. The principle of solidarity, properly understood in its non-political context, is highly relevant here. Corporations should have the right attitude towards those who are affected by their actions and owners should do their best, often in very difficult circumstances, to act with well-informed consciences.

Concluding remarks

The concepts of 'subsidiarity' and 'solidarity' underpin much of Catholic Social Teaching, but their meaning is often misunderstood. The application of the principle of solidarity requires a change of heart, not a change of government. In all that we do, as individuals, families, as employers, or as leaders of voluntary organizations, we should show concern for the poor. Government action to help the poor may also be appropriate in some circumstances. However, the principle of subsidiarity, together with other principles that underpin Catholic Social Teaching, requires that government intervention is limited, takes place at the lowest level of government and is designed in such a way that it assists lower-order communities rather than displaces their initiative.

Notes

1 This chapter draws on a number of papal encyclicals and exhortations, including *Rerum novarum* (Leo XIII, 1891), *Quadragesimo anno* (Pius XI, 1931), *Octogesima adveniens* (Paul VI, 1971) *Familiaris consortio*, *Sollicitudo rei socialis* and *Centesimus annus* (John Paul II, 1982, 1987, 1991 respectively), and *Deus caritas est* (Benedict XVI, 2005). These documents can be obtained from the Vatican website: <http://www.vatican.va/phome_en.htm>.

2 This term has been used frequently in Catholic Social Teaching in the last 40 years (see note 4).

3 See the literature on public choice economics, such as Gordon Tullock et al., *Government: Whose Obedient Servant? A Primer in Public Choice: IEA Readings 51* (London: Institute of Economic Affairs, 2000).

4 See, for example, the encyclical *Sollicitudo rei socialis*, and P. Lamoureux, *Commentary on Laborem Exercens* (On Human Work) in Kenneth R. Himes (ed.), *Modern Catholic Social Teaching: Commentaries & Interpretations* (Washington DC: Georgetown University Press, 2005). It is important to note that even the phrase 'preferential option for the poor' was introduced specifically by Pope Paul VI in the context of charity in *Octogesima adveniens*, and that the discussion of the concept by Pope John Paul II in, for example, *Sollicitudo rei socialis* is wide ranging – including action of both a charitable and political character. Poverty also relates to our spiritual and moral inadequacies, not just material poverty.

5 John Paul II, *Centesimus annus*, 48.

6 *Catechism of the Catholic Church*, 1994.

7 See, for example, *Centesimus annus* and *Quadragesimo anno*.

8 Declaration of the Theological Pastoral Congress, October 1997, 3.12.

9 Pontifical Council for Justice and Peace, *Compendium of the Social Doctrine of the Church* (London: Burns & Oates, 2005), para. 351.

10 *Compendium*, 187–8.

11 Some paragraphs of this chapter, including the following two, are adapted from Philip Booth (ed.), *Catholic Social Teaching and the Market Economy* (London: Institute of Economic Affairs, 2007).
12 An empirical study of how the state crowds out voluntary action can be found in James Bartholomew, *The Welfare State We're In* (London: Politico's, 2004).
13 Pius XI, *Quadragesimo anno*, 49.
14 Pius XI, *Quadragesimo anno*, 50.
15 Pius XI, *Quadragesimo anno*, 137.
16 Rodger Charles, *Christian Social Witness and Teaching: The Catholic Tradition from Genesis to Centesimus Annus* (Leominster: Gracewing, 1998), Vol. 2, p. 396.
17 John Paul II, *Centesimus annus*, 48.
18 *Compendium*, 241.
19 Synod of Bishops, *Justitia in mundo* (1971).
20 *Compendium*, 340, a message emphasized in John Paul II, *Centesimus annus*.
21 *Compendium*, 470.
22 *Compendium*, 360, 486; John Paul II, *Centesimus annus*, 37.
23 *Compendium*, 468.
24 There was a particularly robust defence of private property in *Rerum novarum*, often regarded as the first social encyclical of the Catholic Church, written by Pope Leo XIII in 1891.
25 Roger Bate, *Saving Our Streams: The Role of the Anglers' Conservation Association in Protecting English and Welsh Rivers* (London: Institute of Economic Affairs, Research Monograph 53, 2001).
26 Lydia Polgreen, 'In Niger, Trees and Crops Turn Back the Desert', *The New York Times*, 11 February 2007: accessible at <http://www.nytimes.com/2007/02/11/world/africa/11niger.html?pagewanted=3&_r=1&ei=5087&em&en=d93708af7caaf675&ex=1171342800>.
27 A further example of property rights solutions to environmental problems is discussed on p. 148 in the context of fishing.
28 *Compendium*, 299.
29 It is also important to note that 'private ownership' is not synonymous with purely 'personal' or 'individual' ownership.

There are very many forms of private collective claims on property (often described as 'several property'). These can include properties owned by communities of monks or situations where individuals own buildings that are on land that is owned by a freeholder. The freeholder of the land then has an incentive to impose restrictions on the activities of individual owners of the buildings that benefit the environment enjoyed by the group of owners as a whole. There is not space to develop this point here but, arguably, the concept of 'several property' and the freely negotiated restrictions on use that it leads to, has much to offer environmental preservation in both developed and developing countries. See, for example, Mark Pennington, *Liberating the Land: The Case for Private Land-use Planning* (London: Institute of Economic Affairs, Hobart Paper 162, 2002), and Karol Boudreaux and Paul Aligica, *Paths to Property: Approaches to Institutional Change and International Development* (London: Institute of Economic Affairs, Hobart Paper 126, 2007).

30 Of course, forest destruction is not intrinsically inappropriate. Throughout human history, forests have been developed and destroyed.

31 See Steven F. Hayward and Amy Kaleita, *Index of Leading Environmental Indicators* (San Francisco: Pacific Research Institute, 2007, 12th edition).

32 Many other indicators suggest a positive relationship between the quality of the environment and national income – most notably indicators of air quality. This is likely to be partly because the quality of the environment is a 'luxury good' of which people wish to consume more as they get richer, but also because, as noted, strong property rights go hand in hand with both effective environmental protection and economic development.

33 See Hannes H. Gissurarson, *Overfishing: The Icelandic Solution* (London: Institute of Economic Affairs, Studies on the Environment, No. 17, 2000) and Julian Morris, 'When it Comes to the Sustainability of Marine Resources, Institutions Matter', *Journal of Sustainable Development* 1(2) (Spring 2008).

34 Due to 'transactions costs', to use the economic jargon.

35 I shall ignore the scientific and economic debates here. A minority does not accept the science. Others accept the science but do not believe we can reverse the process at a cost that is worth paying. There is a thorough discussion of one side of the argument in Nicholas Stern, *Stern Review: The Economics of Climate Change* (HM Treasury/Cabinet Office, 2006) and of the other in Bjorn Lomborg, *The Skeptical Environmentalist* (Cambridge: Cambridge University Press, 2001).

36 Charles, *Christian Social Witness and Teaching.* See the chapter by O'Brien in Booth, *Catholic Social Teaching.*

37 Pope Benedict XVI, 'The Human Family, a Community of Peace', World Peace Day message, 1 January 2008.

38 Nor, indeed, should they assume that such a way of living necessarily benefits the environment.

39 The issue is discussed at length in Philip Booth, 'Modern Business and its Moral and Ethical Dilemmas in a Globalized World', in Ian R. Harper and Samuel Gregg (eds), *Christian Theology and Market Economics* (Cheltenham: Edward Elgar, 2008).

7

Government and the common good

CLIFFORD LONGLEY

Introduction: the contemporary relevance of the common good

Will Hutton, doyen of British writers on economics and director of the Work Foundation, returned from a conference in Rome to write a whole-page review of it for *The Observer*. Church seminars on social justice rarely get such headline treatment, and if they do it is usually critical. But Hutton, not himself a Catholic by any means, took a different line. He heaped copious praise on the Vatican for daring to ask the questions politicians were refusing to ask: questions like how capitalism and its market-driven dynamic can be made to serve the good of everyone – the common good – and not just the wealthy. The conference he attended was convened by the Centesimus Annus Foundation, and he was clearly taken by surprise to find how much overlap there was between Catholic Social Teaching (CST) and his own economic ideas, especially his lifelong advocacy of stakeholding. How do you give modern economic systems a human face? He wrote:

> A lot of businessmen and women in Britain share these worries, but our discourse rarely allows them to surface. Any politician who dares to voice them rather than be a

> cheerleader for the superclass, rampant profit-making and 'flexible' wages risks the ludicrous sobriquet of being anti-business.[1]

Perhaps as a result of such influences, Hutton himself has begun to adopt the concept of the common good – 'the global common good' is a phrase he uses – in his own economic and political analysis.

The common good as overarching moral principle

It is hard to exaggerate the extent to which the concept of the common good stands at the heart of Catholic Social Teaching. It is the overarching principle rather than the first in order of priority, which is to say that other principles contained within the tradition – subsidiarity, solidarity, the primacy of labour over capital, the right to organize, the preferential option for the poor – have always to be read in the light of the common good, which permeates all of them. It is itself a representation of the second of the two great commandments – to love God with all one's heart and to love one's neighbour as oneself – and principles do not come any higher than that. That is why the literature occasionally contains striking statements that equate the common good with nothing less than God's will on earth, for which Christians pray in the Lord's Prayer.

Definitions of the common good are many, yet the concept is still elusive. In the social teaching tradition of the Catholic Church, for instance, it is usually defined as 'the sum total of social conditions which allow people, either as groups or as individuals, to reach their fulfilment more fully and more easily'.[2] But such definitions are almost invariably followed by qualifications as to what the common good is not. Thus, from the *Compendium of the Social Doctrine of the Church*:

> The common good does not consist in the simple sum of the particular goods of each subject of a social entity. Belonging to everyone and to each person, it is and remains common, because it is indivisible and because only together is it possible to attain it, increase it and safeguard its effectiveness, with regard also to the future.[3]

Perhaps this flexibility of definition and abundance of qualification is a reassuring sign that nobody owns the common good: it cannot be reduced to a pat formula, its meaning cannot be exhausted, it is universal in scope yet it responds to social circumstances. It is typical of the plastic nature of the concept that it both does and does not answer the question, 'What is the right relationship between God and the government?' It does not provide policy guidelines. Rather, it supplies a test of policy guidelines, which is different; the very simple test, 'Do they serve the common good?'

The debate about the content of the common good in any particular situation is what politics is or ought to be about. Governments may not be moral entities in themselves, but they take on moral qualities in so far as they are committed to the service of the common good, and not otherwise. Indeed, opposition parties may be similarly committed. Yet, far from being so vague as to be useless, the common good does make severe and specific demands, for instance, by transcending nationality, having little time for the nation state, and excluding nobody. It is difficult to see how a government truly committed to the common good could have a policy of deporting illegal immigrants, for example. And as Hutton noted, the common good stands in judgment over free-market economics. As the world has found to its cost, insufficient regulation of finance and business is a threat to the common good. In the name of that common good they must be made to serve the interests of everyone, not just the few.

There are many accounts of the Catholic Social Teaching tradition that make little use of the concept, such as attempts to show that CST is in accordance with classical liberal (or American neoconservative) free-market economics.[4] There is a simple rule of thumb to test how close such accounts of CST come to being a true version of this teaching – how early, and how often, do they mention the common good? If they are mainly concerned to develop and apply the concept, say, of subsidiarity, for instance to justify an argument in favour of small government or against the welfare state, then they are not faithful to the tradition because they do not set the common good as their fundamental governing principle, from first to last. Their claim to be faithful to Catholic Social Teaching must be regarded as dubious.

What the teaching really asserts is the moral truth that the common good is the highest good; in other words, no good can stand above it. As such, its promotion is the true object of all social activity. That applies to individuals, to groups, to society as a whole, and to governments. It applies to the whole human race. There are no national boundaries where the common good is concerned. If it is an expression of the duty to love one's neighbour as oneself, the only possible answer to the question, 'Who is my neighbour?' cannot possibly be 'my fellow citizens' of this country or that, or even of this continent or that. The parable of the Good Samaritan makes clear that the category of 'neighbour' does not mean the people next door or living in the same street. It is universal.

The common good and solidarity

Unlike the economists' concept of the public good, the common good is primarily a moral concept. One is bidden to adhere to it by one's conscience. It is realistic to talk of being 'converted' to the common good, as the moment of *metanoia* when the truth really strikes home that 'we are all responsible for all'. This is expressed by Pope John Paul II in his 1987 encyclical *Sollicitudo rei socialis*:

> The fact that men and women in various parts of the world feel personally affected by the injustices and violations of human rights committed in distant countries, countries which perhaps they will never visit, is a further sign of a reality transformed into awareness, thus acquiring a moral connotation.
>
> It is above all a question of interdependence, sensed as a system determining relationships in the contemporary world in its economic, cultural, political and religious elements, and accepted as a moral category. When interdependence becomes recognized in this way, the correlative response as a moral and social attitude, as a 'virtue', is solidarity. This then is not a feeling of vague compassion or shallow distress at the misfortunes of so many people, both near and far. On the contrary it is a firm and persevering determination to commit oneself to the common good; that is to say, to the good of all and of each individual because we are all really responsible for all.[5]

This makes clear that there is an intimate relationship between the common good and solidarity, which is seen to be the social virtue above all others. It has to take precedence, for instance, over subsidiarity, which can by no means claim to be directly deduced from one of the two great commandments.

It is equally clear, however, that solidarity as a precept is not aimed only, or even primarily, at governments. In so far as governments as such are not moral beings, indeed, it cannot be. Those who make up governments – politicians, legislators and bureaucrats – are, of course, under an obligation to serve the common good; but so are all members of society, equally. It is not a duty that can be sub-contracted or discharged by proxy, so that the individual relinquishes his or her responsibility; but obviously it can be discharged collectively, and in certain circumstances it can only be discharged collectively. We can hire a fire brigade to fight fires for us (or the state can), but by doing so we do not wash our hands of our responsibility to our neighbours when their house is burning. The fire brigade has to answer to us; we have to support it with funds and facilities. Before it arrives at the fire, we must do what we can.

The common good and subsidiarity

As indicated earlier, subsidiarity has sometimes seemed to bedevil the case for Catholic Social Teaching because it seems to lend itself to an ideological attack on 'big government', a particular bête noire of the American right. Therefore it needs to be examined carefully, even a little sceptically. Unlike solidarity, subsidiarity cannot be said to be present as a recommended principle of social organization in either the Old or New Testament. A rather weak argument is sometimes deployed to suggest that it is somehow foreshadowed in Paul's First Letter to the Corinthians, where he expounds on the diversity of ministries in the church:

> But now God hath set the members every one of them in the body as it hath pleased him. And if they all were one member, where would be the body? But now there are many members indeed, yet one body.[6]

Subsidiarity, or something like it, seems to have emerged from Dutch Calvinism in the seventeenth century and found its way into Catholic social doctrine via Catholic social thinkers in Germany in the late nineteenth century.

The word itself is derived, somewhat tortuously, from the practice (*subsidium*) in the Roman Empire of encouraging soldiers to settle in the lands they had conquered. It does not appear at all in the first major social encyclical of modern times, *Rerum novarum* of Pope Leo XIII in 1891. It burst forth fully formed, so to speak, in Pius XI's *Quadragesimo anno* 40 years later. What is significant about that encyclical is that it has forced interpreters of the tradition to recognize that Catholic Social Teaching has been formed spasmodically and not always entirely consistently and coherently, in short bursts separated by substantial intervals; and that each new manifestation, while repeating much of what previous documents have said, also bears the heavy marks of historical circumstances as seen from Rome at the time of writing.

Quadragesimo anno contains a long argument in favour of industry being structured around syndicates of workers and managers. It is significant that no subsequent encyclical refers back to that proposal – it was indeed an idea that was dead almost before it was born. The encyclical was written at a time when the rise of Mussolini's Fascism had both fascinated and frightened the Catholic Church (and pleased it, incidentally, by entering into a concordat or treaty that regularized the position of the Vatican in Italian and international law), and when the dread example of Hitler's Nazism was still in the future. It was probably meant as an attempt to soften and humanize Mussolini's own political creed, which was about the supremacy of the state and the unbounded authority of its leader.

That may well explain why Pius XI thought it so important to include in the encyclical a strong exposition of the doctrine of subsidiarity. It was, above all, an attempt to defend the family and civil society against the inroads of state power. And it was Italian Fascism which represented that threat to the family and society, because of its assertion of the prior claims of the state and of the duty of all citizens to obey the state's leader. The Pope saw that the family was a natural unit, the basic building block of society where the mutual rights and duties of parents and children were not to be interfered with by the state because they were derived from natural law and the teachings of the church, and not from state legislation.

The principle of subsidiarity – a word he did not actually use – was defined by him thus:

> . . . it is an injustice and at the same time a grave evil and disturbance of right order to assign to a greater and higher association what lesser and subordinate organizations can do. For every social activity ought of its very nature to furnish help to the members of the body social, and never destroy and absorb them.[7]

It is an anti-Fascist statement, appropriate to its time, but applied to circumstances very different from Italy at the start of the 1930s it tends to raise more questions than it answers. Unlike syndicalism, subsidiarity did develop into a core principle of Catholic Social Teaching. The 1996 statement of the Catholic Bishops of England and Wales, *The Common Good and the Catholic Church's Social Teaching*, developed the idea like this:

> The human race itself is a 'community of communities', existing at international, national, regional and local level. The smallest such community is the individual family, the basic cell of human society. A well-constructed society will

> be one that gives priority to the integrity, stability and health of family life. It should be a principle of good government, therefore, that no law should be passed with possible social consequences without first considering what effect it would have on family life and especially on children. The principle behind the relationships between the different layers of this 'community of communities' should be that of subsidiarity. In a centralized society, subsidiarity will mainly mean passing powers downwards; but it can also mean passing appropriate powers upwards, even to an international body, if that would better serve the common good and protect the rights of families and of individuals.[8]

This version of subsidiarity says nothing about the relationship between state and private or voluntary provision, an issue to which the concept is sometimes applied in a tendentious and exaggerated way. The teaching insists that governments themselves must attempt to follow its principles as far as possible, in their own structures. Thus it is congruent with the doctrine of subsidiarity that decisions in the public sector affecting the lives of ordinary people should be made as close to those lives as possible. Schools in the state sector should be governed as far as possible by representatives of parents, teachers and the local community. Hospital managements should be answerable as far as possible not to civil servants in Whitehall but to locally elected boards of governors representing patients, care professionals and again the local community. Policing should be done in consultation with, and even to an extent directed by, the concerns and priorities of, once more, the local community.

Subsidiarity does not require schools, hospitals and the police to be privatized, but to be administered as low down the chain of decision-making as possible. But always subject to the common good. Understood in this way, subsidiarity is already a familiar concept in social theory; and indeed it forms a central part of the architecture of a fair and just society. Provided subsidiarity is honoured in this way, the structures of government may be said to be consistent with Catholic Social Teaching: a heavily centralized structure of government could not be.

But to insist on the withdrawal of 'the state' from health, education or welfare provision, as some of the more extreme proponents of subsidiarity advocate, is not a true application of the principle because it could easily undermine, rather than promote, the common good. The notion sometimes heard in this connection – that state welfare must necessarily lack the compassion of the voluntary sector – is an insult to public sector workers who are equally capable of fulfilling a vocation of service as employees of the state as they would be if they were employees of a voluntarily funded charity. It has been a characteristic of the voluntary sector in Britain these last 30 years that it has striven to raise its professional standards to those applying in the state sector. Imitation is indeed the sincerest form of flattery.

The common good, democracy and human rights

The papacy of John XXIII and the Second Vatican Council he inaugurated had a profound influence on Catholic thinking about the relationship of the common good to government. His encyclical *Pacem in terris* and all subsequent papal texts were notable in accepting and applying a doctrine of human rights. Together, human rights and democracy plug what was otherwise a nagging gap in Catholic thinking about the common good. Provided that right-wing Catholic dictators like Franco or Peron could claim to be acting to promote the common good, their political systems seemed beyond the reach of Catholic Social Teaching to criticize. Certainly they would have been prepared to tame the excesses of capitalism. But they would also have been prepared to place their interpretation of the common good above such humanistic considerations as human rights. The suppression of freedom in the name of the common good (wrongly understood) seemed to have been made papally acceptable, and Catholic dictators in Europe and South America particularly seemed content to proclaim as a political creed something like 'The Common Good – *c'est moi*.'

Clearly modern post-conciliar Catholicism, chastened by the experience of the Second World War, could not give such comfort to right-wing dictators, whatever had been its role pre-war. Once democracy and human rights became canonized as fundamental values of the Catholic tradition, the door was closed on fascist leaders and parties who had claimed the sanction of Catholicism while continuing to oppress their people. Indeed, the proper and natural home of the Catholic Social Teaching tradition henceforth seemed to be liberal democracy, as in the West.

The common good became part of a trilogy, alongside democracy and human rights, on which civilized societies depended. Thus in theory a government was elected by the people to pursue the common good, and if it failed to do so it would not be returned to office; one of its primary functions, implicit in upholding the common good, was the defence of human rights, which could not therefore be set aside when the common good appeared to demand it. The solution was to subsume a doctrine of human rights into the notion of the common good itself, to modify the definition, so to speak, in the light of a better understanding. That was the achievement of John XXIII, and it turned the Catholic Church worldwide, once a very uncertain voice when human rights were being violated, into a staunch defender of the rights of oppressed people everywhere.

Nevertheless, there remain tensions between the inner dynamic of liberal democracy and the requirements of the Catholic tradition as so far developed. Democracy in particular gives weight to majority opinion above all else, even natural law. Democracy itself is morally neutral. It is a method of making decisions, not a moral basis for making them. Of course, constitutional democracies have tended to limit what could be achieved by the sovereign will of the people by enshrining codes of human rights, which stood both below and above the law as made and remade by legislatures.

But this merely transferred the debate to other areas, such as who was to be covered by the guarantees of human rights and who was excluded from them. Were human embryos to be regarded as possessing inalienable rights, for instance, or could states legislate to allow their destruction by abortion? Were refugees, asylum seekers or even terrorist 'prisoners of war' covered by human rights guarantees, or did they first have to achieve citizenship? The idea that some rights depended on citizenship and some were universal and inalienable seemed logically necessary, but who was to say which was which? And what happened when, as was inevitable, rights collided? Was there a hierarchy of rights, some absolute and some conditional? The Catholic Church's adoption of human rights language did not offer much insight into how to handle a conflict of rights whenever it arose. This remains an area requiring more development in human rights theory, which is not helped by the tendency for debates about human rights to be taken over by lawyers.

The common good and the state

In his study *Catholic Social Teaching 1891–Present*, the American moral theologian Charles E. Curran drew attention to the limitations of the concept of the common good as applied to nation states per se.[9] He made a distinction between the Leonine tradition that Pope John Paul II seemed to be following, of seeing the common good as the business of the state, and the more limited scope of the role of government that appeared to be envisaged in the Second Vatican Council's *Declaration on Religious Liberty*.[10] The American Jesuit philosopher John Courtney Murray is often hailed as the architect of that declaration, which was pushed for above all by the Catholic bishops of the United States (waking from what had been until that point the sleep of the theologically illiterate).

The *Declaration on Religious Liberty* was indeed safely passed by the Council in its fourth and final session the following year, 1965. It was the singular – and momentous – contribution of American Catholicism to the universal church, with implications that have by no means been exhausted.

The idea that the common good is primarily the business of states belongs, in Murray's analysis, to the age when church and state were usually deemed a unity – a form of political 'monism'. It is a legacy, though he does not say so, of the *ancien régime* mindset still often encountered in the Vatican in the 1960s, which resented being asked to adjust to the world as it has been since 1789. This monist polity was usually said to be according to the teaching of Aquinas, to whom Pope John Paul II in particular was wedded. This teaching said that the state had a duty to align its laws with natural law, and so to promote the good of its citizens. In the spiritual sphere this had to mean steering them into the arms of the Catholic Church and keeping them there.

Thus a state had no duty to provide tolerance for other religions or denominations, which were likely to distract people from the claims of the One True Church. Where a state could do so, therefore, it had to enact laws which, for instance, prevented divorce, prohibited the sale of contraceptives or outlawed abortion. It had no duty to enact laws to protect freedom of worship or even freedom of speech where religion was concerned. The exception would be where the Catholic population was in a minority, when attempts to impose Catholic teaching by law in the moral sphere were ill-advised because it was impractical. Thus a Catholic 'monist' (or '*intégriste*') political system had no scope for dissent or conscience: error had no rights.

The American example sat very uncomfortably with that doctrine, as Murray well knew. He therefore argued for a more restricted role for the state than this all-embracing concern for the common good, confining it instead to the preservation of 'public order'.[11] Promoting the common good remained the priority of society and the duty of all its members – but society and the state were no longer to be seen as coterminous. His definition of public order owed a good deal to the American experience, where 'big government' had always seemed to be some sort of public enemy in a way quite unfamiliar to Europeans. Nevertheless, the notion that the common good is the duty of society rather than just the state has a distinctly modern ring to it, as nations all round the world tried on the clothes of Western-style liberal democracy without necessarily having emerged from a condition where state and society were one. It left scope for the 'unofficial' or 'voluntary' sector, for all the small and big platoons of private or public initiative that constitute the intermediate institutions of civil society. Indeed, commerce and industry too, being largely in private (that is to say non-government) hands, were also planted in that area of society which was not directly organized by the state.

The common good and secularism

This issue has a direct bearing on one of the thorniest constitutional issues of the modern age, namely how to organize the government of a secular society without making it aggressively 'secularist' and therefore anti-religious. This either–or is hard to escape – either religion rules the roost, or it is pressed to the very margins of concern. What is insufficiently developed is a theology of religious and moral pluralism, showing how religion can remain as important as its adherents can make it, but without either suppressing the rights of others or being suppressed in turn. This is the handicap, in the post-modern world, of the meta-narrative – a theory which embraces everything. The English constitutional solution to this dilemma would seem to run along the lines of 'Don't ask theoretical questions, just get on with it', but as such, that is hard to export. In any event, proposals for the disestablishment of the Church of England or even for an English republic, would still require an answer to these state–church questions. How is a secular society to be genuinely plural and not secularist? Can the state remain officially indifferent to religion while society continues to take it seriously? Or does indifference by the state lead to indifference by society?

The American example could be cited on either side of this debate. Its apologists describe the American nation state, as a result of the 'separation of church and state', as secular. In the late eighteenth-century sense that it has no established church, that is true. (It is important to remember that various member 'states' of the USA, such as Massachusetts and Connecticut, actually had established churches both before and after the Revolution and even after the adoption of the 'secular' federal constitution in 1789.)

But the ideology of 'Americanism' is permeated through and through with religious insights and ideas which can be traced directly back to the colonial founders, whether Puritan and republican in New England or monarchist and Episcopalian in Virginia. In that sense the American project can be described as a complete synthesis of church and state (cleverly disguised as the opposite): America is itself a 'church', with its own creed, its own worship, even its own initiation ceremonies. One of the flaws in Murray's depiction of the American church–state 'separatist' solution as a model to be universalized was his failure to see that God was inextricably present in the American social and constitutional woodwork, not detached from it.

Curran's thesis, in his review of Murray's success at Vatican II, was that Catholic teaching under John Paul II remained in captivity to the unexamined assumption that the common good and the responsibility of the state were one and the same. He relates this in part to the fierceness of the Pope's own opposition to abortion, and his determination to insist on a complete ban on it enforced by the criminal law. (A Polish Pope may even have had contemporary church–state tension in Poland over this issue in mind.) Certainly, the notion that Catholic politicians cannot promote, and Catholic electors may not vote for, anything that relaxes the prohibition on abortion was a regular theme of the American Catholic bishops in their interventions in public debate. They had failed to follow the logic of the declaration they (or their predecessors) had so vigorously campaigned for in the Second Vatican Council. This was, in Curran's view, a consequence of regarding it as still the responsibility of the state to promote the common good and all it entails, and not just regarding public order as the outer limit of the functions of government.[12]

To follow the latter course would reduce the vexed question of abortion to a public order issue – to what extent is it conducive to public order to prohibit or to allow abortion? That in turn presupposes that individuals in society might, if they were aggrieved by too lax or too strict an abortion law, become a threat to public order. To relieve that threat the law would be moved in the appropriate direction until it achieved a new equilibrium of maximum public tranquillity, minimum threats to the peace. But this meant that to change the law, all that would be necessary would be to threaten violence. That does not seem a very healthy basis for law-making in a democratic society (though insisting that the law follows exactly the requirements of Catholic moral teaching on this point is not particularly helpful either).

For some reason, possibly the fact that the current situation is set by a judgment of the Supreme Court and not by a vote in Congress, the abortion issue festers in America in a way it hardly still does in Europe and elsewhere. Perhaps this is because Murray's solution – confining the state to upholding public order, leaving the common good to be the responsibility of society (defined as larger than the state) – has already implicitly been adopted without fuss elsewhere in the West, with only Americans still worrying away at it.

But without a theoretical basis for this pragmatic adjustment, it must remain unstable and liable to give way under pressure. It is clear that non-American Western societies are pluralist in theory but deeply unhappy at some of the apparent consequences. Should Western tolerance of Muslim beliefs and customs in the name of pluralism extend to allowing Muslims to practise polygamy, for instance? Should it extend to allowing Muslims to promote female circumcision (notwithstanding that most Muslims in the West would deny it is a practice required by the faith)? Should

Muslims who regard all things Western as satanic (while living in the West all the same) be allowed to behave accordingly towards Western institutions? Should they be allowed the freedom of speech, for instance, to encourage terrorism in the name of Islam (provided, in the name of public order perhaps, that they do their terrorism elsewhere)? Or is it the job of some non-Muslim authority or other – the police, the courts, Parliament – to decide what is or what is not compatible with the Muslim faith, allowing this but prohibiting that? And how does this differ from Pope John Paul II's insistence that state law should follow Catholic teaching on abortion and other moral issues? If Muslims cannot have their way on, say, polygamy, why should Catholics have their way on abortion?

The issue is sharpened for Catholics by the fact that Muslims also see the state and society as coterminous, at least in the Muslim ideal. They have their own concept of the common good, but its basic principles are those of the Qur'an rather than Catholic Social Teaching. How is this mutual incompatibility to be resolved?

These dilemmas are not far below the surface in recent debates about the 'place of God' in the new constitution of the European Union. Formal recognition of such a place implies that religious teachings may from time to time cross over from the private sphere, where most religious activity resides most of the time, to the public sphere, where they may influence public policy. Lack of such recognition (it was feared by some) might amount to a constitutional declaration that religion must stay in the private sphere. In fact, of course, in a democracy electors may be influenced by whatever they want to be influenced by, including their own religious faith or lack of it. What some European framers wanted, it seems, was an aggressive separation of church and state in the American theoretical mould – though without the implicit background of a national religious ideology like Americanism.

Curran, following Murray, sees the Vatican II *Declaration on Religious Liberty* as an important plank of social teaching, even though it is not normally regarded as belonging to that corpus at all. However, as long as Catholic Social Teaching is treated as being concerned with all 'common good' issues rather than purely economic ones, it clearly does belong. The same should be true of Catholic teaching about, say, criminology and penal reform; and must be true about the just war tradition, where a state's responsibility to the common good looms large. But a theology of war and peace does raise a challenge to the common good tradition of a different kind, a challenge also raised by issues like terrorism, genocide, asylum and refugees, and global environmental concerns.

Conclusion: reckoning with pluralism

The Catholic philosophy of politics that says its aim is to advance the common good begs the question: What is the limit of the community whose common good is under consideration? The tradition tends to be uncritically applied to a post late-nineteenth-century world where the political unit is the nation state, and that determines the scope of the common good. While in the process of acting on that automatic assumption, the Catholic tradition also contradicts it. The duty of solidarity, which Pope John Paul II weaves into the concept of the common good, takes its force from the dignity of common humanity, not from shared citizenship or national identity. Similarly, a Catholic doctrine of human rights cannot be confused with a doctrine of local citizenship rights, for human rights pre-exist any notion of the sovereign nation state. For instance, a refugee seeking entry to such a state has the same human rights, but not the same civil rights, as one born into it. A Taliban prisoner held in indefinite detention without trial in Guantánamo Bay has the same human rights as the President of the United States.

The approach set out by Murray also illuminates the role of the politician, particularly one who brings to the public square not only his political principles and the mandate of his election, but also his religious convictions (and if we regard atheism and agnosticism as akin to religious convictions, that describes 100 per cent of them). Ideally, he takes part with his fellow politicians in a search for the common good, in an open discourse to which the public also has access. He will only win the argument if he can persuade a majority to share his view; having done so, however, he then has to safeguard the human rights of those who form the minority. Unless he is a politician in an ideologically or religiously homogeneous society, the emphasis will naturally be on arguments that can appeal across a religious divide, cross platform as it were, which must mean, largely, arguments that do not rest solely on a particular revelation or specific religious authority.

There seems to be no room in this model for any one religious group to be privileged above others, for that would subvert the democratic process by giving extra and unfair influence to one party in the debate. Such a privilege would come about, for instance, if members of a particular religious group had reserved places in a legislature; or if leaders of a religious group claimed to be able to tell politicians who belonged to that group how to act and vote.

But it would be misleading to see such an arrangement as secularist. It represents the open public square, not the empty public square. The more appropriate term for it would be 'plural'. Indeed, this seems to be the model all Western societies are moving towards. There is unlikely to be a better way, in the foreseeable future, of rendering unto Caesar the things that are Caesar's, and to God the things that are God's.

Notes

1 Will Hutton, 'What I told the Pope about how to shape the new capitalism', *The Observer*, 1 June 2008.
2 Paul VI, *Gaudium et spes*, 26.
3 Pontifical Council for Justice and Peace, *Compendium of the Social Doctrine of the Church* (London: Burns & Oates, 2004), 164.
4 See e.g. Michael Novak, *The Catholic Ethic and the Spirit of Capitalism* (New York: The Free Press, 1993).
5 John Paul II, *Sollicitudo rei socialis*, 38.
6 1 Corinthians 12.18–20 (Douay Rheims).
7 Pius XI, *Quadragesimo anno*, 79.
8 Catholic Bishops of England and Wales, *The Common Good and the Catholic Church's Social Teaching*, Part I, para. 21.
9 Charles E. Curran, *Catholic Social Teaching 1891–Present: A Historical, Theological, and Ethical Analysis* (Washington DC: Georgetown University Press, 2002).
10 Paul VI, *Dignitatis humanae.*
11 John Courtney Murray, *Religious Liberty Catholic Struggles With Pluralism*, ed. J. Leon Hooper, SJ (Louisville, KY: Westminster/John Knox, 1993), p. 145.
12 Curran, *Catholic Social Teaching 1891–Present*, pp. 241–3.

8

Government and equality

ANDREW BRADSTOCK

Few soccer fans will forget the moment in the 2008 Champions League final when Chelsea captain John Terry missed the penalty that would have won his team that coveted trophy. Few will also be able to erase the memory of Terry's face in the moments after this disaster, his desolation at letting down his team, his manager, the fans and himself plain for all to see. Media reaction at the time was sympathetic to the tearful Terry, a man who had served his club, country and game well for many years but who would now have to live with this very public moment of failure for the rest of his life. It was only when the dust settled on the match that commentators ventured to point out that Terry earns in a *week* what *six* average British workers take home in a *year*, and suggested that we might expect him, for that sort of money, to do the basics of his job and shoot a ball on target from just 12 yards out.

The question of the salaries paid to top and bottom earners in the UK surfaces from time to time. The BBC is periodically challenged about the sums it pays to some of its DJs and presenters, and the bonuses and payoffs given to leading City executives also raise the occasional eyebrow – especially when, like Terry, they have under-performed and seem to be getting 'rewarded for failure'. Market forces now make it possible for people at the top of some professions to command annual salaries beyond what the average worker would expect to earn in a lifetime, and, as an Organization for Economic Cooperation and Development (OECD) survey in 2008 showed, income inequality in the UK has grown steadily since the 1970s.[1] The earnings gap between rich and poor in 2005 was 20 per cent wider than in 1985, the OECD report noted, and an Incomes Data Services (IDS) survey in 2006 discovered that, in the period 2000–6, the median earnings of FTSE 100 chief executives rose from being 39 times greater than those of all full-time employees to 98 times greater.[2] While the OECD survey showed that the gap between rich and poor in the UK had narrowed 'remarkably' between 2000 and 2005, it also noted that Britain remained one of the most unequal societies in the developed world.[3] The Blair and Brown governments have made strenuous efforts to reduce the number of people in poverty since 1997, yet few leading figures in any of the major political parties have expressed concern about the earnings of those in the top wage bracket, nor the massive gulf that exists between the upper and lower strata of society. Some, even in the Labour Party, have seen the rise of the super-rich as a virtue and consciously declined invitations to condemn the rich–poor gap.

Whether politicians *should* be concerned about this gap is a question I shall address later. First I want to ask what Christian teaching has to say on the matter and whether gross inequality in income is rightly a topic of theological concern. My assumption is that Christians will want to consider the 'principles' of the issue as well as any consequences it may have for their 'neighbour' and the well-being of society as a whole.

Defining the problem

Discussions about equality often get bogged down in arguments over definitions, and some theologians advocate avoiding the term altogether in the interests of bringing greater clarity to the debate. Reinhold Niebuhr,[4] for example, thought 'equal justice' summed up his position better, though even that term might be said to require further qualification since 'justice' can be understood to mean treating people equally without specifying the type of justice or equality one has in mind. Duncan Forrester, Emeritus Professor of Christian Ethics and Practical Theology at Edinburgh University, has also recognized the complexity of the concept and the importance of defining whether we are talking about equality in terms of income, wealth, opportunities, freedom, rights or whatever: he prefers to speak of 'the meanings' rather than 'the meaning' of equality. Yet Forrester does argue that there is a coherence in the idea of equality, that at its heart lies the conviction that each person is of infinite, and hence equal, worth and should be treated as such.[5] And like many Christian writers he finds this idea rooted firmly in the Judaeo-Christian scriptures, and draws from them a Christian imperative to promote equality.

I want to argue two distinct but not unrelated points in this chapter. The first is that the biblical teaching that all people are of equal value because they are created in God's image places certain demands upon communities with respect to their social and economic arrangements – specifically, to ensure that none of their members is unable to meet their basic needs in terms of food, shelter and security. And, second, that there are sound biblical and sociological reasons for governments consciously to pursue policies aimed not simply at relieving poverty but at narrowing the differential between 'rich' and 'poor' in society.

The Bible and inequality: the Old Testament

A core theme in the creation narratives in the book of Genesis is that human beings are endowed with an equality of worth and status by virtue of their being created by God. While all are subject to differences in terms of gender, ethnicity, size or physical or intellectual ability – to be 'equal' is not to be 'the same' and we are to celebrate our differences – all have an inherent equality because they have been made that way in creation. As the Psalmist puts it, all men and women have been made 'a little lower than the angels',[6] all bear to an equal extent the 'image of God'.[7] R. H. Tawney once wrote that 'it is only when we realize that each individual soul is related to a power above other [humans] that we are able to regard each as an end in itself . . . The social order is judged and condemned by a power transcending it.'[8]

When the man created by God in the Genesis 2 account speaks of his companion as 'bone of my bones and flesh of my flesh' he sums up their inherent equality.[9] *In*equality, with one having the power to rule over the other, comes in only after the fall: before that, as the quaint medieval saw put it, 'When Adam delved and Eve span, Who was then the gentleman?'[10] The clear implication of both Genesis 1 and 2 is that, since all humans are made in the image of God, all should reflect that in their life by enjoying the basic gifts that God bestows upon his creation (described in the final verses of Genesis 1). The land and its fruits are freely given to all to enjoy, with none being apportioned a greater share than any other. That *inequality* has been such a feature of human existence since the creation is a consequence of human action, not the outworking of a divine plan. As the fourth-century writer Pelagius rather tellingly put it, reflecting on the 'natural' gifts we enjoy, such as the sun and the air:

> We possess equally with others all the things which are not under our control but which we receive by God's dispensation, and on unjust and unequal terms only the things which are entrusted and subjected to our own rule . . .[11]

A conviction that all human beings have inherent worth as bearers of the image of God, and should reflect that in their lives, runs through the whole of the Hebrew scriptures. While disparities of wealth and status are clearly evident and acknowledged – the riches of certain patriarchs and kings are described uncritically or taken as a sign of divine blessing, and the existence of slaves is accepted – a concern that none should be denied their basic needs pervades every book. For the biblical writers, the fundamental equality of all people before God means that all must have their basic needs met, and many reserve their sharpest invective for those who act unjustly in this respect.[12] God is the creator and sustainer of *life*, and all that operates to diminish or take life is to be resisted. Thus in the earliest Old Testament book, Job, the writer speaks of rich and poor as both being the work of God's hands and condemns as unjust those rulers who favour the former over the latter.[13] The Psalmist talks of God standing alongside the needy and executing justice on their behalf,[14] and the prophets Isaiah and Amos are outspoken in their condemnation of those who exploit the poor:

> What do you mean by crushing my people, by grinding the face of the poor? says the Lord God of hosts.[15]

> Hear this, you that trample upon the needy, and bring to ruin the poor of the land . . . The LORD has sworn by the pride of Jacob: Surely I will never forget any of their deeds.[16]

The connection between having riches and acting justly is strong throughout Scripture. There is a clear sense that all wealth belongs ultimately to God and is not there for people to do with just as they please. 'All that is in the heavens and on the earth is yours . . . Riches and honour come from you, and you rule over all.'[17] 'The land is mine; with me you are but aliens and tenants.'[18]

Creating wealth is good, but it carries with it the responsibility to care for the poor. The 'good wife' described in the book of Proverbs is commended not only for her enterprise and ability to make a profit in her business, but because 'she opens her hand to the poor, and reaches out her hands to the needy'.[19] King Josiah can enjoy his food and drink, but what earns him the favour of the Lord is that he '[did] justice and righteousness' and 'judged the cause of the poor and needy'.[20] Jeremiah also perceives the Lord to be saying:

> Do not let the wealthy boast in their wealth; but let those who boast boast in this, that they understand and know me, that I am the LORD; I act with steadfast love, justice, and righteousness in the earth.[21]

YHWH is also perceived in the Hebrew texts to be against systems that would institutionalize or legalize the exploitation of the poor. This is most clearly seen with respect to the distribution of that most basic commodity, land. In Numbers 26, following a census of the people who had come out from slavery in Egypt, Moses is instructed to divide the land among the tribes in proportion to their size; to ensure that the biggest or most powerful tribes do not secure for themselves the best quality land, the apportioning is to be done by lot.[22] The Jubilee laws in Leviticus make it clear that land was never to be sold in perpetuity, that those who benefited from the poverty of others by buying up their land did not hold on to it permanently.

These laws were not so much geared to creating a fully 'egalitarian' society as to ensuring that a degree of equalization was achieved through workable redistributive mechanisms (though, as commentators always point out, there is no evidence that they were ever put into practice). Thus, if a person reduced to selling his land through poverty was unable to redeem it before the year of Jubilee, when that year came his land would be released by its current owner and he would return to it.[23]

Observing the Sabbath every week also had an equalizing dimension to it, because in so far as it obliged all – rich and poor alike – to abstain temporarily from work it provided, as Christopher Rowland has put it, 'a break in those patterns of relationships which sustain inequality, for those who are used to being served can no longer expect those who serve them to minister to their needs'.[24] References to the land being divided equally also appear in Ezekiel, while Isaiah, Micah and Zechariah all envisage a time when everyone will enjoy the security that comes from having their own access to the necessities of life.[25]

Underpinning the concern that all should have equal access to land is the importance of community: in biblical terms it is fundamental that no one is denied membership of their community on account of their economic circumstances – indeed, such membership is one of the 'basic needs' a person should have fulfilled in order to be 'human'. In the Leviticus 25 passage, the purpose of giving material aid to the impoverished person is so that he may once again be able to live alongside his helpers.[26] Community, for the biblical authors, is predicated on an assumption that every person can maintain his or her own well-being: this seems to be the point of the depiction in Isaiah, Zechariah and Micah of 'all sitting beneath their own vine'. Where even one person becomes dependent upon others the community is deficient, hence the importance of all having access to the land.

The Bible and inequality: the New Testament

The sense that community and 'fellowship' can only truly be said to exist when all members are held to be equal is also evident in the New Testament. In his first letter to the church at Corinth, Paul employs the metaphor of the body to describe the relationship that exists between the followers of Christ, stressing that all limbs and organs are of equal value and equally vital to making the body function. The clear implication here is that, as people join the fellowship of Christ, so any social status or standing they have becomes of no importance. Indeed, in the case of those who might be thought to be 'weaker' or less honourable, their indispensability to the whole is stressed. And as Paul moves on explicitly to discuss the different gifts and abilities people may bring to their fellowship, so he underlines how diversity with respect to functions does not mean diversity in terms of worth or status. True fellowship cannot exist where some members are held in higher esteem than others. The epistle of James also contains warnings against showing favouritism, on account of their outward appearance, to people who attend church.[27]

Another example of equality being demonstrated among the early Christians is described in Acts 4.32–35, where the practice of the Jerusalem church seems to have been for no one to consider anything as their own private possession but for everything to be shared. Those who owned lands or houses sold them and the apostles distributed the proceeds to those in need. Again, the requirement that basic needs be met seems to have been fulfilled in that 'there was not a needy person among them' – an echo of the situation that it was believed would obtain if the people of Israel followed the Jubilee principles.[28] Equality *between* churches was also important for Paul, as his call to the Corinthian fellowship to share their goods with a poorer community suggests.[29] He does not want to see a reversal of fortunes but suggests that from their present abundance they should supply the wants of others so that, on another occasion, their need may be met by the abundance of others 'then there will be equality' (NIV).

In 2 Corinthians 8.15 Paul harks back to the account in Exodus 16 of the provision of the manna in the wilderness, where the principle was again that the basic needs of all were met: 'those who gathered much had nothing over, and those who gathered little had no shortage'.[30] The early Christian practice of sharing to ensure that basic needs were met would also have been informed by the teaching of Jesus himself – for example, his instruction to 'give to everyone who begs from you' – and perhaps also John the Baptist, with his call to those with two coats to give one away to those with none.[31]

Yet Paul also uses the powerful image of Christ's incarnation, his rejection of riches and adoption of poverty, to underline his point about giving to ensure the well-being of others.[32] This thought is echoed in another letter Paul wrote around the same time, to the church at Philippi, Christ being described there as laying no claim to equality with God but making himself nothing, taking the nature of a servant and being made in human likeness.[33] It is when speaking of the 'Word becoming flesh' that Scripture most clearly attests to the equality of all people for, as Timothy Gorringe says, 'in taking "flesh" God assumed all human beings – black, white, female, male, Dalit and high-born, cognitively disabled and others – into a full filial relation, and therefore into equality'.[34]

The Communion service, Eucharist or Mass also affirms the equality of all before God. Paul strongly rebukes those in the church at Corinth who broke the spirit of fellowship underpinning this meal by taking more than their fair share – becoming drunk while others went hungry – and his exhortation to the members to wait for one another when they eat together suggests that the point of their meal was to share. Allowing some to eat and drink more than others amounted to a denial – perhaps even a parody – of what the Lord's Supper stood for, and Paul tells his readers as much.[35]

The Eucharist powerfully anticipates the heavenly banquet, when none shall be distinguishable by rank or status. It is celebrated in memory of the One who ate with the social outcasts of his day and taught that, while in society people might pull rank on one another, 'it is not so among you' for 'whoever wishes to become great among you must be your servant, and whoever wishes to be first among you must be slave of all'.[36] 'The last will be first, and the first will be last.'[37]

In his own teaching and practice Jesus reflected the tenor of the scriptures in which he was immersed. At the beginning of Luke's account he affirms his call to proclaim the year of the Jubilee, and a leitmotif of his teaching was that, in the kingdom which he had come to announce, the poor and humble would be raised up and the rich and important brought down.[38] In her song of praise during her pregnancy, Mary prefigures her son's mission by speaking of God as one who fills the hungry with good things and sends the rich away empty,[39] and Jesus quite literally does this by challenging people who come to him to sell their possessions and give to the poor,[40] telling parables which show the rich in a bad light and poverty in a good,[41] and suggesting that entry into the kingdom will not be possible without the abandonment of wealth – presumably because in the kingdom the categories of 'rich' and 'poor' will not exist.[42]

Jesus also appears to have approved of sharing possessions, some commentators suggesting that the 'real' miracle in the story of the feeding of the five thousand was that, by using the example of the small boy with his loaves and fishes, Jesus got the people to share what they had brought. He might also have envisaged his promise to his disciples that, if they left all for his sake, they would 'receive a hundredfold', being fulfilled by their sharing of their surplus wealth.[43]

Applying the principles

If the Scriptures acknowledge the fundamental equality of all before God, and suggest that all should be able to meet their basic needs and be 'agents of their own well-being', how can we who want to see biblical principles inform our national life bring them to bear on our own situation? How can we relate the concepts of 'fellowship', 'community' and 'sharing' to our own economic system, and translate into workable policies the principle that no one should permanently benefit from the poverty of others and that a community's economic structures should not permit an ever-widening gap between rich and poor?

Clearly it is unwise to try to take economic principles that may or may not have been adopted by nomadic tribespeople in the Middle East 15 centuries before the birth of Christ, and apply them immediately in our own day. Yet if we believe that the Bible should inform our thinking about all areas of life we will want to hear what it says about issues relating to wealth, poverty and justice. Given the importance attached in some Christian circles to the relatively small number of references in Scripture that appear to touch on issues such as embryo research, assisted dying and same-sex relationships, it would be strange to ignore its much more extensive treatment of what we would now call economic matters, including inequality.

Arguably the most influential Christian advocate of economic equality in the twentieth century was R. H. Tawney. Tawney saw inequality as the 'lion in the path' to the development of a common culture, and he was in no doubt that if Scripture encouraged us to see all people as equal in God's eyes, and impelled us to love our neighbours equally, that equality should be reflected in our social and economic structures. For Tawney this implied a powerful role for the state, which had a duty to operate in the public interest and to use the levers of taxation and social security to ensure that differences of wealth and income were gradually narrowed. Many of Tawney's readers in the 1920s and 1930s would have shared his assumption that a degree of central control was essential in any serious search for equality, and another great architect of the welfare state, Archbishop William Temple, argued that the state had a duty to ensure that all families had an adequate income, good housing and access to education. Certainly the post-war Labour government, with a vision of a more equal Britain, enjoyed widespread public support when it nationalized key utilities and centrally administered a whole raft of services including education, health and housing.

Today the issue is arguably less clear-cut. While some still see the state as pivotal in the quest for equality, and taxation as a vital lever in the project, others argue that the greater freedom given to the market since the 1980s has raised living standards across the board and made the very notion of 'inequality' seem outdated. While government control of the 'commanding heights' of the economy in the public interest may have been welcomed by a people shattered by the ravages of war, today the idea that 'Whitehall knows best' about providing services is seen as hopelessly outdated. (At the time of writing, it remains to be seen whether government intervention to shore up some UK banks during the economic crisis of October 2008 will serve to change this way of thinking.)

It is true that Tawney – and for that matter his contemporary William Beveridge – did not see the state as the *only* agency with the power to promote equality, arguing that local authorities, individual citizens and what we would now call the 'third sector' (voluntary bodies and community groups) also had a crucial role. Now, however, the received wisdom on both the 'left' and 'right' is that the era of the 'big state' and government welfare as the 'institutional expression of altruism' has long passed, replaced by the concept of 'stakeholder welfare' and an emphasis on individual responsibility and the role of the voluntary sector.

These twin features of stakeholder welfare make it appealing from a Christian perspective. It is never suggested in Scripture that people should be dependent on 'benefits' or 'charity' if they are able to work, and Christian agencies and churches have increasingly played a vital role in providing services to local communities. Greater diversity in welfare provision, and the introduction of the concept of 'choice', have improved the quality of life for many. Yet the case for pressing toward greater equality, and for this to be a consciously shared project under government direction, still seems compelling.

Take the idea, which I have argued is strongly scriptural, that everyone should receive an income sufficient to live on – an ideal also reflected in the 1948 Universal Declaration of Human Rights with its assertion that 'everyone has the right to a standard of living adequate for the health and well-being of himself and his family, including food, clothing, housing and medical care'. While we will heed Paul's injunction that anyone who will not work should not eat – noting that it says will not work, not cannot work – we will want to argue that the mark of a godly society must be its commitment to see that every person receives sufficient to enable them to meet their basic needs.[44] The question then raised is, how is 'a society' to fulfil this function unless through some centrally administered apparatus?

Unlike 'relieving poverty', the business of ensuring that every person or family has the basic necessities for survival must involve some central coordination. To argue this is not to advocate a return to the heavily bureaucratic 'command economy' models of the old Soviet bloc, nor to rule out a vital role for the voluntary or business sectors or for local authorities or other agencies. But it is to rule in a 'managing' or 'coordinating' role for the state, rooted in a conscious commitment to achieve basic equality. While some will find the argument for a 'direct' role for the state in providing for basic needs compelling, it is possible to conceive of government maintaining a 'mixed' approach to service provision, reflecting modern, progressive attitudes to the state, within a well-defined framework for tackling inequality. One of the key lessons of history (the latter half of the nineteenth century being a prime example) is that, for all its merits, spontaneous voluntary charitable provision cannot *guarantee* a standard of living adequate for the health and well-being of all, and therefore some degree of government intervention will be required if this is to be achieved. The challenge for politicians is to set the balance between direct central provision and state-supported voluntary provision.

Pushing governments farther

In our own context we have seen some government-coordinated action in the direction of greater equality. In 1999

Prime Minister Tony Blair gave a concrete commitment that child poverty would be eradicated within 20 years, and by the end of the first quarter (2004) the target was on course to being met (though progress has been slower since). The Blair government also brought in a minimum wage, a system of pension credits to guarantee everybody over the age of 60 an agreed minimum income, and schemes to create new jobs and help people back into work. These measures, driven from the centre, have played their part in lifting young and old, families and single people, out of poverty, but we have yet to see a political party commit to introducing a *living* wage or to setting the minimum wage and welfare rates and pensions by taking into account research into minimum income standards.

Our vision of a more equal society should compel us to press for agreement on where a living wage should be fixed, and for the means to be found to achieve it. This is to wade into deep political waters, of course, because the standard response of the government when challenged about the perceived inadequacy of the minimum wage, or the level at which benefit payments or incentives to train for work are pitched, is 'this is what we can afford and things will improve for individuals when they find work (or better work)'. From a biblical perspective, however, we might ask whether 'affordability' should be the chief criterion for setting a minimum level of income, and whether a realistic figure should not first be set and then the resources found to meet it.

Some will argue that the extra revenue needed to ensure a decent standard of living for all should be raised through taxation – particularly taxation, at a higher level than at present, of the highest incomes. This could be one way of meeting the twin biblical imperatives of getting the rich to 'share' their wealth with the poor and achieving a greater level of economic equality within society. However, increasing taxation is now perceived to be deeply unpopular with voters and is seldom advocated by the mainstream parties. Tax is now seen almost universally in negative terms, as something punitive and restrictive of freedom rather than serving a positive function, so perhaps there is scope for a fresh debate (which could be initiated by the churches) about its purpose.[45] This could involve re-examining both its potential as a contributor to the promotion of 'social justice' and greater equality, and also the relative merits of direct and indirect taxation. Reflection on the Muslim concept of 'Zakah', which requires wealth redistribution in order to achieve social justice, could be instructive. Zakah derives from a theological understanding of wealth as something to be shared, and places a responsibility on the producers of wealth to distribute a portion of their wealth so as to ensure that all in the community receive their 'fair share'.[46]

If taxing the incomes of the living provokes lively debate, so, too, does the question of taxing the dead. Whenever inheritance tax is discussed, politicians – aware of its unpopularity[47] – will usually promise either to abolish it or raise the threshold so that only the super-rich will be caught. Yet the biblical model of Jubilee challenges us to adopt a more creative approach to this form of taxation – such as increasing it substantially in order to fund a national dowry to benefit those starting out in life. Through such a mech-anism, as one of its advocates has put it, the state would 'do for *all* young citizens what the comfortable do already but only for their own offspring – redistribute wealth on death so that everyone gets a dowry'.[48] If one of the main contributors to the persistence of inequality is inheritance, a radical reform of the laws enshrining 'the right of privilege to breed privilege' must be a priority for those committed to the equality agenda.

Andrew Bradstock

Saying difficult things

If seeking a more equal society leads us to question the received wisdom of our day, we might observe that Jesus himself did nothing less when challenging those he met about their attitude to their possessions and responsibility to the poor. Of course Christians should take into account the world of *realpolitik* when translating their vision of a fairer society into hard-edged policies, but it is difficult to see how some engagement with questions of taxation and redistribution can be avoided. In the face of the widespread assumption that poverty can be reduced without materially affecting the standard of living of the better off, Christians will be among those saying that people (including often themselves) who enjoy a comfortable lifestyle do so, to some extent, because some in our society receive low wages. They will want to extend the conversation about building an inclusive society by stressing the importance of 'community' and 'partnership' over against greed and individual consumption as foundation stones for this society, and be honest about what this may mean for a tax system which still allows the bottom fifth of workers to pay a higher proportion of their income in tax than the top fifth. They will stress that to be 'human' involves more than just having enough to remain alive: it encompasses being able to share in and feel one belongs to a society, and therefore what other people take home *does* matter. And they will be clear that this has nothing to do with the 'politics of envy', but rather has to do with the creation of a society that seeks materially to acknowledge that all its members are made in God's image and should live in a way which reflects that status.

Christians may also want to argue that extending the 'opportunity society' will only be possible when there is a more equal distribution of resources. Politicians often speak of increasing social mobility and making it possible for people to reach the top through merit rather than factors such as class, gender, ethnic group or wealth. But by definition 'meritocracy' only provides a route to the top for the few, often those who are able to benefit from the best education and enjoy the healthiest living environments. Promoting 'equal opportunity' only makes sense when all have the same chance to access the new opportunities – something that can never happen under the current public school system. As Tawney once put it:

> The existence of such opportunities in fact, and not merely in form, depends, not only upon an open road, but upon an equal start . . . equality of opportunity is fictitious without equality in the circumstances under which people have to develop and exercise their capacities.[49]

Being creative

If our concern to see greater equality leads us down the well-worn path of campaigning for tax reform and an end to 'privileged education', it should also inspire us to seek creative ways forward. One would be to stimulate a public debate around the values of generosity and giving, acknowledging that the UK is some way behind countries such as the USA in developing a 'giving culture', a sense of putting something back into the community. No society can legislate to make people generous, but Christians can do much to highlight the moral issues involved and seek to change the culture with potentially far-reaching consequences. Encouraging wealthy individuals and institutions to be more publicly linked with poverty reduction, including through corporate social responsibility programmes, could well meet with a ready response at a time when these bodies are increasingly perceived to be 'part of the problem' on account of the high profits and bonuses that attend their activities.

Another practical way forward would be to increase awareness about the 2019 target for eliminating child poverty and secure an all-party consensus around it to ensure that any personnel changes in Downing Street before that date do not imperil progress towards it. It seems vital that, as with the 2015 target for meeting the Millennium Development Goals, tackling inequality in the UK moves beyond being a party political issue: could not all parties now undertake to 'poverty proof' all their policies to ensure that they are consistent with eradicating *child* poverty? And could not the existing commitment to eradicate child poverty be developed into a commitment endorsed by all political parties to see poverty eliminated *across the generations* by 2020?

A further way forward would be for governments to ensure that incomes – especially those of people on the minimum wage – rise in line with average earnings. This would act as a brake on inequality and ensure that earners at the very bottom of the scale did not get left even further behind.

Another development with potentially far-reaching consequences would be the establishment of a 'commission on inequality', perhaps as part of the existing Equality and Human Rights Commission. Such a body could focus specifically on the economic dimension of inequality, examining the costs and impacts of growing wealth inequality and identifying remedies that would attract broad public support. Central to such a commission's work must be consideration of the growing body of independent research which, by comparing data from a number of different countries, and different states across the USA, has indicated that narrowing the gap between rich and poor in a society produces a stronger and more stable community, one more likely to generate trust, reduce violence and crime, increase life expectancy and improve social mobility. Spearheaded by Professor Richard Wilkinson and Dr Kate Pickett, this research provides the first real evidence that inequality is the most important explanation of why, despite their extraordinary material success, advanced societies are often social failures, and how, when income differences between rich and poor are smaller, outcomes are invariably better.[50] If narrowing the gap between rich and poor really can be proven to have a positive effect on the major causes of social breakdown then it behoves us to force it higher and higher up the political agenda.

Does it matter?

So, does it matter that John Terry and his Premier League colleagues earn more in a month than most British workers will earn in a lifetime? In one sense no, for a degree of inequality of income will always exist in society. The Bible acknowledges that some will enjoy greater wealth than others, and nowhere does it advocate economic equality – what we might now define as 'equalized after-tax real income' – even if that were practically and politically possible.

Yet where that conspicuous wealth exists alongside material poverty the Bible does have much to say, both about the fact of that poverty and the structures of a society that allow such gross inequality to exist. And much of the empirical data available to us today confirms the continuing relevance and applicability of the Bible's concerns.

Clearly we should not be concerned about inequalities which result from our natural differences, but we can find in Scripture imperatives for a society to tackle those rooted in its own organization, which prevent the development of a 'common life'. In our own society, where hundreds of people still die every year because they cannot afford to heat their homes, where tens of thousands of families live in temporary accommodation because they cannot afford to get on to the property ladder and there is a shortage of affordable rented housing, action could be taken to bring about a greater 'levelling' of income and to ensure the basic needs of all are met. And such action, as we have noted, will bring benefits for society in terms of greater cohesion, higher levels of trust and a better quality of life for all.

But it will need a government committed consciously to tackling inequality, as governments have been in the past, and to using the levers of power to achieve this; and therein lies the challenge for those, including Christians, who see this issue as worth pursuing. Critics of wealth redistribution to achieve social good claim that such a policy stifles ambition and drive and represents a loss of freedom, yet the relatively small reduction in the range of choices open to the richest 10 per cent of the population when subjected to, say, a higher level of personal taxation, compared to the enormous increase in 'freedoms' the redistribution of that wealth would mean for the very poor, makes that argument less than convincing. When redistribution is effected to enable the hitherto poor and disempowered to increase their chances of realizing their God-given potential through access to education, healthcare, housing and employment, the 'freedom' enjoyed by the society actually increases. 'Freedom' has to encompass freedom *from* (poverty, powerlessness and dependency) as well as freedom *to* (spend one's resources as one chooses), and the ability to exercise freedom should be available to all, not just a minority. And the importance of pursuing a society where all are treated justly cannot be exaggerated for Christians. It is, after all, the 'nations' who are gathered before the Son of Man when the separation of those who have acted justly towards the poor and those who have not is made.[51]

Challenging inequality has never been a mainstream concern in the UK. Matthew Arnold once went so far as to suggest that inequality was almost a 'religion' in England, and while we have made considerable progress since the nineteenth century – no one now seriously questions the principle of 'one person, one vote' or 'equality before the law' – equality is still a divisive issue. Yet there are signs that it might be returning to the political agenda. In a succession of opinion polls, from British Social Attitudes to the *Guardian* ICM, three-quarters of voters in the UK say that the income gap is too wide. The work of Wilkinson et al. is gradually gaining purchase among the policy community, and all three main parties are indicating a growing concern that 'inequality matters' and must be addressed – even if none is yet prepared to commit to using tax as a mechanism.[52] With their firm belief in a God who sees all people as of equal worth, Christians will want to contribute to that debate, both because their faith impels them to see their values reflected in society and because they believe that these values, as expressed in a concern for a more equal society, will take us nearer to realizing the 'abundant life' for all that Jesus came to announce.

Notes

1 Cited in Robert Booth, 'Gap between rich and poor narrows, but UK is still one of the world's most unequal countries', *The Guardian*, 22 October 2008.

2 Caroline Muspratt, 'Top bosses earn 98 times employee wage', Telegraph.co.uk, 7 November 2006: accessible at <http://www.telegraph.co.uk/finance/2950229/Top-bosses-earn-98-times-employee-wage.html>.

3 Booth, 'Gap between rich and poor'.
4 Cited in Stephen Charles Mott, *A Christian Perspective on Political Thought* (New York: Oxford University Press, 1993), p. 82.
5 Duncan Forrester, *On Human Worth* (London: SCM, 2001), p. 30.
6 Psalm 8.5.
7 Genesis 1.26.
8 R. H. Tawney, *'The Attack' and Other Papers* (London: George Allen & Unwin, 1953), pp. 67–8; cited in Forrester, *On Human Worth*, p. 141.
9 Genesis 2.23.
10 Genesis 3.16.
11 Pelagius, 'On Riches', in Andrew Bradstock and Christopher Rowland (eds), *Radical Christian Writings: A Reader* (Oxford: Blackwell, 2002), p. 18.
12 Nicholas Sagovsky, *Christian Tradition and the Practice of Justice* (London: SPCK, 2008), appeared after this chapter was drafted, but several sections deal in detail with the 'basic needs' argument from Scripture – for example, Chapters 3 and 9.
13 Job 34.17–19.
14 Psalms 109.31; 140.12.
15 Isaiah 3.15.
16 Amos 8.4, 7.
17 1 Chronicles 29.11–12.
18 Leviticus 25.23.
19 Proverbs 31.10–31.
20 Jeremiah 22.15–16.
21 Jeremiah 9.23–24.
22 Numbers 26.52–56.
23 Leviticus 25.23–28.
24 Christopher Rowland, '"The First Will Be Last, and the Last First": Practical Theology and Equality', in William F. Storrar and Andrew R. Morton (eds), *Public Theology for the 21st Century* (London: T. & T. Clark, 2004), p. 345.
25 Isaiah 65.17–25; Ezekiel 47.13ff.; Micah 4.4; Zechariah 3.10.
26 Leviticus 25.35–36.

27 James 2.1–7.
28 Deuteronomy 15.4.
29 2 Corinthians 8.13–14.
30 Exodus 16.18.
31 Matthew 5.42; Luke 3.11.
32 2 Corinthians 8.9.
33 Philippians 2.5–7.
34 Timothy Gorringe, 'Slouching Towards Jerusalem: Achieving Human Equality', in Storrar and Morton, *Public Theology*, p. 327.
35 1 Corinthians 11.17–34.
36 Mark 10.43–44.
37 Matthew 20.16.
38 Luke 4.18–21.
39 Luke 1.46–55.
40 Matthew 19.21; Luke 12.33; 19.1–10.
41 Luke 12.16–21; 16.19–31; cf. Matthew 6.19–21.
42 Mark 10.25; Luke 6.24.
43 Matthew 19.29; Mark 10.29–30.
44 2 Thessalonians 3.10.
45 One Christian organization which has done some useful work on taxation is the Cambridge-based Jubilee Centre. See <http://www.jubileecentre.org/document.php?id=33&topicID=3>.
46 See Zahid Hussain, 'Contours of an Islamic Political Economy', in John Atherton and Hannah Skinner (eds), *Through the Eye of a Needle: Theological Conversations over Political Economy* (Peterborough: Epworth, 2007), pp. 102–18.
47 See S. White and W. Paxton, *A Citizens' Stake: Exploring the Future of Universal Assets Policies* (Bristol: Polity Press, 2005), cited in Nick Pearce and Will Paxton (eds), *Social Justice: Building a Fairer Britain* (London: IPPR, 2005), p. 13.
48 John Collins, 'Not Mine But Thine: A Christian Approach to the Redistribution of Wealth and the Reform of Inheritance Tax' (unpublished dissertation, 1999), p. 72.
49 R. H. Tawney, *Equality* (London: Allen & Unwin, 1952; 4th edn), p. 106. Equality of *opportunity* was the chief focus of the report produced by John Smith's Social Justice Commission (the 'Borrie Report') in 1994.

50 See most recently, Richard Wilkinson and Kate Pickett, *The Spirit Level: Why More Equal Societies Almost Always Do Better* (London: Allen Lane, 2009).

51 Matthew 25.31–46.

52 Interestingly, as it wrestled with the severe global economic crisis in the latter half of 2008, the Brown administration adopted measures to increase the tax commitment of 'those who have done best in the last decade' in order to be able to spend to protect jobs.

Conclusion
Christian political wisdom

JONATHAN CHAPLIN

This conclusion will not seek to present either a summary or a synthesis of the rich, varied and sometimes contrasting ideas expounded in this book. Each chapter speaks clearly enough, and the contributors speak for themselves alone. Its aim is to offer an interpretive commentary: identifying and developing some central affirmations recurring throughout the book, exploring some outstanding questions further, and suggesting the possible cash value of the book's insights for contemporary British policymaking. First, however, we need an important caveat about the nature of political theology itself.

Principle and policy

Taking its cue from the incomparable Homer Simpson, the Introduction assured readers that this book would not offer any straightforward or precise answers to its central question, and the subsequent chapters have lived up to this promise. This is not intended as a criticism, for it has been recognized throughout that political theology does not pretend to generate the sort of detailed policy prescriptions found in party manifestos or White Papers.

It should be recognized that in this respect political theology is not essentially different from political theory generally. Comprehensive principled frameworks, of whatever ideological stripe, can offer broad understandings of political reality and broad orientations for the direction of government policy, but not 'Homeric' answers to concrete policy questions such as the 'right' level of interest rates or the 'correct' solution to transport congestion.

Political theologians should not feel apologetic over the apparent lack of policy specificity in the biblical or theological reflections they offer (which is not to say that political theologians cannot get quite specific, as several of our contributors have). Equally, political practitioners should not feel frustrated or let down by political theologians who fail to deliver such specificity. Liberals whose 'Bible' is John Stuart Mill's *On Liberty* don't expect to find in it a blueprint for a contemporary law on hate speech, and conservatives who revere Edmund Burke's classic *Reflections on the Revolution in France* don't turn to it for advice on whether the UK should join the euro – though we could hazard a decent guess as to which way Mill or Burke might lean on such issues were they sitting in Parliament today.

The purpose of political theology is rather to *help form practical Christian political wisdom*. To be sure, it is not the only source of such wisdom – there is no substitute for seasoned experience – but it is an indispensable, and today a sadly neglected, one. Our modest hope is that the essays gathered here will function as a useful resource and stimulus for Christian, and perhaps other, practitioners as they seek to reflect more deeply and rigorously on the core question confronting every political actor every day: what is the *unique* role of government in society and how may it better discharge that role on behalf of its citizens?

It is very easy to lose sight of that fundamental question when immersed in the bear-pit of political campaigning, the messy scramble of coalition-building, the twists and turns of policy-making, the tedium of late-night legislative committee work, or the complexities of managing some small corner of a labyrinthine bureaucracy. But this isn't a problem only for politicians. Most people don't hold the 'mission statement' of their institutions (if they work in one) at the forefront of their minds for most of the time; mostly they simply get on with the job at hand as best they can. There are only so many hours in the day.

Imagine, however, how business performance could change if every manager, employee and shareholder regularly asked him or herself how this particular act – of pricing, hiring, marketing, producing, investing, restructuring – served the purpose of, for example, 'supplying socially valuable and environmentally sustainable goods to those who need them at a price they can afford'.

Equally, consider how government performance might be enhanced if every political actor – individuals, campaigning groups, parties, government departments and agencies – continually held before them the mandate of government to 'render just judgment' and to 'advance the common good' – to use the weighty terms introduced by David McIlroy.

Government performance would not change comprehensively: a good deal of what government does already pursues that mandate, as a result of the sound intuitions and motivations guiding those who work in it, or of existing procedures for promoting such goals (e.g. extended debates on Second Readings where many viewpoints are canvassed, or the Register of Members' Interests). But it could change substantially. Concentrating minds on the priority of justice and the common good would, for example, help mitigate narrow sectionalism or electoral expediency; ward off spurious or self-interested justifications for this or that new policy; discourage misrepresenting the views of opponents, who (alarmingly!) might turn out to have the occasional true insight into the justice of one's tax proposal; raise the quality of debate within government and Parliament – perhaps even in the media; and, generally, encourage 'joined-up government'.

This is not at all to imply that consensus on the content of implications of 'just judgment' or 'the common good' is easily attainable. Clifford Longley reminds us of the inescapable diversity of views of the common good in today's secularized and plural society. On the contrary, arguments over what the terms 'justice' and 'common good' actually mean and what they imply for policy are the very lifeblood of democratic political debate (even when the words themselves are not used). As Polly Toynbee has said, 'Every day in parliament, fundamentally different worldviews do battle. Politics is all about the clash of moral universes.'[1] It also involves pointed debate between adherents of the same vision: witness the contending readings of 'solidarity' and 'subsidiarity' in the chapters by Clifford Longley and Philip Booth, who draw on the same sources in Catholic Social Teaching.

Christians will often bring a distinctive interpretation or range of interpretations of justice and the common good to political life. In democratic debates, they will then find themselves alongside advocates of other interpretations and will have to argue their case like anyone else. Where consensus is attainable, well and good: it should be seized upon and made the most of. Where it is out of reach, debate continues until a decision must be taken, and all sides must then accept the constitutional (if not the moral) validity of the outcome, at least until it is formally reopened.

There is, of course, no guarantee that democratic debate will, in fact, issue in policies that promote 'just judgment' or 'the common good': political truth is not validated by parliamentary majorities. But today the practical meaning of justice and the common good can only be discerned *amid* such debates: it cannot be handed down from on high, either by Christians or secularists. So Christians, like others, must remain fully committed to the demanding task of democratic deliberation, through which alone the contemporary imperatives of justice and the common good can be identified.

Disagreement, then, is endemic to political debate. But this cannot mean that the only Christian contribution to politics is the mere elaboration of principles so general that no one could possibly disagree with them. In fact, we will not have succeeded in explaining the meaning of a principle until we can specify how it should be concretely applied. R. H. Tawney went so far as to say that 'to state a principle without its application is irresponsible and unintelligible'.[2] Since political practitioners are the ones best placed to specify the applications of principles, this means that they actually share in the task of identifying the meaning of principles like justice, the common good, accountability, the rule of law, equality and many more. They don't just take them fully formed from theorists and then 'apply' them. The process is as much inductive as deductive.

Some practitioners may already have grown fidgety waiting to remind us that terms like 'justice' or 'the common good' are just abstract ideas, operating at a high level of generality, which in themselves don't tell anyone what to do. It is only as they begin to get specified in more concrete guides to action that they begin to shape policy choices. Political theologians whose advice to politicians stops at 'do justice' or 'promote the common good' evoke justified consternation: politicians think they are doing that anyway all the time. R. H. Tawney again states the point bluntly. Churchmen who think they have something distinctive to say about society, he chides, should 'state fearlessly and in unmistakable terms what precisely they think that distinctive contribution to be. If they do not, then let them cease reiterating secondhand platitudes, which disgust sincere men, and bring Christianity in contempt.'[3]

This process of specification is complex and hard to map in advance. For example, it involves formulating a series of middle-level objectives such as 'adhering to the rule of law' (discussed by Julian Rivers) or 'equal satisfaction of basic human needs' (proposed by Andrew Bradstock). But then it calls for yet more concrete directives such as 'innocent until proven guilty' or 'healthcare free at point of use', or the 'Seven Principles of Public Life' drawn up by Lord Nolan to guide public officials (cited by David McIlroy). And as any parliamentarian knows, consensus on even *these* more specific notions doesn't yet secure policy agreement, for it is still necessary to determine what counts as 'proof' in a court of law (e.g. by specifying 'rules of evidence'), or what exact types of healthcare should be free at point of use (dental care currently isn't for many). Nor should it be thought that such questions are 'technical', non-partisan and, so, easy to resolve. On the contrary, deciding what types of healthcare should be free at point of use has been and remains a major political tussle given the constant pressure on health budgets. To rephrase Tawney's point, it is sometimes only when we get 'down and dirty' on such policy details – when we are engaged in what David McIlroy calls 'wise execution of just judgment' – that the force of our political principles comes to be really felt.

Yet, notwithstanding the limits of the 'principles' offered up by political theology, the conviction of this book is that

Christian practitioners will be aided significantly by sustained reflection on such principles, as they engage in this indispensable, tough, often bad-tempered, and frequently exhausting front-line task of putting principles to work on behalf of their fellow citizens. Political practitioners themselves actually shape the meaning of the principles they (and we) must live by politically. And recognizing this serves both to enhance the dignity of their office and to underline the gravity of their responsibility. They need our critical support as they discharge that heavy burden on behalf of the rest of us. It is in that spirit that we offer them this book.

Political wisdom: skill and substance

The contribution of political theology, we have proposed, is to help form practical Christian political wisdom. Political wisdom consists both of skill and substance. The previous section spoke mainly about wisdom as skill: a virtue or art acquired as a body of principle is brought to bear upon, indeed brought to clarity within, concrete political experience. As David McIlroy defined it, this is 'the skill of rightly adjudicating among the competing and legitimate demands constantly made on government'. What follows is more about the body of principle itself. For it would be a serious mistake to construe political wisdom only as a kind of internal Global Positioning System enabling individuals to negotiate their way successfully through the thickets of political life. We sometimes witness political practitioners seeming to operate with such an internal GPS as they manoeuvre and manipulate (harsher critics would say smarm and elbow) their way up the greasy pole. We might call them shrewd, but not wise.

Political wisdom involves discerning how a *body of political principle* is to assume concrete form in policy-making and statesmanship at a particular time and place. The chapters of this book have identified several core political principles which seem to have won widespread recognition and displayed continuing traction over the centuries of (mainly Western) Christian engagement in politics. In other words, they have acquired something like the status of 'tradition'. But like the only Christian traditions worthy of the name, their authority lies not in their mere momentum (the 'traditionalist' fallacy) but in their evident rootedness in biblical revelation. And like all valid Christian traditions they must continually be tested by exposure to fresh biblical scrutiny in every generation, and rearticulated or dispensed with as appropriate.

A 'body of political principle' is not a mere *assortment of political principles*, a ragbag into which just anything can be thrown. It should display a broad coherence, reflecting its origins in a coherent worldview. We do not claim that the chapters assembled here offer anything more than a rough approximation of such coherence. In any case they represent only some strands of 'the Christian political tradition', and they only speak from a British (and male) location. Nevertheless, with those limitations acknowledged, something like the following overall sketch of the role of government has begun to take shape.

Government under God: core principles

Government is created, fallen, open to redemption

We begin with the nature of government: what kind of beast is it? The book of Revelation, of course, does refer to it as a 'beast', in a chilling warning of how government – in this case a violent and predatory first-century Roman imperial government – can acquire idolatrous characteristics. As Nigel Wright, Tom Wright and Julian Rivers all make clear, the Bible is, to say the least, 'ambivalent' about government. But, as both Nigel Wright and Tom Wright's chapters also make clear, we must view government against the encompassing panorama of the entire biblical story and not just from the standpoint of one book, theme or passage.

Government, Nigel Wright explains, must be read through the wide-angle lens of 'creation, fall and redemption'.[4] It is, in the first place, one outworking of the 'cultural' mandate given to humanity at creation, a mandate to realize the many potentials of created life by establishing institutions that serve human needs. But, second, it is also as thoroughly corrupted by sin and evil as anything else in the human creation. Indeed, as one of the 'powers' it forms part of what Nigel Wright starkly calls a 'Domination System of general malignance' – the threatening sway of the powers insofar as they are in rebellion against the Creator. Yet, third, government, again like everything else in the human creation, remains open to the restraining and elevating influence of redemption, whereby, as Nigel Wright puts it, state power is drawn 'towards the service of justice and kindness'.

In this sense, as he points out, we can say that government is employed providentially by God within the 'order of preservation', restraining sin, disorder and violence and protecting the weak. This is in line with Oliver O'Donovan's account of government (cited by McIlroy) as an institution established to exercise 'public judgment' on 'wrong'. This specific assignment places a vital limit around the scope of its authority, since God has chosen other means, centrally the church, as his agents within the 'order of redemption'.

The same distinction is highlighted in other terms by Nicholas Townsend. The gospel of redemption is not advanced by the 'ordinary means of political power' but by the regenerative work of the Spirit. The 'temporal' common good, that part of the common good open to realization in this age, is advanced by God in two ways: primarily and directly by the church and only secondarily and indirectly by government. Government must therefore know its place and respect its limits. We explore that important distinction below.

As several contributors point out, maintaining this balanced theological vision can help practitioners who are caught up in the whirlwind of government both to keep their spirits up and to keep their heads level. On the one hand, such insights can help ward off those who would downplay the moral dignity of government as if it were comprehensively sinful or (literally) irredeemable. They can sustain our confidence that governmental justice can be infused with, or at least tempered by, the effects of grace. On the other hand, such insights warn against unrealistic expectations of what government – 'the hard edge of society', as Nigel Wright puts it – can actually achieve, and against naivety in the face of government's seemingly inexhaustible capacity to perpetrate evil: to commit wrong rather than correct it.

Government is legitimate, limited, accountable, diffused and representative

Several chapters reiterate the longstanding Christian view that government is an institution authorized by God. Theologically, the office of government has almost always been seen as legitimate, even if particular governments or governmental acts may not be. Julian Rivers' chapter spells out the biblical basis for that view. Here we can immediately anticipate the potential rejoinder that claiming God as the source of political authority plays into the hands of those who would favour an authoritarian view of the state, according to which political authority is self-validating and legally limitless. And historically, the Bible has been enlisted to do exactly that. So it is necessary to emphasize three crucial affirmations aired in the foregoing chapters. First, government's legitimate authority extends only so far as its divinely assigned purpose. Second, government is to be held accountable for its discharge of that authority. Third, in the divine ordering of society many other centres of legitimate authority exist which circumscribe the authority of government.

There is also an important fourth affirmation which has not been so clearly aired so far, largely because it lay beyond the brief assigned to our contributors. Government must also be representative of its citizens. That theme is picked up later on (see pp. 220–3).

The first affirmation is that *government's legitimate authority extends only so far as its divinely assigned purpose.* To pre-empt a possible early misunderstanding, to say that government's purpose is assigned by God is obviously not to say that government itself must explicitly acknowledge God or that only Christians (or theists) can have a right view of its purpose. That disclaimer entered, the central point is this: theologically, authority is only ever given by God to humans pursuant to a clearly demarcated purpose. God doesn't hand out blank cheques to those in office. Parental authority extends only so far as parents' duty to nurture children into independent adulthood: at the age of majority, children are bound to honour their parents, but not to obey them. The authority of businesses extends only as far as the proper purpose of business: where employees are required to sacrifice their family life out of exaggerated corporate loyalty, we know a moral limit has been breached.

The question of how we might go about specifying the proper purpose (and so the role) of government is addressed below. It is worth underlining the contemporary relevance of the question. The question of the proper scope of government's role is not put today with anything like enough frequency or precision. Politicians often speak of the purpose of government very loosely and imprecisely. Sometimes this doesn't matter all that much: after all, what governments do is more important than what they say they are doing.

Nevertheless, what they say (or, rather, think) they are doing – *and may do* – is, in the final reckoning, extremely important. All too often, when asked about the purpose of government, leading politicians resort to platitudinous generalizations, soundbites or rigid dogmatic certainties, and sometimes all of the above in the same breath. Precision about what government should and may do is critical. It needs continually to be repeated that good government is not the same as promoting just anything that happens to be good for society (the statist fallacy), or advancing anything that might be good for the nation (the nationalist fallacy), or merely refereeing the individual pursuit of self-chosen goods (the libertarian fallacy).

The incoherence of our view of the role of government today is often expressed in the frequent inconsistencies of our demands on government. In one breath we complain at what we take to be illegitimate government interventions (too much 'red tape' for business; the 'nanny state'; the 'surveillance state'), and in the next we chastise government for not intervening enough ('too little, too late' in a banking crisis; not enough grit on the roads in a weather crisis). It is true that for government to fulfil its proper role it will sometimes need to do more, and sometimes less, than is currently the case. Certainly the chapters in this book do not propose opting simplistically for either bigger or smaller government, as if only size mattered (though it does matter). What Nicholas Townsend calls the 'fourth way' emerging from Christian political theology amounts to a distinctive view not so much of the size of government but of its ends and means. But in order to know when we need more government and when less, we need a clear conception of what those proper ends and means are. We return to that question shortly.

The second affirmation in the foregoing chapters is that *government is to be held accountable for the discharge of its authority*. This is most forcefully stated by Tom Wright, who expounds the radically important but badly neglected assertion resounding throughout the pages of the New Testament: Caesar is not Lord of this world, but Jesus is. All authority has been given by the Father to the ascended Christ, and in his kingly authority Christ commands all human governments to serve his good purposes of establishing justice, peace and order in a world still deeply prone to disorder and violence. And it is not only patently evil empires like that of ancient Rome that stand under his judgment: every national government today is summoned to the same humble task of serving its people and not its own interests.

It is also vitally important to note that, contrary to superficial impressions of the Christian tradition, the principle of governmental accountability has almost always meant accountability both to God *and* to some human agent. As Julian Rivers notes, already in the Old Testament it meant the accountability of rulers not only to YHWH but also to the prophets. This is crucial because merely declaring a government accountable to God for some wrong has no practical effect unless the ruler concerned voluntarily changes his or her ways (which is rare), or is persuaded to do so by other members of the ruling elite (which is more common, though not always for principled reasons).

Over time, however, the notion of a religious accountability of government to God underwent two far-reaching transformations. First, it came to imply accountability to a universal moral framework which, while derived from God, was not dependent for its force on a shared faith or on the authority of the church – 'the natural law'. Next, it came to imply accountability to a formal constitutional framework which was legally binding on rulers – 'the rule of law'. The fundamental principle of the rule of law was obviously not only produced by Christian political theology. It took clear shape in the modern world also as a result of distinctively Enlightenment notions such as the doctrines of 'natural rights', 'popular sovereignty' and the 'separation of powers'. Yet it emerged clearly – perhaps uniquely – out of a political culture permeated by the confession that human political authority is a 'servant' of God rather than a master of society.

The gradual implementation of the basic constitutional principle of the rule of law was a momentous achievement in the evolution of Western political orders. Julian Rivers rightly notes that 'the Bible does not contain a theory of the Rule of Law' but concludes nevertheless that it does suggest that 'forms of government which are located within and not above law are preferable'.[5]

The third affirmation is that *in the divine ordering of society many other centres of legitimate authority exist which circumscribe the authority of government.* Rivers refers to this as the principle of the 'diffusion' of authority. He points out that the overall direction of biblical material on government points both to the dangers of excessive concentrations of power in any one institution and also to the positive mandates given to non-governmental offices such as family or tribe, priest, prophet. Likewise, as David McIlroy claims, 'The insistence that government has limits may be one of the most important services the church offers society.'[6]

Many have argued, in fact, that the most radical contribution of Christianity to Western political thought was the assertion that the church represented a completely alternative authority to that of government. As Tom Wright points out, the church's earliest confession, 'Jesus is Lord', was intentionally directed against the worship of Caesar, who in Romans 13 is radically downgraded to the status of a mere 'servant' of God.

The political thinker Eric Voegelin has acclaimed this historic achievement as the 'de-divinization of politics', the rolling back of the ancient belief that the political community was the supreme horizon of human loyalty.[7]

As Nigel Wright shows, this is the foundation for the modern doctrine of the 'separation of church and state'. This does not mean an absolutely watertight compartment between them; each institution quite legitimately shapes the other in particular ways. Rather, it reflects 'a clear desire to distinguish between the order of preservation secured by government and the order of redemption secured by the church'. Tom Wright assumes a broadly similar distinction but argues by contrast that it need not rule out an arrangement in which an established church occupies a guaranteed place at the heart of public life. The English model of establishment, he suggests, implies neither church control of government nor government control of the church.

It is not only the independent mandates of other institutions that serve to check the scope of governmental authority. The freedom of individual citizens has the same effect. Several contributors point out that among the deepest springs of this principle is the biblical claim that each human being is made in the image of God and thus worthy of an incomparable dignity that civil orders must respect and protect. This confession in time helped nurture a recognition that law must stand back in the face of religious conscience, thus paving the way for freedom of thought, speech and expression.[8]

The fourth affirmation, which lay beyond the scope of the contributions to this book, is that *government must be representative of its citizens*. Contributors were asked to address the role of government, not its responsiveness to citizens. But since the two cannot really be separated, certainly not under democratic governance, some pointers are appropriate.

It is important to get the relationship between the authority of government and the consent of the people right, especially because a Christian view of popular consent stands in tension with the modern secular liberal view. Modern secular liberalism sees this relationship as a one-way street: political authority originates with the 'sovereign' people and is transferred to government in acts of consent. But stated so simplistically this has the fatal implication that the 'office' of government lacks any inherent moral purpose or limit. Its purposes are only those given to it by the people. In theory, and too often in practice, these might include any goal that current political majorities happen to desire: destroying non-renewable energy resources in defence of one's standard of living, discriminating against resented minorities (blacks, gypsies, gays, religious believers, disabled people), or waging war on envied neighbours.[9] It is this democratic absolutism that Tom Wright warns against in his critique of the modern adulation of the 'vox populi'. He rightly observes that in the Christian tradition more attention has been concentrated on what governments do than on how they came to power.[10]

Actually, most secular liberals generally don't state the point so simplistically. They acknowledge that there are some things the people are not permitted to will, such as violations of human rights, or abolishing an independent judiciary. This is why they promote not simply 'democracy' but 'liberal democracy', the term 'liberal' referring to constraints on democratic majorities intended to safeguard people's liberty. Secular liberalism does, after all, acknowledge that there are sources of moral authority that do not proceed from individual human *will*. Democratic majorities can't be allowed to give their consent to just anything. But then they usually go on to identify such sources as individual human 'rights' or 'interests' or 'needs'. By contrast, Christian political theology ascribes the limits on what democratic majorities can will to the divinely assigned purpose of government (which includes protecting certain individual rights, interests and needs but isn't exhausted by these).

This is not to suggest that Christian political theology is essentially cool towards democracy. For many centuries, of course, it was cool to the point of indifference or hostility, but in the last two centuries it has gradually come not only to tolerate democratic institutions as the 'least bad' option (to paraphrase Winston Churchill's famous aphorism) but to embrace them enthusiastically.[11] Two comments on this outcome may be helpful.

First, the modern Christian embrace of democratic institutions has its roots in a much older Christian notion of 'representation', reaching back as far as the Middle Ages. Rulers, it was held, were not only to represent God to the people, but also to represent the people's judgment in their own acts of judgment. For many centuries this was not thought to require anything like popular election. Yet the notion that government should govern on behalf of the people, what David McIlroy calls 'the ideal of public service', and that it should do so in ways that honoured the inherited customs and mores of the people, emerged in political theology long before the modern era. Over time it fed wider notions of popular consent, participation and, eventually, election.[12] The crucial shift was from a passive, organic theory of representation to an active, constitutional one in which the formal consent of the people was seen as a necessary (but not sufficient) basis of the legitimacy of current office-holders (although not of the office of government itself).

Second, this active theory of representation is not an alien, secular intrusion into the Christian political tradition as some have suggested.[13] It can be seen as flowing from the tradition's longstanding view of government as guardian of the common good. If the very purpose of government is 'common' or public, it is a natural, indeed a necessary, step to conclude that 'the public' ought to play a role in identifying what the requirements of the common good are. As several contributors point out, the common good is not something other than the good of the whole people. It is not, as Oliver O'Donovan puts it, like a 'giant millennium dome' standing above and apart from them.[14]

Political theologians were increasingly willing to take this step as they began to appreciate the full ramifications of the principle of equality. As Julian Rivers points out, while the Bible does not explicitly endorse modern representative democracy, it nevertheless suggests that 'forms of government which reflect equal citizenship . . . are preferable'.[15]

From a Christian standpoint, then, institutions of popular representation, such as elected assemblies or local councils, should be seen in a very different light from that in prevailing opinion: not as mere instruments for the obtaining of our own interests but rather as avenues for the people's active participation in discerning the common good.[16]

The right to vote and participate in other ways in the political process thereby acquire a new and deeper significance. Such opportunities do not first of all derive from an inherent *individual right* to consent to one's governors, but rather from a *corporate responsibility* to take up the task of deliberating on what the common good requires. If more citizens, Christians among them, shared such a view of political participation, the quality of public debate and the conduct of elections might be significantly elevated. The question staring at voters in the polling booth would not be, 'How can I and my kind get more out of the system?' but, 'What does the public good require?'

Government is established to secure justice and the common good

The foregoing chapters offer extended reflections on the meaning of the terms 'justice' and 'the common good' (the latter being the wider notion, embracing the former).[17] There is no need here to summarize their various definitions of these terms or to rehearse the contrasting ways contributors work them out. What may be helpful for practitioners, however, is to explore further why it is that principles like the common good and justice with such deep roots in a shared tradition nevertheless lead to such different policy prescriptions today. Two sources of disagreement can be noted.

The first source is the way that different political theologians relate these terms to the broader biblical themes of creation, fall and redemption. For example, those holding a corrective or remedial view of government – the view that government is occasioned by the fall – tend to define its essential purpose as corrective justice: the 'righting of wrongs'. Such a view does not necessarily imply 'minimal government'.[18] But it can depress our expectations of what government can achieve in this age and so lead to narrower understandings of the scope of the common good or the claims of justice than are held by those who favour a creation-based, directive view of government. The result can be policies requiring the least government intervention possible (though, as we will note, Philip Booth's chapter makes clear that one can reach that conclusion by another route).

A directive view of government typically does lead to wider conceptions of the scope of the common good and justice, thereby potentially legitimizing more government intervention than would the corrective view. Yet as several authors point out, even such a view does not imply 'big government'. For, as several contributors crucially note, the responsibility of government *does not extend to the whole of the common good.* As Nicholas Townsend has noted, it is limited in the first place to the 'temporal common good'.[19] More specifically, he suggests, government's role is only to create 'social infrastructure', 'to secure the social conditions necessary for the possibility of the [temporal] common good'. Not only can government not save us, it also cannot exercise our varied social responsibilities on our behalf; it can only create the conditions in which we can exercise them. Viewed in this way, the difference between the corrective and the directive views of government begins to narrow. There is scope here to explore further whether the public policy implications of the two views can already be brought into closer alignment or whether the debate has to be conducted at the level of deeper differences over the very meaning and scope of the doctrines of creation, fall and redemption.

The second source of disagreement arises from the different interpretations put upon, and weightings attached to, principles like common good, justice, solidarity, subsidiarity and equality.

An initial point is that the common good is, as both McIlroy and Townsend explain, not an aggregative but a qualitative concept. As Townsend puts it, it refers to those goods that are 'irreducibly held in common'. It is noteworthy that all our contributors accept the possibility of at least some 'irreducibly common goods'. An important difference between some of them arises from contrasting views of the respective powers and capacities of institutions, individuals and governments to realize common goods.

Julian Rivers suggests that while the Bible clearly teaches the principle of limited government, and favours a 'diffusion of powers', it does not specify exactly where the limits of government vis-à-vis individuals or other institutions lie. While this seems clear, Townsend, Booth and Longley nevertheless explain how notions like solidarity and subsidiarity, deriving from Christian political theology rather than directly from the Bible, enable us to identify those limits more precisely.

In spite of their contrasting policy sympathies, Philip Booth, Clifford Longley and Nicholas Townsend agree that, properly understood, the principles of solidarity and subsidiarity do help specify the role of government. But they read the content of and connections between these principles differently. Booth especially emphasizes that solidarity is not in the first instance a political norm, but rather a universal norm of Christian love, to be taken up by every individual and all institutions in many different ways. For example, businesses should not simply meet but exceed their legal obligations for caring for the environment. There is such a thing as political solidarity and government has a role in establishing it – but only after other communities of solidarity have first attempted to address whatever problem is at hand.

The contrasting readings of the principle of subsidiarity in Philip Booth's and Clifford Longley's chapters are also instructive in regard to public policy questions. These authors endorse a common set of principles but differ in the substance they attach to them and in the relative weighting each receives in specific contexts. For example, Longley holds that solidarity 'takes precedence' over subsidiarity (and questions whether the latter has an obvious biblical foundation), while Booth claims that the two principles are essentially consistent with each other and will only very rarely conflict in practice.

The difference becomes clear in their contrasting evaluations of the relation between government and markets. Clifford Longley starts from an attitude of hesitation about the capacity of markets to deliver socially necessary outcomes. The common good, he suggests, 'stands in judgment over free-market economics'. Booth starts from a general presumption against government intervention and in favour of market solutions to social problems. Because of the propensity of fallen humans towards a centralization of power, he warns, government intervention can be justified only on the basis of a compelling argument, and a crucial step in that argument is a clear demonstration that no other agency is able to redress the wrong in question. These two presumptions are not finally incompatible with each other – both accept that governments and markets have limits – but they do generate quite different strategic policy tendencies.

This is at its clearest in Booth's extended analysis of environmental policy. For him, the crucial agents for workable environmental solutions are property-holding individuals and institutions. He argues that the widespread private (i.e. non-governmental) ownership of property is a clear implication of the principle of subsidiarity. This principle argues not only for the right of self-government for non-government institutions, but also for the right of both individuals and institutions to dispose of their own resources freely. His argument here is actually twofold. On the one hand, he points out that the principle of subsidiarity is not a mere pragmatic principle but a principle of justice. The proper allocation of responsibilities among different agents (persons, intermediate institutions, governments) is a matter of the rightful distribution of authority, not only of 'what works'.

Transferring responsibilities upwards to government thus requires a compelling justification. On the other hand, he holds that private ownership also creates a powerful incentive to manage property with care, and supports this claim with empirical studies of the management of rivers and fisheries. If environmental goods are privately owned, then their owners have a strong motivation towards stewarding them responsibly.

Booth does not rule out a legitimate role for government in addressing this or other large-scale social problems. But in his example of how to sustain fish stocks in EU waters, his preferred solution is not for the public ownership of the North Sea by the EU but for the legal regulation by the EU of a system of private fishing rights. Similarly, his preferred response to climate change is for governments to institute market-based solutions such as tradable quotas and carbon taxes, harnessing the incentives created by individual freedom for the common good.[20]

The same debate arises in other areas of policy. For example, those who look primarily to the principle of subsidiarity to indicate the limits of government may part with Julian Rivers, who seems to imply that the question of government's role in education is essentially a pragmatic one arising from circumstances ('even the most ardent supporters of "voluntaryism" had to admit defeat'). But the Catholic principle of subsidiarity, like the Calvinist principle of 'sphere sovereignty',[21] counsels that government's role in education should always be to aim to support non-governmental (voluntary or private) initiatives rather than to establish an alternative to them.

Rivers is probably right to venture that 'few would deny that universal education is a component of the common good'. Yet contributors differ over the precise role of government in realizing this laudable goal. Should that role be to create, fund and manage a single, uniform, centralized system of national education, or rather to facilitate and fund a diversity of educational providers (including, perhaps, both parent-controlled and private schools) within a regulatory framework for teacher qualification, curricular standards, health and safety standards, non-discrimination and so forth? As Rivers asks while explaining the principle of the 'diffusion of authority': 'Are we paying too high a price for the efficiency and equity of modern government in terms of national and international centralization?'[22] Those for whom the principle of subsidiarity looms largest in their thinking would tend to argue for the latter while those for whom the principle of equality looms largest would tend to favour the former. Booth argues that for the state to refuse to fund non-state schools would amount to 'an injustice', while Bradstock implies that it is precisely the 'privilege' generated by private education that counts as unjust.

The contrasting usages of the term 'equality' deserve further comment. Informed in part by the Christian socialist R. H. Tawney, Andrew Bradstock presents a powerful, robustly egalitarian reading of the Bible.[23] His proposals are certainly not a revival of a now discredited old-fashioned state socialism, yet he insists on a very active role for government in redressing the continuing, indeed on some measures increasing, economic inequalities in British society.

There is no dispute in the book over Christian support for the basic constitutional principles of political and legal equality as summarized by Julian Rivers.[24] But there is a real divergence, especially between Booth and Bradstock, over both the propriety and the capacity of government to redress economic inequality.

Rivers crisply states the point at issue: 'How can we pursue a fully rounded conception of equality without constructing an unlimited state?' The disagreement about how to diminish avoidable economic inequality emerges again from the relative weight accorded to governmental and non-governmental responsibilities. Booth does accept a role for government in redistributing income in order to secure the 'necessities of life' for those who would otherwise lack them, but only where non-governmental remedies have been exhausted. For Booth, this hesitation is justified in part by an insistence, not shared by most other contributors, that government is structurally incapable of exercising virtues like charity and mercy, since, he claims, they 'have no limit in their application'.

At the same time, the disagreement over the capacity of government to address economic inequality also arises from differing empirical judgments regarding the administrative capacities of government (what it can factually achieve), and the potentially debilitating impact of governmental action on non-governmental providers (its tendency to 'crowd out' voluntary provision). The same divergence explains the contrasting prescriptions regarding taxation between Booth and Bradstock.

The differences are, of course, far from complete. Bradstock does not expect government to secure complete economic equality, only an equal satisfaction of basic economic and social needs. This is a demanding but a much more modest goal. He embraces the notion developed since the 1990s of 'stakeholder welfare', in which government provision works alongside voluntary initiative and arrangements to promote individual responsibility for welfare. His preferred model is for government to perform a 'managing' or 'coordinating' role in a 'mixed' welfare system. Yet he also wishes to hold the British government to higher standards of achievement than it has currently reached. To that end, he proposes a government commission on inequality, which would monitor and drive progress towards governmental targets for reducing inequality. He also proposes the more radical measure of a 'living wage' which would exceed that of the mere minimum wage and would need to be funded by higher taxation.

It is not the aim of this book to suggest a way to reach agreement on such contested issues. But a critical issue for Christian political thinkers and practitioners in the next generation, as in former ones, is whether these contrasting and at least partly incompatible policy orientations in the economy, welfare, education, the environment and so forth express a perfectly legitimate diversity of political viewpoint which we should simply reconcile ourselves to, or whether they indicate regrettable and avoidable fractures in the Christian political mind that could at least be mitigated. Our hope is that Christian practitioners will consider the latter possibility. Both denominational and party affiliations place significant barriers to even recognizing such a possibility. Our challenge is that Christian practitioners will make time and space for the kind of dialogue about principle and policy necessary to conclude whether it is at least worth exploring.

Government: is a moral vision possible at all?

Yet there may be some who still wonder whether the whole enterprise in which this book has been engaged is after all based on a dubious assumption: that it is actually possible at all for government to pursue 'moral' purposes like justice or the common good. Too often, what seems to come first to the lips of senior political leaders when at the despatch box or in the glare of the media is the language of economic growth or strategic national advantage, rather than that of larger moral purposes. So an educational policy might be wrongly justified in terms of material objectives such as 'sustaining prosperity', 'improving global competitiveness' or 'creating wealth', instead of the properly educational objective of nurturing children towards moral and social maturity. Or a policy on international trade or defence might be defended primarily as a contribution to 'defending national security', 'promoting British interests' globally or 'retaining our seat at the table', instead of that of advancing the cause of the global common good.

In themselves, any of the aforementioned objectives could be seen as legitimate goals. They might find some degree of justification under the broad umbrella of the principles of 'just judgment' or 'the common good', for these principles don't counsel us to shrink our economies or marginalize our global standing. But the point is that more often than not that connection is simply not spelled out, and too often we suspect it cannot be. The impression is given that objectives like economic growth or national advantage are self-evident and self-validating. And the accompanying tacit message is that such 'hard' objectives won't be obstructed by 'soft' ones such as redressing economic inequality (because it would be just) or ceding greater global power to developing countries in international institutions (because it would enhance their contribution to the global common good).

There are, of course, many encouraging exceptions: Robin Cook's announcement of an 'ethical foreign policy' in 1997;[25] Tony Blair's Chicago speech spelling out 'the Doctrine of the International Community' in 1999;[26] Gordon Brown's account of a British 'national narrative' in 2006;[27] David Cameron's speech to the Conservative Party conference in 2008;[28] the Centre for Social Justice's documents *Breakdown Britain* and *Breakthrough Britain*;[29] *Faith in the Future*, written by a cross-party group of MPs.[30] Whether or not we agree with the particular contents of these statements, we can recognize them as laudable attempts to lift political debate above narrowly materialist or nationalist goals and point it to wider horizons of justice and the common good.

Citizens, however, often wonder how far such lofty sentiments actually control public policy when the going gets rough (as it usually does): Robin Cook's ethical foreign policy statement seemed to have been dropped even before the ink was dry. And he was one of only two ministers to resign over the invasion of Iraq even though we can reasonably conjecture that many others had deep conscientious reservations about it.[31]

The thrust of the chapters of this book is that governments should make much greater effort consistently and explicitly to explain their policies as intended to defend some specific aspect of justice or to promote some particular component of the common good (or at least as contributions to middle-level principles or concrete directives deriving from them). The impoverished language of getting rich or protecting interests diminishes us all by reducing citizenship to mere consumption or security.

How should such articulations emerge? It is obviously too much to expect each individual office-holder to do this kind of serious reflective work alone, least of all on the hoof. In the British context, the task falls in the first instance to *political parties*. It is their role not simply to mobilize an electoral majority but to ask and answer the basic question as to why they would want to win an election at all. Their challenge is to formulate a clear political vision, a coherent 'body of principle', and to work it out in successive policy documents, major speeches by leaders, manifestos and in other ways. Citizens then rightly expect parties once in government to continue to articulate this body of principle and to seek as far as possible to put it demonstrably into practice in specific policies. If this were done, the result would be less pandering to narrow and short-term populist instincts, and more commitment to longer-term, strategic, principled policy-making.

Political parties are an easy target for political cynics. And when their representatives engage in self-interested public spats over issues such as whether parties should receive state funding or whether MPs should declare all their expenses, they place themselves squarely in the firing line. But if British governments are to promote justice and the common good better than they do now, we will need not only many vigorous campaigning groups outside formal politics (and we certainly need plenty of those) but also stronger, more cohesive, more intelligent, more visionary political parties within it.[32]

To get those, we will need, as Margaret Thatcher famously and rightly put it, more 'conviction politicians'. And to nurture more conviction politicians we will also need what Nigel Wright calls 'communities of constructive dissent . . . to incubate new ways of living together and to stimulate social change' – communities, whether faith-based or not, to imagine creative and challenging alternatives to conventional political thinking. Taking a cue from Clifford Longley, we can say that such communities will contribute to establishing a vital precondition for Christian political influence – they will generate resistance to the secularist model of a 'naked public square' and nurture the possibility of an 'open public square' in which contrasting political faiths (religious and secular) contend respectfully and vigorously.[33]

If this book has at least alerted readers to the need to produce more politicians of Christian conviction or, to be more accurate, *more articulate* members of that already well-populated species, it will not have failed entirely. We hope it has demonstrated that there is a wealth of biblical and theological resources available to assist them in that goal. But the book's more ambitious hope is that it will spur Christian practitioners on as they seek to forge new, closer and more critical linkages between their theological convictions and their policy commitments – and so to manifest practical Christian political wisdom in ways that promote justice and the common good for a contemporary Britain crying out for much more of both. This book has tried to show that what lofty and demanding principles like justice and the common good require in politics isn't esoteric, elusive or mysterious: it's practical and it's available – as Moses reminded the assembled people of Israel as they were about to embark on the daunting task of nation-building:

> 'For this commandment that I command you this day is not too hard for you, neither is it far off . . . But the word is very near you. It is in your mouth and in your heart, so that you can do it.'[34]

Notes

1 Polly Toynbee, 'Religion doesn't rule in this clash of moral universes', *The Guardian*, 25 March 2008.
2 R. H. Tawney, *'The Attack' and Other Papers* (London: George Allen & Unwin, 1953), p. 178. Quoted in Duncan Forrester, *Beliefs, Values and Policies: Conviction Politics in a Secular Age* (Oxford: Oxford University Press, 1989), p. 33.
3 Quoted in Forrester, *Beliefs, Values and Policies*, p. 32.
4 For further discussions of the relation between these three fundamental motifs, see: Paul Marshall, *God and the Constitution: Christianity and American Politics* (Lanham, MD: Rowman and Littlefield, 2002); David Koyzis, *Political Visions and Illusions: A Survey and Christian Critique of Contemporary Ideologies* (Downers Grove, IL: IVP, 2003); Nigel Oakley, *Engaging Politics: The Tensions of Christian Political Involvement* (Milton Keynes: Paternoster, 2007).
5 For more on this point see Julian Rivers, 'Government', in Michael Schluter and John Ashcroft (eds), *Jubilee Manifesto* (Leicester: IVP, 2005), pp. 138–53.

6 In the same vein he suggests that the kind of justice government can hope to deliver can only ever be 'shallow justice', the legal regulation of external behaviour, never the 'deep justice', the inner moral renewal, available only by the grace of God, dispensed centrally through the church.

7 Eric Voegelin, *The New Science of Politics* (Chicago: University of Chicago Press, 1952), p. 106.

8 It hardly needs saying that Christian practice has not always advanced these principles enthusiastically. But it is equally necessary to counter the reigning but one-sided secularist historical narrative in which individual freedom is the exclusive achievement of the triumph of reason over faith and of the state over the church. See e.g. A. C. Grayling, *Towards the Light: The Story of Struggles for Liberty and Rights That Made the Modern West* (London: Bloomsbury, 2007).

9 For further discussion of this point, see Jonathan Chaplin, 'A Christian-democratic Vision – Foundations and Futures', Kuyper Lecture, University of Villanova, 23 October 2008, available at <http://www.cpjustice.org/files/KuyperLecture2008.pdf>. See also Koyzis, *Political Visions*, Chapter 5.

10 The same point is made by Oliver O'Donovan in *The Ways of Judgment* (Grand Rapids: Eerdmans, 2005), Chapter 10.

11 See e.g. Graham Maddox, *Religion and the Rise of Democracy* (London: Routledge, 1996).

12 See e.g. John De Gruchy, *Christianity and Democracy* (Cambridge: Cambridge University Press, 1995); Maddox, *Religion and the Rise of Democracy*.

13 See e.g. Robert P. Kraynak, *Christian Faith and Modern Democracy: God and Politics in a Fallen World* (Notre Dame, IN: University of Notre Dame Press, 2001).

14 O'Donovan, *Ways of Judgment*, p. 75.

15 In a similar vein, Kenneth Grasso, reflecting on the cumulative teaching of the Roman Catholic Church into the twentieth century, concludes that such teaching today expresses a 'preferential option for constitutional democracy'. Kenneth L. Grasso, 'Beyond Liberalism', in Grasso et al. (eds), *Catholicism, Liberalism, and Communitarianism* (Lanham, MD: Rowman & Littlefield, 1995), pp. 29–58.

16 And if this is so, democracy would not after all be 'morally neutral', as Clifford Longley implies in his chapter. See e.g. Jonathan Chaplin, 'Christian Justifications for Democracy', *Ethics in Brief* 11(3) (August 2006).

17 O'Donovan, *Ways of Judgment*, Chapters 1–4. See also Nicholas Sagovsky, *Christian Tradition and the Practice of Justice* (London: SPCK, 2008); Raymond Plant, *Politics, Theology and History* (Cambridge: Cambridge University Press, 2001), Part II; Duncan Forrester, *Christian Justice and Public Policy* (Cambridge: Cambridge University Press, 1997).

18 Oliver O'Donovan, for example, holds a corrective view of government but includes a wide range of governmental tasks in that category, including aspects of the contemporary welfare role of government, indeed, even establishing transport infrastructure (since to suffer geographic isolation would be a 'public wrong'). See *The Ways of Judgment*, Chapter 3.

19 Clifford Longley also proposes it be limited yet further to what John Courtney Murray called 'political order', leaving 'the common good' to be realized by the wider society.

20 His argument here has parallels with that developed by Michael Novak in *Free Persons and the Common Good* (Lanham, MD: Madison Books, 1989). See also Philip Booth (ed.), *Catholic Social Teaching and the Market Economy* (London: Institute of Economic Affairs, 2007).

21 See e.g. Jonathan Chaplin, 'Subsidiarity and Sphere Sovereignty: Catholic and Reformed Conceptions of the Role of the State', in Francis P. McHugh and Samuel M. Natale (eds), *Things Old and New: Catholic Social Teaching Revisited* (Lanham, MD: University Press of America, 1993), pp. 175–202; David McIlroy, 'Subsidiarity and Sphere Sovereignty', *Journal of Church & State* 45 (2003), pp. 739–64; Jeanne Heffernan Schindler (ed.), *Christianity and Civil Society: Catholic and Neo-Calvinist Perspectives* (Lanham, MD: Lexington Press, 2008).

22 See also his 'The Abuse of Equality', *Ethics in Brief* 11(1) (Summer 2006).

23 David McIlroy, however, holds that in the tradition the common good has always been understood as set against 'permanent social exclusion'.

24 Clifford Longley also points out the expression of this idea in the modern Catholic doctrine of human rights.

25 Accessible at <http://www.guardian.co.uk/world/1997/may/12/indonesia.ethicalforeignpolicy>.

26 Accessible at <http://www.pbs.org/newshour/bb/international/jan-june99/blair_doctrine4-23/html>.

27 Accessible at <http://fabians.org.uk/index.php/20070915219/Events/Speeches/The-future-of-Britishness.html>.

28 Accessible at <http://www.guardian.co.uk/politics/2008/oct/01/davidcameron.toryconference>.

29 Accessible at <http://www.centreforsocialjustice.org.uk/default.asp?pageRef=266>.

30 Alistair Burt et al., *Faith in the Future: Working Towards a Brighter Future. A report by a cross-party Committee of Inquiry* (published by the authors, 2008).

31 The point being made here is not that the invasion was wrong (Christians disagreed about that) but that many ministers seemed to have allowed pragmatic considerations of party unity or relations with the USA to override what they believed to be politically just.

32 Here, faith-based groups within the parties (such as the Christian Socialist Movement, Conservative Christian Fellowship, Liberal Democrat Christian Forum, etc.) are positioned to play a crucial 'leavening' role. Faith-based campaigning, research or policy groups can and do provide vital support for political practitioners generally (e.g. Theos; the Jubilee Centre; the Von Hügel Institute).

33 On this see e.g. Nick Spencer, *Doing God: A Future for Faith in the Public Square* (London: Theos, 2006); Nick Spencer, *Neither Private Nor Privileged: The Role of Christianity in Britain Today* (London: Theos, 2008); Jonathan Chaplin, *Talking God: The Legitimacy of Religious Public Reasoning* (London: Theos, 2009); Roger Trigg, *Religion in the Public Square: Must Faith Be Privatized?* (Oxford: Oxford University Press, 2007).

34 Deuteronomy 30.11, 14.

Index

abortion 102, 174–5
Abraham 70
Acts of the Apostles 37 n26, 41–2, 67, 75, 187
Adam 74
Ahab 34–5, 54, 55
Ambrose of Milan 83
Amos 184
anarchy 76–8
Anglers' Conservation Association (ACA) 145–6
Apringius, proconsul 83
Aquinas, Thomas 86, 92–3, 99–100, 171
Arnold, Matthew 201
ascension the 67
association 91–2
atonement 69–72
Augustine of Hippo 96–7, 106 n27, 117; *City of God* 83, 97
authority: human 47–8; political 53–4, 122, 218–19, 228

Babel 53
Babylon 53
Baptists 37 n21
Barth, Karl 88
basic liberties 124
Bate, Roger: *Saving Our Streams: The Role of the Anglers' Conservation Association in Protecting English and Welsh Rivers* 145–6
BBC 180
Becket, Thomas 86
Benedict XVI: *Deus caritas est* 139; World Peace Day 152
benefaction 24
benefit rights 124–5
Blair, Tony 82, 194, 231
Booth, Philip 9–10, 208, 223, 225, 226–7, 228, 229
Bradstock, Andrew 11–12, 228
Breakdown Britain (Centre for Social Justice) 231
Breakthrough Britain (Centre for Social Justice) 231
Brown, Gordon 204 n52, 231
Burke, Edmund: *Reflections on the Revolution in France* 206
Bush, George W. 85
business 125–6, 132 n21; and the environment 144, 153–4; and equality 193; as love of neighbour 126–7

Caesar 64–5, 115; and Jesus Christ 28, 40, 63
Calvin, John 84–5, 86–7
Calvinism 88, 165, 227
Cameron, David 231
Campbell, Alastair 82
capitalism: and common good 159–60
Catechism of the Catholic Church 136, 151
Catholic Social Teaching (CST) 9, 10, 109, 162, 208; on charity 140–1; on common good 110–11, 112–13, 117, 122, 131 n18, 160–2; on the environment 143–4; formation of 165; and liberal democracy 169; on political authority 122; on solidarity 135–6; on subsidiarity 166–7
Cavanaugh, William 115

Cavour, Camillo 39 n39
Centesimus Annus Foundation 159
Chaplin, Jonathan 12–13
charity 84–5, 139–43, 155 n8
Charles I 92–3
Charles, Rodger 151
child poverty 194, 198
Christian belief, nature of 17–18
Christian Democrats 135
Christianity: and counter-imperialism 63–4
Chronicles, books of 102
church 49, 219; citizenship of 44–5; and equality 187–8; independence of 32, 54; limited role of 87–8; served by government 102–3; and society 31–2; and state 30–6, 48–9, 71, 88, 171; *see also* separation of church and state
Church of England 77
civil liberty 90
civil service 92
civil society 89
climate change 10, 149–51, 227
Colossians, letter to 68
commission on inequality 198–9
common good 10–11, 90–5, 129 n3, 177, 213–14, 230, 236 n19, 236 n23; and capitalism 159–60; Catholic Social Teaching (CST) on 110–11, 112–13, 117, 122, 131 n18, 160–2; *Compendium of the Social Doctrine of the Church* on 110–11, 131 n18, 161; defining 131 n18, 160–1; and democracy 168–70; and education 227–8; and government 112–13, 119–20; and human rights 168–70; and human well-being 111; and justice 207–11, 223–30; moral principle 160–2; and the reign of God 117; and representation 222–3; and secularism 173–7; and solidarity 163–4; and the state 170–2; and subsidiarity 164–8
Common Good and the Catholic Church's Social Teaching, The (Catholic Bishops of England and Wales) 166–7
commonwealth 92
communication 91–2
Communion service 188–9
communitarian position 112
community 186, 233; *see also* society
Compendium of the Social Doctrine of the Church (Pontifical Council for Justice and Peace) 109, 128 n1, 132 n21, 138, 146, 151; on common good 110–11, 131 n18, 161
Confessing Church 88
Congregationalists 37 n21
conscience 27
consent, popular 220–2
conservatism 128
Constantine, Emperor 82
constitution 56–7
consumers: and the environment 144
Cook, Robin 231, 232
Corinthians, letters to 51, 164, 187
Cornelius, centurion 41–2
counter-imperialism 63–7; in the Synoptic Gospels 67–8
creation 21, 213, 223–4; equality in 183; liberation of 46–7; nature of the world 73–9; and redemption 66–7, 74
Cromwell, Oliver 89
cross, the 66, 69–72
Curran, Charles E. 174, 177; *Catholic Social Teaching 1891–Present* 170–1

Daniel, book of 67, 68
David, King 41, 55
defence 92
democracy 168–70, 220–3, 235 n15, 236 n16
Deuteronomy, book of 51
divorce 99
doctrine of the two 89
Domination System 20, 35, 213

dominion 21–2, 24
Donatists 106 n27

ecological sustainability 130 n16
economy 109–10, 125–6; and the environment 151–2; and equality 191, 199; and government 266
education 49, 137, 142–3, 227–8
Elijah 34–5, 55
environment, the 226–7; business and consumers 144, 153–4; Catholic Social Teaching (CST) 143–4; and the economy 151–2; and income 147, 157 n32; international problems 147–51; juridical framework 3, 144–5; and private property 145–7, 157 n29; and property rights 151–2, 153; reductionist approach to 144; subsidiarity and solidarity 143–54
Ephesians, letter to 75
equality 11–12, 50–1, 222, 228; and the church 187–8; in creation 183; defining 182; economic 191, 199; in income 180–1; Jesus Christ on 188, 189–90
establishment, the 77–9
Esther 41
eternal realm 86
Eucharist 188–9
European Union 176–7
Eusebius 82
Eve 74
Exodus, book of 188
Ezekiel 52, 186

Faith in the Future 231
fall, the 223–4
family, the 47–8, 166–7
Fascism 165–6
feeding of the five thousand story 190
fishing rights 148–9, 227
forest destruction 146, 147, 157 n30
Forrester, Duncan 182
Franco, Francisco 168–9
free will 137
free-church tradition 26, 30–5, 37 n21
freedom 85, 110, 124, 125, 200, 219, 235 n8
freedom rights 124, 125

Galatians, letter to 114, 117, 118
Gallio, proconsul 41
Gelasius I 85–6
Genesis, book of 18, 42, 53, 70, 73–4, 183
giving culture 197
global warming *see* climate change
God: government accountable to 82–5; government as work of 45, 214–15; kings accountable to 89; and the poor 185; and the powers 28–30, 116–17; reign of 113–14, 117; supremacy of 44
Good Samaritan, the 162
Gorringe, Timothy 188
gospel, Christian 113–17
government 8, 40–1, 213; accountability of 54–6, 217–18; accountable to God 82–5; and common good 112–13, 119–20; coordinating role of 87, 123–4, 224; corrective role of 86–7, 236 n18; diffusion of authority 53–4, 218–19, 228; and the economy 226; global 77–8; as legitimate 44–5, 215–17; limits of 27–8, 46–50, 85–90, 132 n19, 225; remedial role of 123, 132 n19, 223–4; and representation 220–3; serving the church 102–3; as social infrastructure: practice 122–8, 131 n19; as social infrastructure: theory 117–22; work of God 45, 214–15
Grasso, Kenneth 235 n15
Gregory of Nazianzus 8, 82, 104 n3
Gregory the Great 83–4, 96, 104 n7
Gross Domestic Product (GDP) 4, 14 n3, 147, 157 n32

Haman 41
Hauerwas school 115, 129 n11
Hauerwas, Stanley 115
healthcare 210
Henry II 86
Henry VIII 37 n23
heretics, persecution of 106 n27
Herod, King 42
Hitchens, Christopher 38 n33, 107 n39
Hitler, Adolf 165
Hobson, Theo: *Against Establishment* 77
Holy Spirit 114
Hosea 41
Hubmaier, Balthasar 37 n28; 'On Heretics and Those Who Burn Them' 38 n28
Huckabee, Mike 85
human beings 19–20, 21, 73–4
human rights 125, 128, 168–70, 177–8
humanism 38 n31
Hutton, Will 159–60, 161

imperialism 7–8, 53, 61–3
income 180–1, 194, 198, 199
Incomes Data Services (IDS) 181
inequality *see* equality
Iraq, invasion of 232, 237 n31
Isaiah, book of 68, 71, 74
Isaiah, the prophet 65, 184, 186
Israel 23, 50, 53–4

James, disciple 67
James, epistle of 187
Jefferson, Thomas 32, 38 n32
Jehoshaphat 102
Jeremiah 185
Jerusalem church 187
Jesus Christ 17–18, 77; authority over death 114; and Caesar 28, 40, 63; collaboration of church and state 48–9; on equality 188, 189–90; exercise of dominion 24; life in 114, 117–18; as Lord 63–4, 71–2, 75, 82, 118–19, 217, 219; as Messiah 44; Paul on 44, 68–72; and Pilate 41, 64–7, 77; political message 115; and reign of God 113–14; resurrection of 75; salt and light 34–5
Jezebel 35
Job 184
John, disciple 67
John, Gospel of 64–7, 70
John the Baptist 188
John of Salisbury 89
John Paul II 11, 109, 136, 171, 174, 176, 177; *Centesimus annus* 109, 139, 141; *Familiaris consortio* 142; *Sollicitudo rei socialis* 155 n8, 163
John XXIII 95, 169; *Pacem in terris* 132 n21, 168
Josiah, King 185
Jubilee laws 185, 189, 195
judgment 84–5, 90, 103, 131 n19
just judgment 91, 95–102
justice 122, 128, 214; charity in 84–5; and common good 207–11, 223–30; deep justice 99, 235 n6; equal justice 182; possibility of 230–4; shallow justice 99, 103, 235 n6

kingdom of God 46–7, 65
kings 54, 55, 86, 89
Kings, books of 34–5, 54, 55
kingship 23, 41, 50, 54
Knox, John 88

Labour Party 181; *see also* New Labour
land, distribution of 185–6
Late Scholastics 140
Laurence, deacon 95
law 4–5, 52–3, 55, 98–102, 144–5; rule of law, 52–3, 85, 218
Leo XIII 140; *Rerum novarum* 156 n24, 165

Leviticus 185, 186
liberal democracy 169, 220–1
liberalism 110, 128, 162, 220–1
Longley, Clifford 10–11, 208, 225, 226, 233, 236 n19
Lord's Prayer 160
love of neighbour 126–7
Luke, Gospel of 28, 70
Lutheran Reformation 87

manna, provision of 51, 188
Mark, Gospel of 28, 67–8, 70
Marxism 76
Mary, mother of Jesus 189
Mass 188–9
Matthew, Gospel of 28, 67, 70
McIlroy, David 8, 207, 210, 211, 218, 221, 224, 236 n23
meritocracy 197
messiah, meaning of term 115
Messiah, the 44, 74
Methodists 37 n21
Micah 186
military, the 92
Mill, John Stuart 127; *On Liberty* 206
minimum wage 194, 198
mishpat 96
Monbiot, George 151
morality and law 98–102
Mordecai 41
Moses 185, 234
Mugabe, Robert 89
Murray, John Courtney 171–2, 174, 175, 178, 236 n19
Muslims: concept of Zakah 195; tolerance of beliefs 175–6
Mussolini, Benito 165–6

Naboth 54
Nathan 55
natural law 99, 100, 171–2, 218
Nazism 88, 165
Nebuchadnezzar, King 44
neighbour as universal, category of 162
neoliberalism 126–7, 128
new Jerusalem 117
New Labour 110; *see also* Labour Party
New Statesman 72–3
Niebuhr, Reinhold 182
Nolan, Lord 93, 210
Nolan Report on Standards in Public Life 93
Numbers, book of 185

Obadiah 34–5
O'Donovan, Joan Lockwood 97–8
O'Donovan, Oliver 87, 89, 95, 96, 101, 130 n11, 213, 222; corrective view of government 236 n18; government as social infrastructure 131 n19; rights and responsibilities 97–8
Olson, Roger 17–18
order, maintenance of 28–30
order of preservation, the 30, 33
order of redemption, the 33
Organization for Economic Cooperation and Development (OECD) 181

parousia, the 69
Paul 41–2, 48, 55; on atonement 69–72; counter-imperialism 62, 67, 68–72; on equality 51, 187, 188–9; on Jesus Christ 44, 68–72; life in Christ 114, 117–18; on secular rule 118–19; on subsidiarity 164; on vengeance 130 n15; on work 192–3
Paul VI: *Gaudium et spes* 131 n18; *Octogesima adveniens* 143, 155 n8; *Populorum progressio* 109
Pelagius 183–4
pension credits 194
Peron, Juan 168–9
Peter, first letter of 45
Philippians, letter to 69
Pickett, Kate 199
Pilate, and Jesus Christ 41, 64–7, 77

Index

Pilgrim, W. 118
Pius XI 140; *Quadragesimo anno* 165–6
pluralism 173–7, 178
police, the 92
political order 236 n19
political parties, role of 178, 232–3
political theology, application of 206–11
political wisdom 211–12
politics 108, 113–17
poor, the: and God 185; preferential option for 134–5, 155 n8
poverty 155 n8, 194, 198
powers, the 20–1, 74; as created 21–3; and equality 51; as fallen 23–5; and God 28–30, 116–17; as to be redeemed 25–7, 213–14; religious validation of 31
Presbyterians 37 n21
priests, and kings 86
private property 148, 156 n24, 156 n29; and the environment 145–7, 157 n29
property rights 149, 151–2, 153, 157 n32, 226–7
prophets 50, 54, 55, 217
Protestant Reformation in England 37 n23
Protestantism 26–7, 109
Proverbs, book of 185
Psalms 52
public life and religion 32–3
public order 175
public service 92–3
public wrong 87
pulpit, speaking from 133 n22

Rawls, John 127
redemption 25–7, 66–7, 74, 213–14, 223–4
reforestation 147
religion and public life 32–3
representation 220–3
resurrection 46, 70, 75
Revelation of John 42, 53, 63, 212
Rio Declaration on the Family 136
Rivers, Julian 7, 212, 214, 217, 218, 222, 225, 227–8
Roma, goddess 69
Roman Empire 45, 53, 61, 62, 165
Romans, letter to 19, 45, 63, 68–9, 85, 96, 108, 117–18, 130 n14
Rowland, Christopher 186

Sabbath, the 186
Sacks, Jonathan 132 n21
Sagovsky, Nicholas: *Christian Tradition and the Practice of Justice* 202 n12
salvation 17–18, 33
Samuel, books of 55
Samuel, the prophet 23
Saul 55
Second Vatican Council 168; *Declaration on Religious Liberty* 11, 171–2, 177
secularism 33, 38 n31, 38 n34, 118–19, 173–7
self-government 48
separation of church and state 30–5, 173–4, 176–7, 219; *see also* state
servanthood 29–30
simultaneity 20–1, 25
sin 213
sins: of commission 123, 124, 127; of omission 123, 124–5, 127
social assistance state *see* welfare state
social exclusion 94–5, 120–1, 236 n23
social infrastructure 9, 224; government as, in practice 122–8, 131 n19; government as, in theory 117–22
social mobility 197
socialism 128
society 31–2, 166–7; *see also* community
Society of Biblical Literature 64

solidarity 9–10, 177, 208, 225–8; Catholic Social Teaching (CST) 135–6; and common good 163–4; and the environment 143–54; taxation and charity 139–43
specification 210
sphere sovereignty 227
stakeholder welfare 229
state, the: and church 30–6, 48–9, 71, 88, 171; and common good 170–2; *see also* separation of church and state
subsidiarity 9–10, 162, 163, 166–7, 208, 225–8; Catholic Social Teaching (CST) 166–7; and common good 164–8; and the environment 143–54; and private property 146; and service provision 167–8; taxation and charity 139–43
sword, the 48, 118

Tawney, R. H. 183, 191, 192, 197, 209, 210, 228
taxation 139–43, 194–5, 196–7
Temple, William 191
Terry, John 180, 199
Thatcher, Margaret 233
Theodosius, Emperor 83
Thessalonians, letters to 62, 69
Timothy, letters to 48–9
torture 100, 107 n39
Townsend, Nicholas 8–9, 213–14, 216, 224, 225
Toynbee, Polly 208
Treaty of Maastricht 137
Trinity, the 17–18, 82
tsedeq 96
Tutu, Desmond 103
two kingdoms doctrine 63
tyranny 76–8

United Reformed Church 37 n21
United States 61, 71, 173–4
Universal Declaration of Human Rights (1948) 192

Valerian, Emperor 94–5
vengeance 130 n15
Villa-Vicencio, C. 130 n11
Voegelin, Eric 219
voluntary sector 192, 193
vox populi 62, 76, 220

water-boarding 100, 107 n39
wealth 184–5; redistribution of 194–7, 200
welfare state 141–3, 167–8, 191–2, 229
well-being: and common good 111–12
Wells, Samuel 115
Widdecombe, Ann 102
Wilkinson, Richard 199, 201
Williams, Roger 38 n32
Williams, Rowan xi
Wink, Walter 20, 24
wisdom 98, 101
Wisdom of Solomon 70
'Word becoming Flesh' 188
world, the: nature of 18–19, 73–9
Wright, Nigel 6–7, 212, 213, 214, 219, 233
Wright, Tom 7–8, 118, 130 n15, 212, 213, 217, 219, 220

Xerxes, King 41

YHWH *see* God
Yoder, J. H. 130 n14
Yunus, Muhammad 132 n21

Zakah 195
Zechariah 186